READING AND NO

STUDY GUIDE

THE WESTERN HERITAGE

SINCE 1300

TWELFTH EDITION

AP® Edition

Donald Kagan

Yale University

Frank M. Turner

Yale University

Steven Ozment

Harvard University

Gregory F. Viggiano

Sacred Heart University

AP® is a trademark registered and/or owned by the College Board, which was not involved in the production of, and does not endorse, this product.

AP® is a trademark registered and/or owned by the College Board, which was not involved in the production of, and does not endorse, this product.

Printed in the United States of America

ISBN-10: 0-13-526044-2
ISBN-13: 978-0-13-526044-9

www.pearsonhighered.com

9 2022

CONTENTS

PART 3: Toward the Modern World, 1850–1939

PART 4: Global Conflict, Cold War, and New Directions, 1939 to Present

Chapter 1
The Late Middle Ages: Social and Political Breakdown (1300–1453)

Complete the following exercises *as you read* this chapter.

Section 1 The Black Death

Focus Question

What were the social and economic consequences of the Black Death?

Social Consequences	Economic Consequences
•	•
•	•
•	•
•	•

Using the information in your flowchart, write a brief answer to the Focus Question.

OUTLINE

Read the section topic entitled "Preconditions and Causes of the Plague" and create an outline of the section below. Note the key words that reflect the main ideas in each paragraph as well as the key words that inform those ideas.

I. Preconditions and Causes of the Plague

A. Population and food production

1.

2.

3.

4.

B. Crop failures and famine

1.

2.

3.

C. Rats, fleas, and trade routes

1.

2.

3.

4.

5.

6.

7.

Section 2 The Hundred Years' War and the Rise of National Sentiment

Focus Question

How did the Hundred Years' War contribute to a growing sense of national identity in France and England? Complete the flowchart to outline the causes and effects of the Hundred Years' War.

Causes	Effects
•	•
•	•
•	•
•	•

Using the information in your flowchart, write a brief answer to the Focus Question.

OUTLINE

Read the section topic entitled "The Causes of the War" and create an outline of the sections below. Note the key words that reflect the main ideas in each paragraph as well as the key words that inform those ideas.

I. The Causes of the War
   A. Edward III of England
      1.
      2.
   B. Friction between the French and English
      1.
      2.
      3.
      4.

REVIEW QUESTIONS

Write a brief answer to the following questions. Each answer should highlight a primary idea using key words and supporting details.

1. What were the underlying and precipitating causes of the Hundred Years' War?

2. What advantages did for each side in the Hundred Years' War have?

3. Why were the French finally able to drive the English almost entirely out of France?

SECTION 3 ECCLESIASTICAL BREAKDOWN AND REVIVAL: THE LATE MEDIEVAL CHURCH

FOCUS QUESTION

How did secular rulers challenge papal authority in the fourteenth and fifteenth centuries?

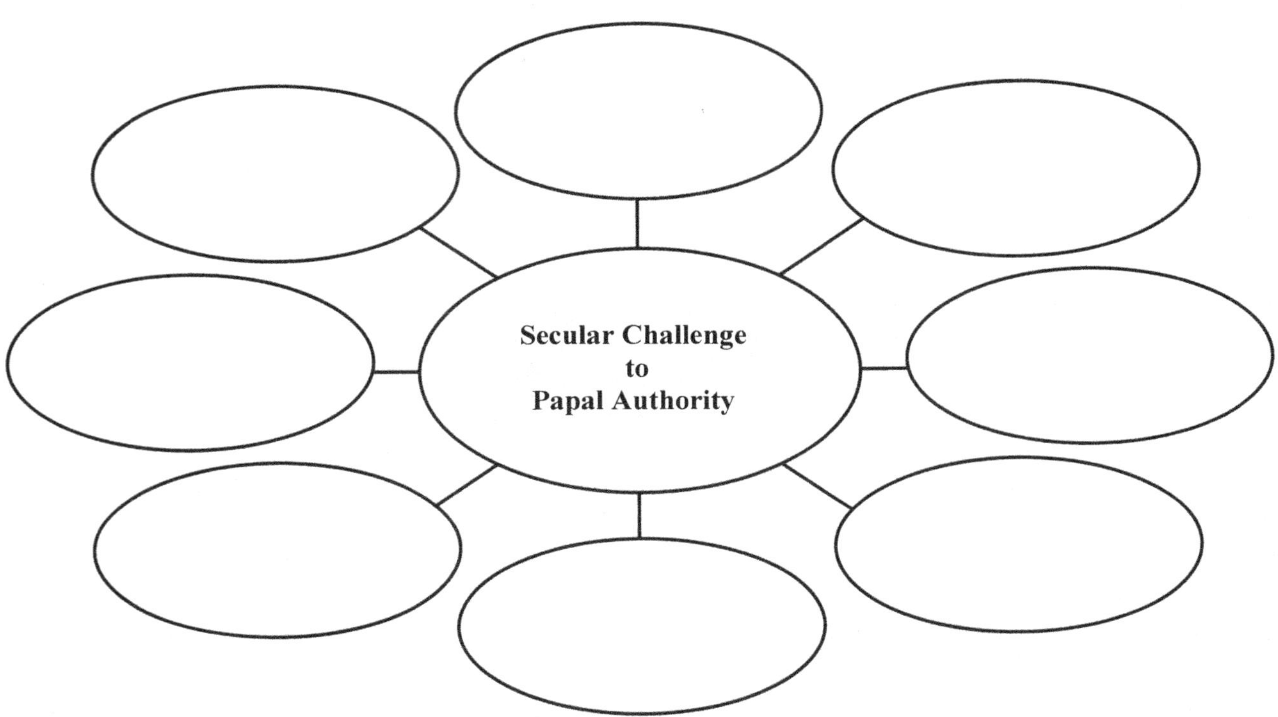

Using the information in your concept web, write a brief answer to the Focus Question.

Outline

Read the section topic entitled "The Thirteen-Century Papacy" and create an outline of the section below. Note the key words that reflect the main ideas in each paragraph as well as the key words that inform those ideas.

I. The Thirteenth-Century Papacy

   A. Precedent: Innocent III (1198-1216)

      1.

      2.

   B.

      1.

      2.

      3.

   C.

      1.

      2.

      3.

   D.

      1.

      2.

      3.

   E.

      1.

      2.

      3.

      4.

Reading Skill: Summarize

Complete the Venn diagram below summarizing the main ideas held by Lollards and Hussites.

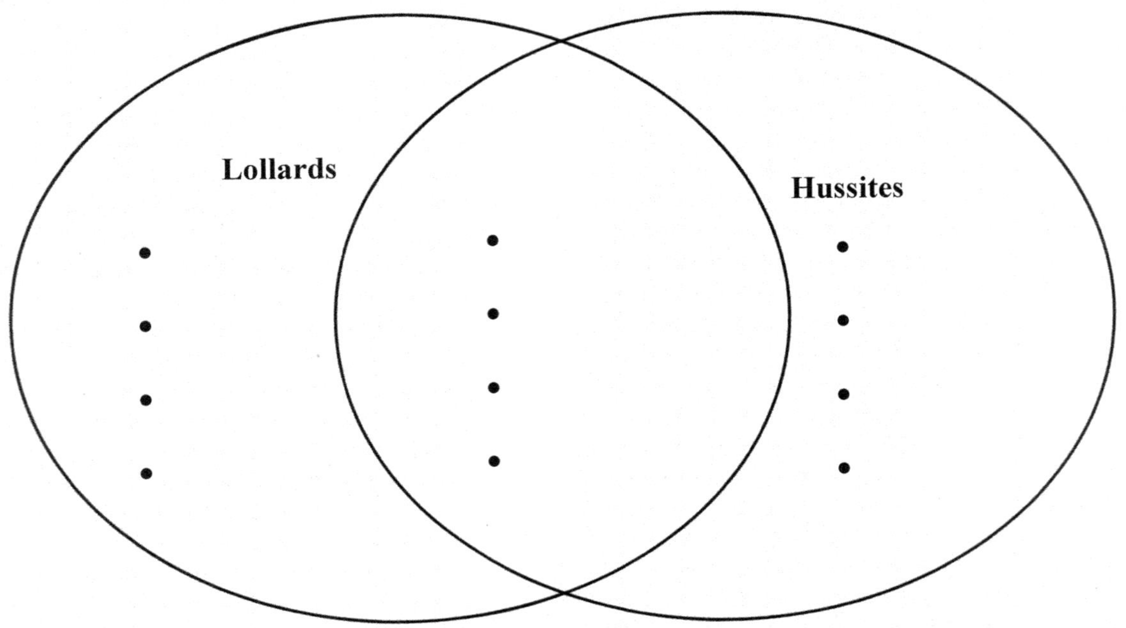

REVIEW QUESTIONS

Write a brief answer to the following questions. Each answer should highlight a primary idea using key words and supporting details.

1. Why did Pope Boniface VIII quarrel with King Philip the Fair? Why was Boniface so weak in the conflict?

2. How did the church change from 1200 to 1450? What was its response to the growing power of monarchs?

3. What was the Avignon papacy, and why did it occur? How did it affect the papacy?

4. How did the church become divided and how was it reunited?

5. What was the conciliar movement? Why was it a setback for the papacy?

SECTION 4 MEDIEVAL RUSSIA

FOCUS QUESTION

How did Mongol rule shape Russia's development?

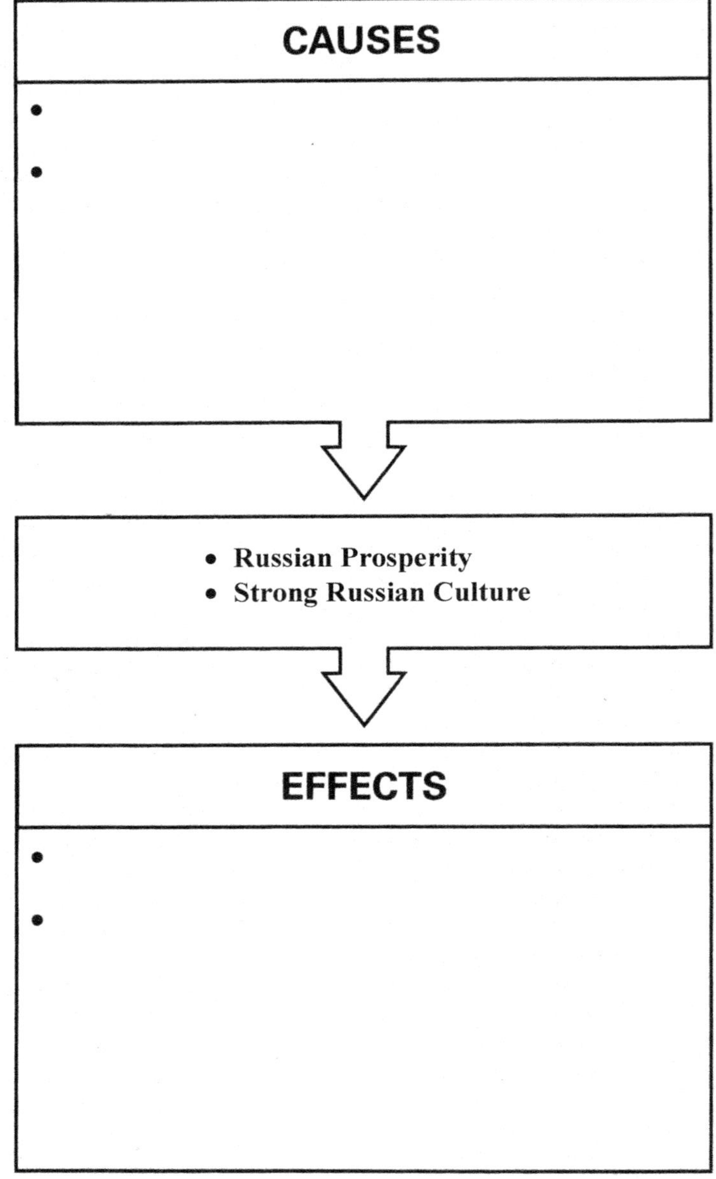

Using the information in your flowchart, write a brief answer to the Focus Question.

OUTLINE

Read the section entitled "Mongol Rule (1243–1480)" and create an outline of the section below. Note the key words that reflect the main ideas in each paragraph as well as the key words that inform those ideas.

I. Mongol Rule (1243–1480)
   A. Mongol Invaders
      1.
      2.
      3.
   B.
      1.
      2.
   C.
      1.
      2.
      3.
      4.
   D.
      1.
      2.
   E.
      1.
      2.
      3.
      4.
         a.
         b.
      5.
         a.
         b.
   F. The "third Rome"
      1.
      2.

Review Questions

Write a brief answer to the following questions. Remember, each answer should highlight a primary idea using key words and supporting details.

1. Why is it significant for Russian history that Mongol overlords used tribute as the principal means of subjecting the Russian people to their rule?

2. Why did the Russian victory at Kulikov Meadow mark the beginning of the decline of the Mongol hegemony?

REVIEW: KEY TERMS AND PEOPLE

Complete your review of the chapter by writing a brief definition of the following terms and people.

Black Death
flagellants
taille
Jacquerie
Hundred Years' War
Estates General
Joan of Arc
Avignon papacy
Pope John XXII
John Wycliffe
John Huss
Great Schism
Church Councils
Mongol
Genghis Khan
Golden Horde
Tribute
Kulikov Meadow
Ivan III, the Great

MY KEY TERMS

Write down terms that are unfamiliar. How are the words used? Do other words or examples reveal their meaning? Try to figure out meaning from the context.

CHAPTER 2
RENAISSANCE AND DISCOVERY

Complete the following exercises *as you read* the chapter.

SECTION 1 THE RENAISSANCE IN ITALY (1375–1527)

FOCUS QUESTION

How did humanism affect culture and the arts in fourteenth- and fifteenth-century Italy?

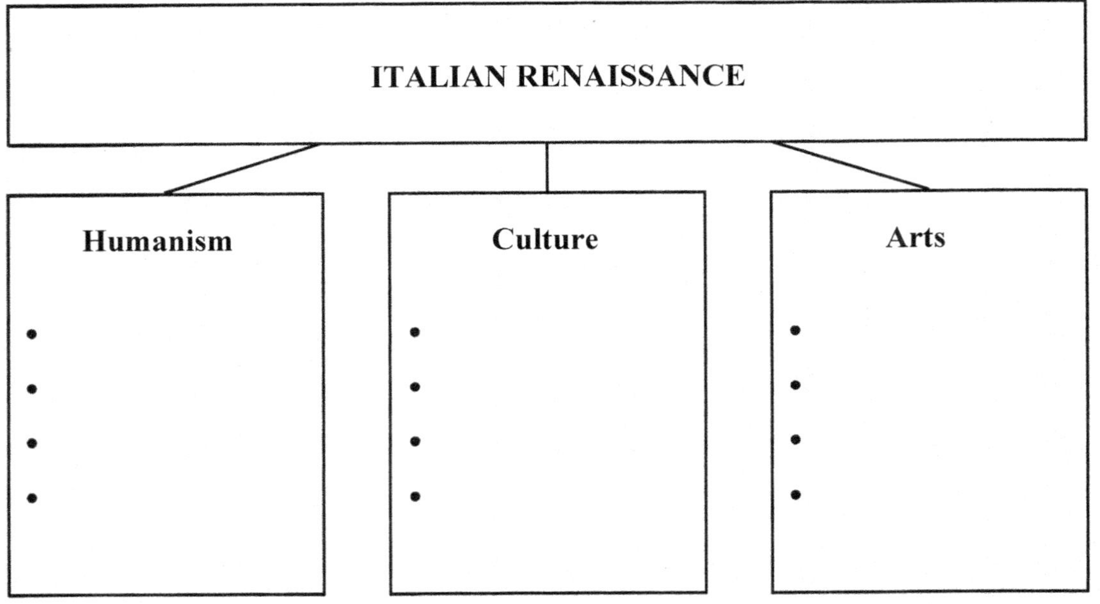

Using the information from your chart, write a brief answer to the Focus Question.

OUTLINE

Read the section topic entitled "High Renaissance Art" and create an outline of the section below. Note the key words that reflect the main ideas in each paragraph as well as the key words that inform those ideas.

I. Renaissance Art
   A. Power of laity
      1.
      2.
      3.
      4.
   B.
      1.
      2.
      3.
      4.
   C.
      1.
      2.
   D.
      1.
      2.
      3.
      4.

Review Questions

Write a brief answer to the following questions. Remember, each answer should highlight a primary idea using key words and supporting details.

1. What did the term "Renaissance" mean in the context of fifteenth- and sixteenth-century Italy?

2. How would you define Renaissance humanism?

3. In what ways was the Renaissance a break with the Middle Ages, and in what ways did it owe its existence to medieval civilization?

4. Who were some of the famous literary and artistic figures of the Italian Renaissance? What did they have in common that might be described as "the spirit of the Renaissance"?

Section 2 Italy's Political Decline: The French Invasions (1494–1527)

Focus Question

What were the causes of Italy's political decline?

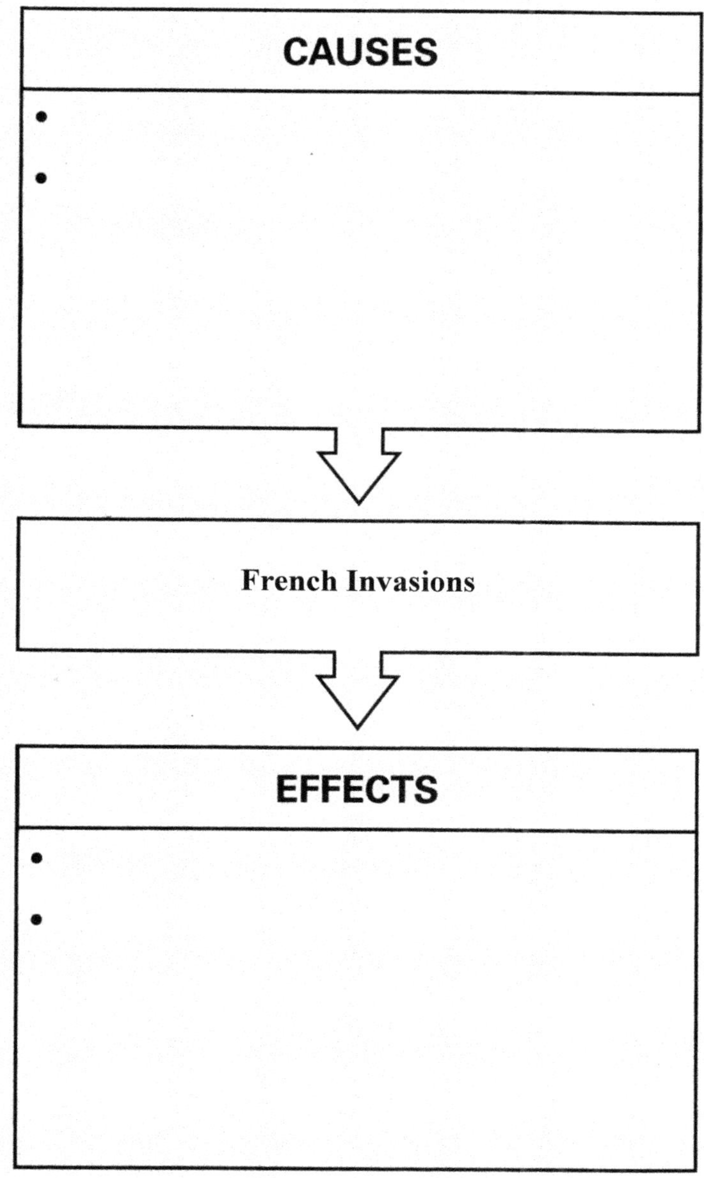

Use the information in your flowchart, write a brief answer to the Focus Question.

OUTLINE

Read the section topic entitled "Pope Alexander VI and the Borgia Family" and create an outline of the section below. Note the key words that reflect the main ideas in each paragraph as well as the key words that inform those ideas.

I. Pope Alexander VI and the Borgia Family
   A. Context: loss of Papal authority in the Romagna
      1.
      2.
   B.
      1.
      2.
   C.
      1.
      2.
      3.
   D.
      1.
      2.
      3.

Review Questions

Write a brief answer to the following questions. Remember, each answer should highlight a primary idea using key words and supporting details.

1. Why did the French invade Italy in 1494? How did this event trigger Italy's political decline?

2. How did the actions of Pope Julius II and the ideas of Niccolò Machiavelli signify a new era in Italian civilization?

3. A common assumption is that creative work will proceed best in periods of calm and peace. Given the combination of political instability and cultural productivity in Renaissance Italy, do you think this assumption is valid?

SECTION 3 REVIVAL OF MONARCHY IN NORTHERN EUROPE

FOCUS QUESTION

How were the powerful monarchies of northern Europe different from their predecessors?

Feudal Monarchy	National Monarchy
•	•
•	•
•	•
•	•

Using the information in your table, write a brief answer to the Focus Question.

OUTLINE

Read the section topic entitled "France" and create an outline of the section below. Note the key words that reflect the main ideas in each paragraph as well as the key words that inform those ideas.

I. France
    A.
        1.
        2.
        3.
        4.
    B.
        1.
        2.
    C.
        1.
        2.
        3.
        4.
    D.
        1.
        2.
        3.

REVIEW QUESTIONS

Write a brief answer to the following questions. Remember, each answer should highlight a primary idea using key words and supporting details.

1. How were the respective developments of the silk and sheep industries relevant to the ascension of strong national monarchies in France and Spain?

2. In what way was religion key to the success of newly unified Spain?

SECTION 4 THE NORTHERN RENAISSANCE

FOCUS QUESTION

How did the northern Renaissance affect culture in Germany, England, France, and Spain?

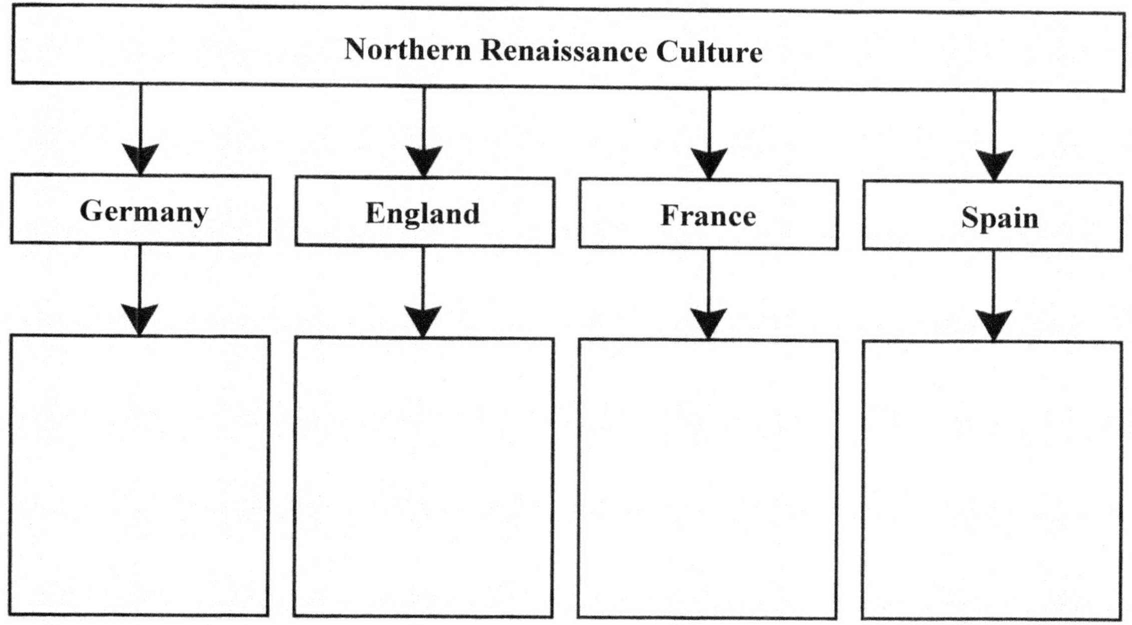

Using the information in your flowchart, write a brief answer to the Focus Question.

Outline

Read the section topic entitled "The Printing Press" and create an outline of the section below. Note the key words that reflect the main ideas in each paragraph as well as the key words that inform those ideas.

I. The Printing Press
    A. Conditions for invention
        1.
        2.
        3.
    B.
        1.
        2.
        3.
    C.
        1.
        2.
        3.
    D.
        1.
        2.
        3.
    E.
        1.
        2.
        3.

Review Questions

Write a brief answer to the following questions. Remember, each answer should highlight a primary idea using key words and supporting details.

1. How did the Renaissance in the north differ from the Italian Renaissance?

2. In what ways was Erasmus the embodiment of the northern Renaissance?

Section 5 Voyages of Discovery and the New Empires In the West and East

Focus Question

What were the motives for European voyages of discovery, and what were the consequences?

Motives	Consequences
•	•
•	•
•	•
•	•

Using the information in your chart, write a brief answer to the Focus Question.

OUTLINE

Read the section topic entitled "The Church in Spanish America" and create an outline of the section below. Note the key words that reflect the main ideas in each paragraph as well as the key words that inform those ideas.

I. The Church in Spanish America

  A. Philosophy of Christ

    1.

    2.

  B.

    1.

    2.

    3.

    4.

  C.

    1.

II.

  D.

    1.

    2.

    3.

    4.

  E.

    1.

    2.

READING SKILL: SUMMARIZE

Complete the chart below listing the impact of the European voyages of discovery on native peoples and on Europe.

Impact on Native Peoples	Impact on Europe
•	•
•	•
•	•
•	•

Review Questions

Write a brief answer to the following questions. Remember, each answer should highlight a primary idea using key words and supporting details.

1. What factors led to the voyages of discovery?

2. Why were the Portuguese interested in finding a route to the East?

3. Why did Columbus sail west across the Atlantic in 1492?

Review: Key Terms and People

Complete your review of the chapter by writing a brief definition of the following terms and people.

Humanism
Christine de Pisan
Platonism
Civic Humanism
Pico della Mirandola
Chiaroscuro
Treaty of Lodi
Ludovico il Moro
Julius II
Niccolò Machiavelli
gabelle
Isabella of Castile
Mesta
Tomás de Torquemada
Wars of the Roses
Golden Bull
Northern humanism
Erasmus
Reuchlin affair
Thomas More
Jiménez de Cisneros
Henry the Navigator
Ferdinand Magellan
Tiano
Aztec
Atahualpa
Conquistadores
Hacienda
Encomienda

My Key Terms

Write down terms that are unfamiliar. How are the words used? Do other words or examples reveal their meaning? Try to figure out meaning from the context.

CHAPTER 3
THE AGE OF REFORMATION

Complete the following exercises in order *as you read* this chapter.

SECTION 1 SOCIETY AND RELIGION

FOCUS QUESTION

What was the social and religious background of the Reformation?

Social and Political Conflicts	Religious Movements
•	•
•	•
•	•
•	•

Using the information in your chart, write a brief answer to the Focus Question.

OUTLINE

Read the section topic entitled "Popular Religious Movements and Criticism of the Church" and create an outline of the section below. Note the key words that reflect the main ideas in each paragraph as well as the key words that inform those ideas.

I. Popular Religious Movements and Criticism of the Church
   A. Spiritual crisis in the medieval church
      1.
      2.
      3.
      4.
      5.
      6.
   B.
      1.
      2.
      3.
   C.
      1.
      2.
      3.
   D.
      1.
      2.

Review Questions

Write a short response to the following review questions. Remember, each answer should highlight a primary idea using key words and supporting details.

1. What problems in the church contributed to the Protestant Reformation?

2. What was the role of city magistrates in creating a welcoming context for reformation?

Section 2 Martin Luther and the German Reformation to 1525

Focus Question

Why did Martin Luther challenge the church?

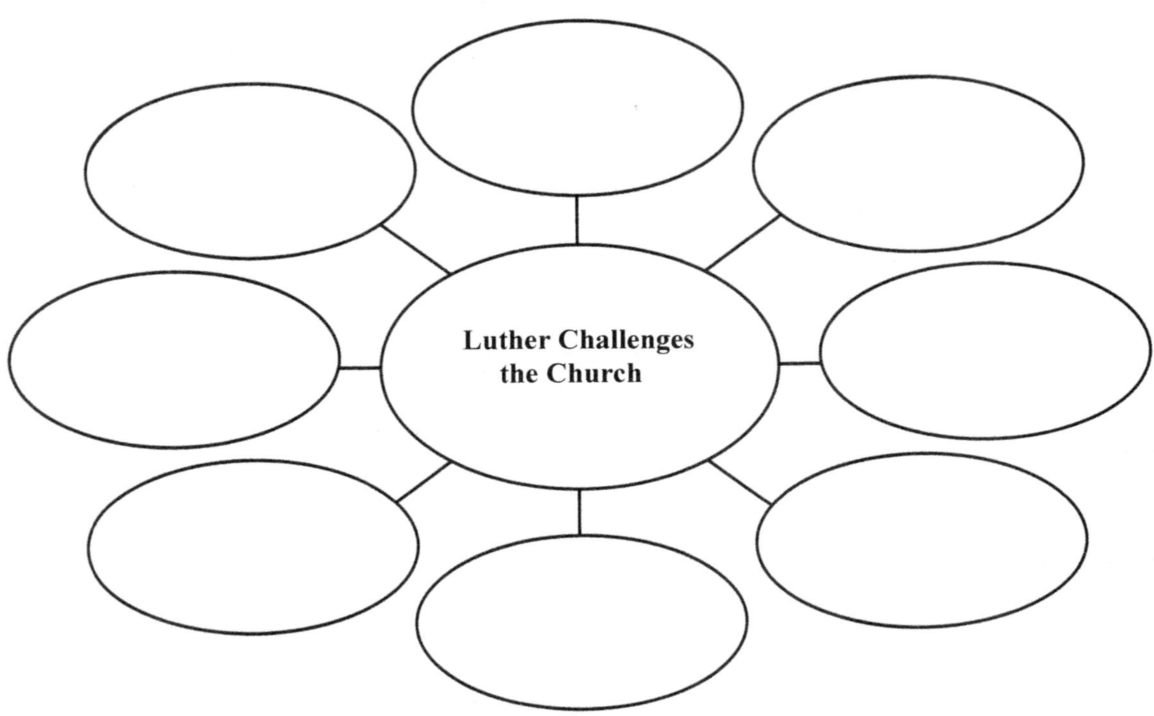

Using the information in your concept web, write a brief answer to the Focus Question.

REVIEW QUESTIONS

Write a short response to the following review questions. Remember, each answer should highlight a primary idea using key words and supporting details.

1. Why was the church unable to continue to suppress dissent as it had earlier?

2. What was the role of Imperial politics in the success of the Protestant Reformation?

SECTION 3 HOW THE REFORMATION SPREAD

FOCUS QUESTION

Where did other reform movements develop and how were they different from Luther's?

Movement	Goals/Characteristics	Major Figures
Luther		
Zwingli		
Anabaptists		
Spiritualists		
Antitrinitarians		
Calvinists		

Using the information in your table, write a brief answer to the Focus Question.

Review Questions

Write a short response to the following review questions. Remember, each answer should highlight a primary idea using key words and supporting details.

1. What were the basic similarities and differences between the ideas of Luther and Zwingli?

2. What were the basic similarities and differences between the ideas of Luther and Calvin? How did these differences tend to affect the success of the Protestant movement?

Section 4 Political Consolidation of the Lutheran Reformation

Focus Question

What were the political ramifications of the Reformation?

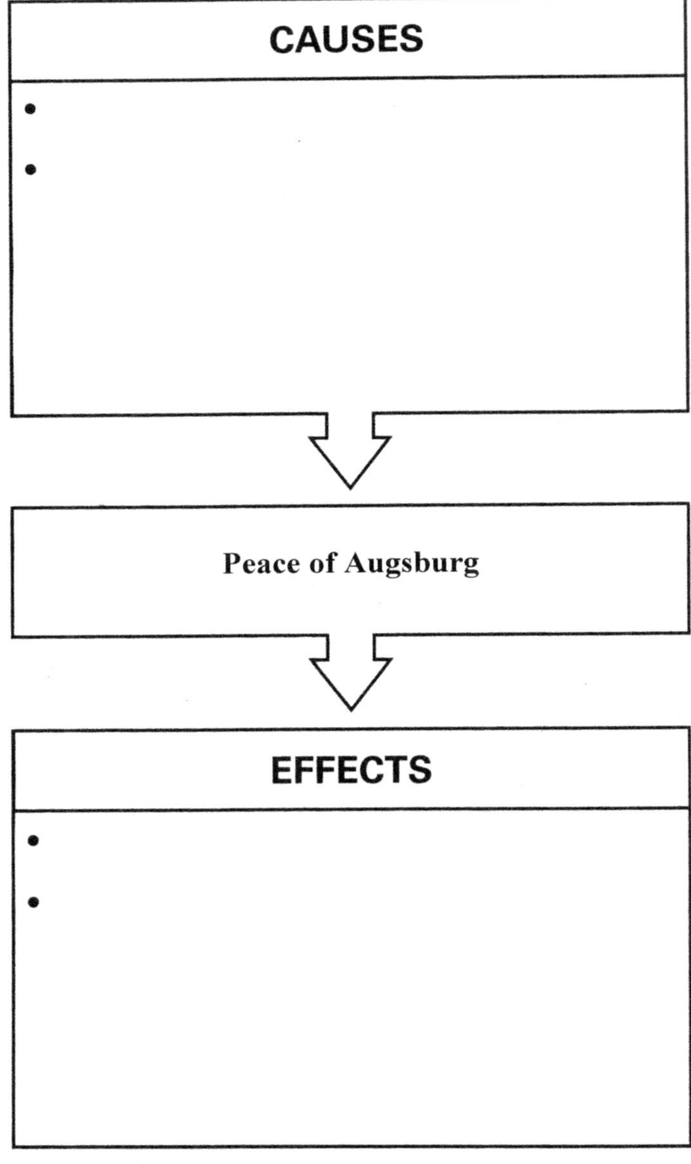

Using the information in your chart, write a brief answer to the Focus Question.

OUTLINE

Read the section topic entitled "The Expansion of the Reformation" and create an outline of the section below. Note the key words that reflect the main ideas in each paragraph as well as the key words that inform those ideas.

I. The Expansion of the Reformation
   A. Regional consistories composed of theologians and lawyers replace episcopates
   B.
      1.
      2.
      3.
      4.
   C.
      1.
      2.
      3.
   D.
      1.
      2.
   E.
      1.
      2.
      3.
      4.
      5.

Reading Skill: Summarize

Complete the chart below identifying what the Peace of Augsburg did and didn't accomplish.

Peace of Augsburg	
Did Accomplish	**Did Not Accomplish**

Review Questions

Write a brief answer to the following questions. Remember, each answer should highlight a primary idea using key words and supporting details.

1. Why did the Reformation begin in Germany?

2. What political factors contributed to its success there as opposed to in France, Spain, or Italy?

SECTION 5 THE ENGLISH REFORMATION TO 1553

FOCUS QUESTION

How did royal dynastic concerns shape the Reformation in England?

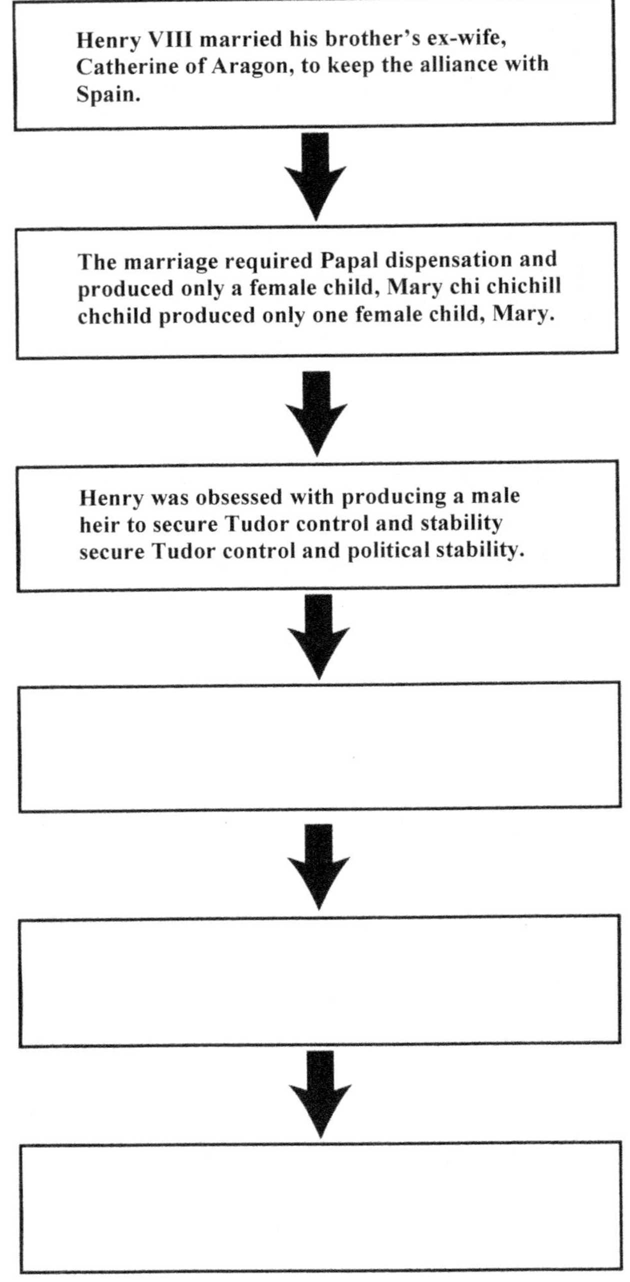

Using the information in your flowchart, write a brief answer to the Focus Question

Outline

Read the section topic entitled "The Reformation Parliament" and create an outline of the section below. Note the key words that reflect the main ideas in each paragraph as well as the key words that inform those ideas.

I. The "Reformation Parliament"

   A. Bringing clergy under English, not papal, jurisdiction

      1.

      2.

      3.

      4.

   B.

      1.

      2.

      3.

      4.

      5.

      6.

Review Questions

Write a brief answer to the following questions. Remember, each answer should highlight a primary idea using key words and supporting details.

1. Why did Henry VIII break with Rome? Was the "new" church he established really Protestant?

2. How did the English church change under his successors?

SECTION 6 CATHOLIC REFORM AND COUNTER-REFORMATION

FOCUS QUESTION

What was the Counter-Reformation and how successful was it?

Characteristics	Successes	Failures

Using the information in your table, write a brief answer to the Focus Question.

Outline

Read the section topic entitled "Ignatius Loyola and the Jesuits" and create an outline of the section below. Note the key words that reflect the main ideas in each paragraph as well as the key words that inform those ideas.

I. Ignatius Loyola and the Jesuits

A. Society of Jesus, new order of Jesuits

1.

2.

3.

B.

1.

2.

3.

4.

C.

1.

2.

D.

1.

2.

3.

4.

REVIEW QUESTIONS

Write a brief answer to the following questions. Remember, each answer should highlight a primary idea using key words and supporting details.

1. What was the Catholic Counter-Reformation?

2. What reforms did the Council of Trent introduce?

3. Was the Protestant Reformation healthy for the Catholic Church?

SECTION 7 THE SOCIAL SIGNIFICANCE OF THE REFORMATION IN WESTERN EUROPE

FOCUS QUESTION

What was the social significance of the Reformation and how did it affect family life?

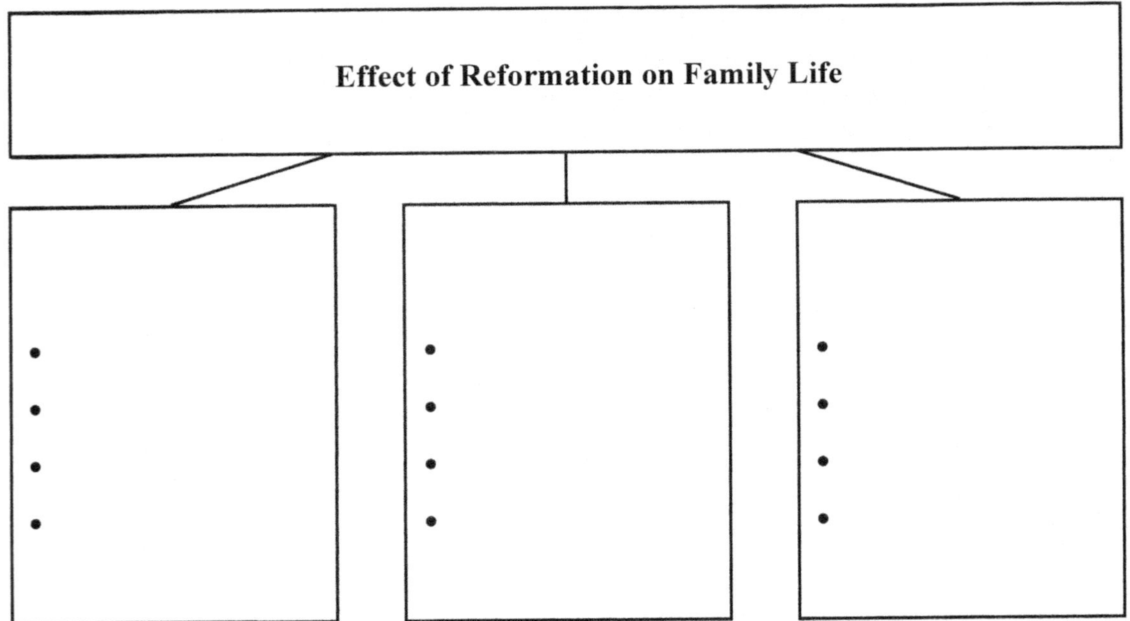

Using the information in your flowchart, write a brief answer to the Focus Question.

OUTLINE

Read the section topic entitled "The Revolution in Religious Practices and Institutions" and create an outline of the section below. Note the key words that reflect the main ideas in each paragraph as well as the key words that inform those ideas.

I. The Revolution in Religious Practices and Institutions
   A. Fifteenth-century church: presence and role of church leaders
      1.
      2.
   B.
      1.
      2.
   C.
      1.
      2.
      3.
      4.
      5.
      6.
      7.
      8.
      9.
   D.
      1.
      2.
   E.
   F.
      1.
      2.
      3.
      4.

REVIEW QUESTIONS

Write a brief answer to the following questions. Remember, each answer should highlight a primary idea using key words and supporting details.

1. How did the Reformation affect women in the sixteenth and seventeenth centuries?

2. What was the connection between the Protestant Reformation, Humanism, and educational reform in the early sixteenth century?

SECTION 8 FAMILY LIFE IN EARLY MODERN EUROPE

FOCUS QUESTION

What was family life like in early modern Europe?

Early Modern Family Life	
Factors	**Results and Conditions**
• Later Marriages	

Using the information in your table, write a brief answer to the Focus Question.

Outline

Read the section topic entitled "Wet Nursing" and create an outline of the section below. Note the key words that reflect the main ideas in each paragraph as well as the key words that inform those ideas.

I. Wet Nursing

    A. Condemned by church and physicians

        1.

        2.

        3.

        4.

    B.

        1.

        2.

        3.

    C.

        1.

        2.

        3.

Review Questions

Write a brief answer to the following questions. Remember, each answer should highlight a primary idea using key words and supporting details.

1. How did relations between men and women, family size, and child care change during the sixteenth century?

2. What were some of the key considerations involved in accepting a marriage proposal during the sixteenth century?

SECTION 9 LITERARY IMAGINATION IN TRANSITION

FOCUS QUESTION

How was the transition from medieval to modern reflected in the works of the great literary figures of the era?

Literary Transition to Modernity		
Authors	**Medieval Characteristics**	**Modern Characteristics**
Cervantes		
Shakespeare		

Using the information in your table, write a brief answer to the Focus Question.

Outline

Read the section topic entitled "Miguel de Cervantes Saavedra: Rejection of Idealism" and create an outline of the section below. Note the key words that reflect the main ideas in each paragraph as well as the key words that inform those ideas.

I. Miguel de Cervantes Saavedra: Rejection of Idealisms
   A. Influence of Catholic Church on Spanish literature
      1.
      2.
      3.
   B.
      1.
      2.
   C.
      1.
      2.
      3.
   D.
      1.
      2.
   E.
      1.
      2
      3.
      4.
      5.

Review Questions

Write a brief answer to the following questions. Remember, each answer should highlight a primary idea using key words and supporting details.

1. In what way can Cervantes' Don Quixote be characterized as satire? How not?

2. What aspects of Shakespeare's dramas represent a clear departure from the medieval mindset?

Review: Key Terms and People

Complete your review of the chapter by writing a brief definition of the following terms and people.

Reformation
Modern Devotion
Indulgence
Benifice
Martin Luther
Ninety-five theses
Charles V
Frederick the Wise
Diet of Worms
Canton
Anabaptist
Antitrinitarian
Predestination
Calvinism
Magdeburg
Peace of Augsburg
William Tyndale
Henry VIII
Anne Boleyn
Act of Supremacy
Six Articles
Act of Uniformity
Counter-Reformation
Jesuit
Council of Trent
Genevan Academy
Apprentice
Miguel de Cervantes Saavedra
William Shakespeare
Christopher Marlowe
Tragedy

My Key Terms

Write down terms that are unfamiliar. How are the words used? Do other words or examples reveal their meaning? Try to figure out meaning from the context.

CHAPTER 4
THE AGE OF RELIGIOUS WARS

Complete the following exercises *as you read* this chapter.

SECTION 1 RENEWED RELIGIOUS STRUGGLE

FOCUS QUESTION

How did religious conflict in Europe evolve over the course of the second half of the sixteenth century?

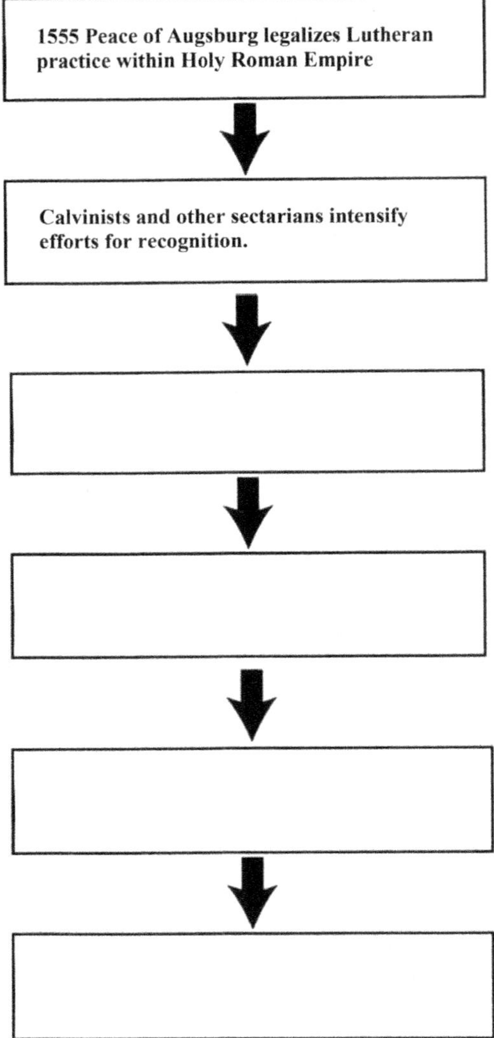

Using the information in your flowchart, write a brief answer to the Focus Question.

OUTLINE

Read the section topic entitled "Renewed Religious Struggle" and create an outline of the section below. Note the key words that reflect the main ideas in each paragraph as well as the key words that inform those ideas.

I. Renewed Religious Struggle
   A. Struggle for recognition of non-Lutheran Protestants
   B.
   C.
   D.
      1.
      2.
   E.
      1.
      2.
      3.
   F.
      1.
      2.
   G.
      1.
      2.

REVIEW QUESTIONS

Write a brief answer to the following questions. Remember, each answer should highlight a primary idea using key words and supporting details.

1. In what way did the Peace of Augsburg precipitate the religious strife and civil wars of the last half of the sixteenth century?

2. How did art and architecture exemplify the political and religious struggles of the last half of the sixteenth century?

Section 2 The French Wars of Religion (1562–1598)

Focus Question

What caused the civil war between the Huguenots and the Catholics in France and what was the outcome?

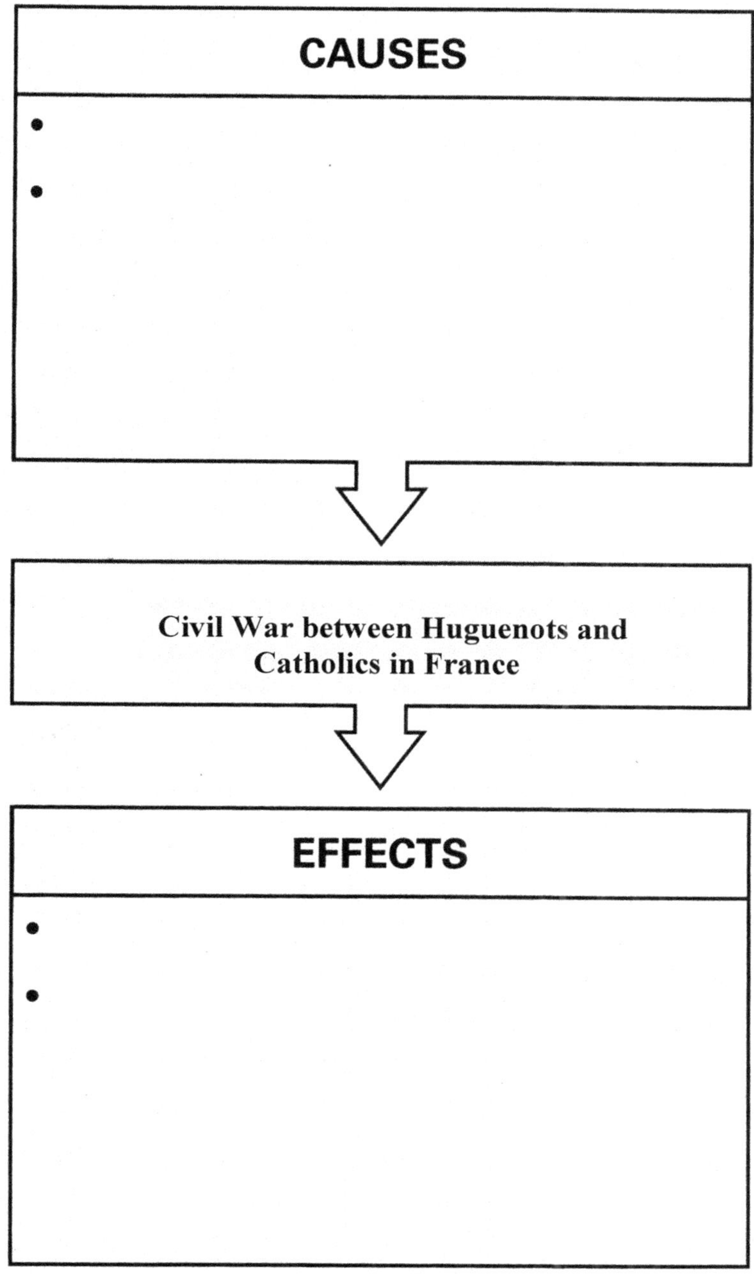

Using the information in your chart, write a brief answer to the Focus Question.

OUTLINE

Read the section topic entitled "Appeal of Calvinism" and create an outline of the section below. Note the key words that reflect the main ideas in each paragraph as well as the key words that inform those ideas.

I. Appeal of Calvinism (French Huguenots)
   A. Opposition to Guise-dominated French monarchy
      1.
      2.
      3.
      4.
   B.
      1.
      2.
   C.
      1.
      2.
      3.

Review Questions

Write a brief answer to the following questions. Remember, each answer should highlight a primary idea using key words and supporting details.

1. How did politics shape the religious positions of the French leaders?

2. What led to the Saint Bartholomew's Day Massacre and what did it achieve?

SECTION 3 IMPERIAL SPAIN AND PHILIP II (1556–1598)

FOCUS QUESTION

How was Philip II able to dominate politics for much of the latter half of the sixteenth century?

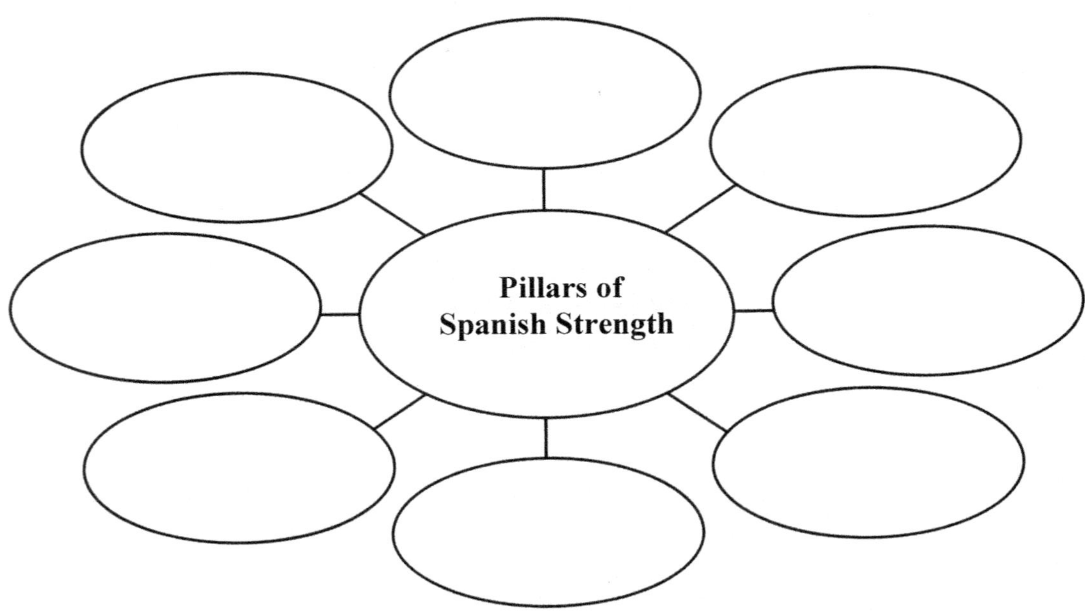

Using the information in your concept web, write a brief answer to the Focus Question.

Outline

Read the section topic entitled "The Revolt in the Netherlands" and create an outline of the section below. Note the key words that reflect the main ideas in each paragraph as well as the key words that inform those ideas.

I. The Revolt in the Netherlands
  A. Philip II wished to impose his authority on the Netherlands
    1.
    2.
  B.
    1.
    2.
  C.
    1.
    2.
  D.
  E.
    1.
    2.
  F.
    1.
    2.
    3.
    4.
    5.
  G.
    1.
    2.
    3.
    4.
    5.
  H.
    1.
    2.

READING SKILL: SUMMARIZE

Complete the chart below identifying supporting details related to the "Pacification of Ghent" and the "Union of Utrecht."

Pacification of Ghent	**Union of Utrecht**
• • • •	• • • •

Review Questions

Write a brief answer to the following questions. Remember, each answer should highlight a primary idea using key words and supporting details.

1. How did Spain gain a position of dominance in the sixteenth century?

2. What were Philip II's successes and failures?

Section 4 England and Spain (1553–1603)

Focus Question

What role did Catholic and Protestant extremism play in the struggle for supremacy between England and Spain?

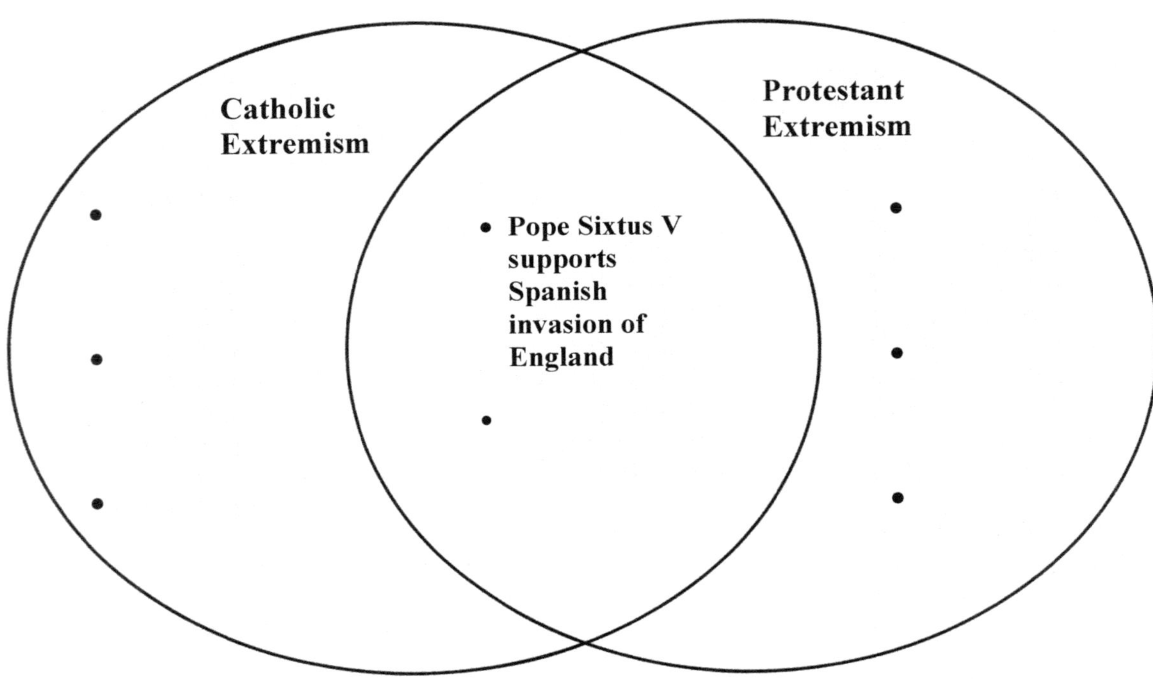

Using the information in your Venn diagram, write a brief answer to the Focus Question.

Review Questions

Write a brief answer to the following questions. Remember, each answer should highlight a primary idea using key words and supporting details.

1. What led to the establishment of the Anglican Church in England?

2. Why did Mary I fail?

3. What was Elizabeth I's settlement, and why was it difficult to impose on England? Who were her detractors and what were their criticisms?

Section 5 The Thirty Years' War (1618–1648)

Focus Question

What toll did the Thirty Years' War take on Germany?

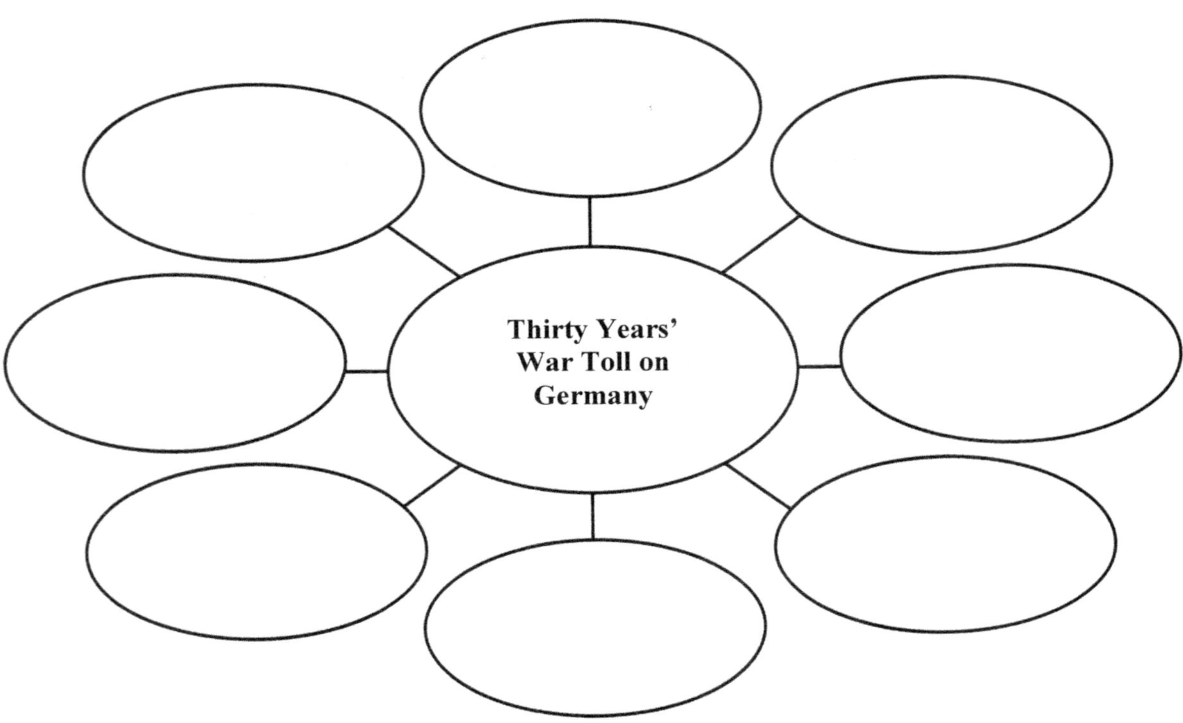

Using the information in your concept web, write a brief answer to the Focus Question.

OUTLINE

Read the section topic entitled "Preconditions for War" and create an outline of the section below. Note the key words that reflect the main ideas in each paragraph as well as the key words that inform those ideas.

I. Preconditions for War

   A. Fragmented Germany

      1.

      2.

      3.

   B.

      1.

      2.

      3.

      4.

      5.

   C.

      1.

      2.

      3.

      4.

   D.

      1.

      2.

Review Questions

Write a brief answer to the following questions. Remember, each answer should highlight a primary idea using key words and supporting details.

1. Why was the Thirty Years' War fought?

2. Was politics or religion more important in determining the outcome of the war?

3. What were the main terms of the Treaty of Westphalia in 1648?

4. Why has the Thirty Years' War been called the outstanding example in European history of meaningless conflict? Is this true? Were the results worth the cost of the war?

REVIEW: KEY TERMS AND PEOPLE

Complete your review of the chapter by writing a brief definition of the following terms and people.

Counter-Reformation
Presbyter
Baroque
Politiques
Huguenots
Catherine de Médicis
Saint Bartholomew's Day Massacre
Protestant Resistance Theory
Henry of Navarre
Edict of Nantes
Philip II
Bullion
William of Nassau the Prince of Orange
Spanish Fury
Pacification of Ghent
Union of Arras
Union of Utrecht
Mary I
Elizabeth I
Thirty-Nine Articles
Presbyterians
Congregationalists
Mary Queen of Scots
Armada
Palatinate
Edict of Restitution
Gustavus Adolphus II
Peace of Prague
Treaty of Westphalia

MY KEY TERMS

Write down terms that are unfamiliar. How are the words used? Do other words or examples reveal their meaning? Try to figure out meaning from the context.

CHAPTER 5
EUROPEAN STATE CONSOLIDATION IN THE SEVENTEENTH AND EIGHTEENTH CENTURIES

Complete the following exercises *as you read* this chapter.

SECTION 1 THE NETHERLANDS: GOLDEN AGE TO DECLINE

FOCUS QUESTION

What was the Dutch Golden Age and what led to its decline?

Social and Political Organization

-
-
-
-

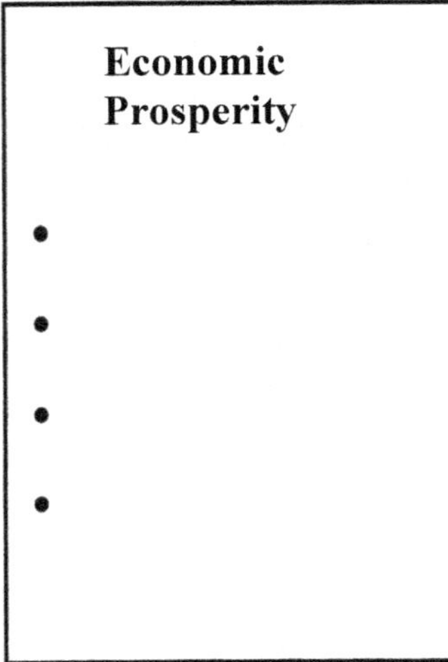

Using the information in your flowchart, write a brief answer to the Focus Question.

Outline

Read the section topic entitled "Urban Prosperity" and create an outline of the section below. Note the key words that reflect the main ideas in each paragraph as well as the key words that inform those ideas.

I. Urban Prosperity
    A. High urban consolidation
        1.
        2.
    B.
        1.
        2.
        3.
    C.
        1.
        2.
        3.
        4.
        5.
    D.
        1.
        2.

REVIEW QUESTIONS

Write a brief answer to the following questions. Remember, each answer should highlight a primary idea using key words and supporting details.

1. What were the sources of Dutch prosperity, and why did the Netherlands decline in the eighteenth century?

2. In what way was Dutch political organization connected to Dutch prosperity?

SECTION 2 TWO MODELS OF EUROPEAN DEVELOPMENT

FOCUS QUESTION

What factors led to the different political paths taken by England and France in the seventeenth century?

Cost of Warfare	Source of Revenue
•	•
•	•
•	•

Using the information in your concept web, write a brief answer to the Focus Question.

Outline

Read the section topic entitled "Two Models of European Development" and create an outline of the section below. Note the key words that reflect the main ideas in each paragraph as well as the key words that inform those ideas.

I. Two Models of European Development
   A. Underlying political forces
      1.
      2.
   B.
      1.
      2.
   C.
      1.
      2.
   D.
      1.
      2.

READING SKILL: SUMMARIZE

Complete the chart below defining the difference between a republic, a parliamentary monarchy, and political absolutism.

Seventeenth Century European Models of Government		
Republic	**Parliamentary monarchy**	**Political absolutism**
•	•	•
•	•	•
•	•	•

REVIEW QUESTIONS

Write a brief answer to the following questions. Remember, each answer should highlight a primary idea using key words and supporting details.

1. Why did England and France develop different systems of government and religious policies?

2. Why were military expenditures at the root of these divergent histories?

Section 3 Constitutional Crisis and Settlement in Stuart England

Focus Question

How did conflicts over taxation and religion lead to civil war in Stuart England?

Conflicts Leading to Civil War	
Conflicts over Taxation	**Conflicts over Religion**

Using the information in your chart, write a brief answer to the Focus Question.

Outline

Read the section topic entitled "Charles I" and create an outline of the section below. Note the key words that reflect the main ideas in each paragraph as well as the key words that inform those ideas.

I. Charles I

   A. Charles' extra-parliamentary measures to fund war with Spain

      1.

      2.

      3.

      4.

   B.

      1.

      2.

      3.

      4.

   C.

      1.

      2.

      3.

      4.

   D.

      1.

      2.

   E.

      1.

      2.

      3.

   F.

      1.

      2.

REVIEW QUESTIONS

Write a brief answer to the following questions. Remember, each answer should highlight a primary idea using key words and supporting details.

1. Why did the king and Parliament quarrel in the 1640s? What were the most important issues behind the war between them, and who bore more responsibility for it?

2. What was the Glorious Revolution and why did it take place?

3. What role did religion play in seventeenth century English politics?

4. Do you think the victory of Parliament over the monarchy in England was inevitable?

SECTION 4 RISE OF ABSOLUTE MONARCHY IN FRANCE: THE WORLD OF LOUIS XIV

FOCUS QUESTION

Why were efforts to establish absolute monarchy successful in France but unsuccessful in England?

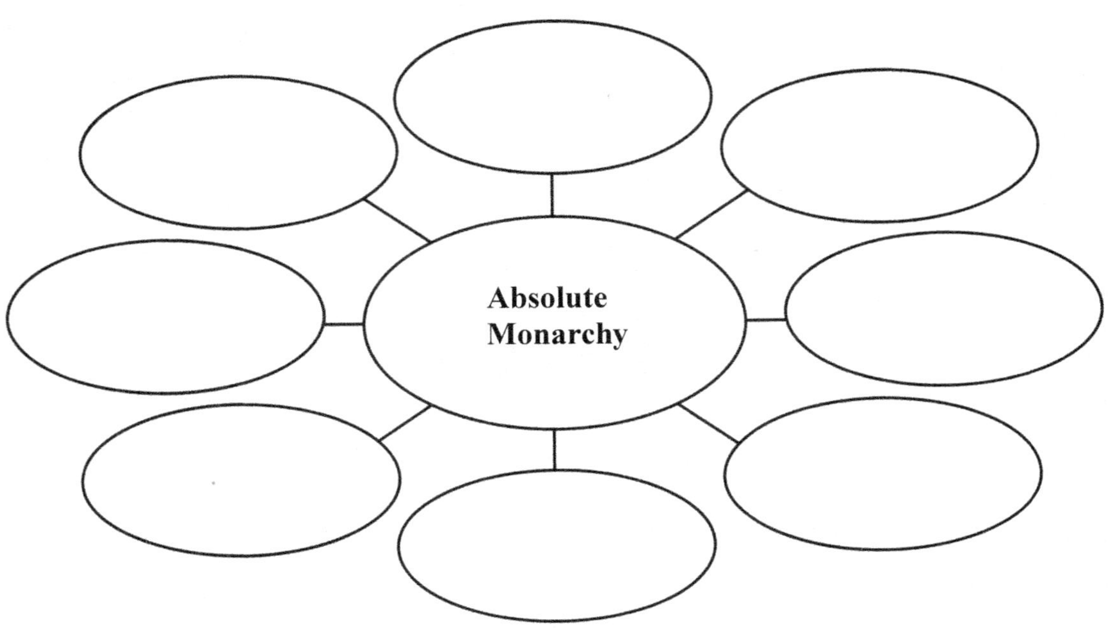

Using the information in your concept web, write a brief answer to the Focus Question.

OUTLINE

Read the section topic entitled "Versailles" and create an outline of the section below. Note the key words that reflect the main ideas in each paragraph as well as the key words that inform those ideas.

I. Versailles
   A. Louis XIV: master of propaganda
      1.
      2.
      3.
   B.
      1.
      2.
      3.
      4.
   C.
      1.
      2.
      3.
   D.

Review Questions

Write a brief answer to the following questions. Remember, each answer should highlight a primary idea using key words and supporting details.

1. Why did France become an absolute monarchy?

2. How did Louis XIV consolidate his monarchy? How did he use ceremony and his royal court to strengthen his authority? What limits were there on his authority?

3. What was Louis's religious policy?

4. What were the goals of his foreign policy?

5. What features of French government might Europeans outside of France have feared?

SECTION 5 CENTRAL AND EASTERN EUROPE

FOCUS QUESTION

What were the main characteristics that defined Polish, Austrian, and Prussian states in the seventeenth and eighteenth centuries?

Poland	**Austria**	**Prussia**
•	•	•
•	•	•
•	•	•
•	•	•

Using the information in your table, write a brief answer to the Focus Question.

OUTLINE

Read the section topic entitled "The Habsburg Empire and the Pragmatic Sanction" and create an outline of the section below. Note the key words that reflect the main ideas in each paragraph as well as the key words that inform those ideas.

I. The Habsburg Empire and the Pragmatic Sanction

   A. Habsburg Holy Roman Empire

      1.

      2.

      3.

      4.

      5.

      6.

   B.

      1.

      2.

      3.

      4.

   C.

      1.

      2.

   D.

      1.

      2.

   E.

      1.

      2.

      3.

Review Questions

Write a brief answer to the following questions. Remember, each answer should highlight a primary idea using key words and supporting details.

1. How were the Hohenzollerns able to forge their diverse landholdings into the state of Prussia?

2. Who were the major figures involved in this process and what were their individual contributions?

3. Why was the military so important in Prussia?

4. What major problems did the Habsburgs face, and how did they seek to resolve them?

5. Which family—the Hohenzollerns or the Habsburgs—was more successful and why?

SECTION 6 RUSSIA ENTERS THE EUROPEAN POLITICAL ARENA

FOCUS QUESTION

How did Peter the Great transform Russia into a powerful, centralized nation?

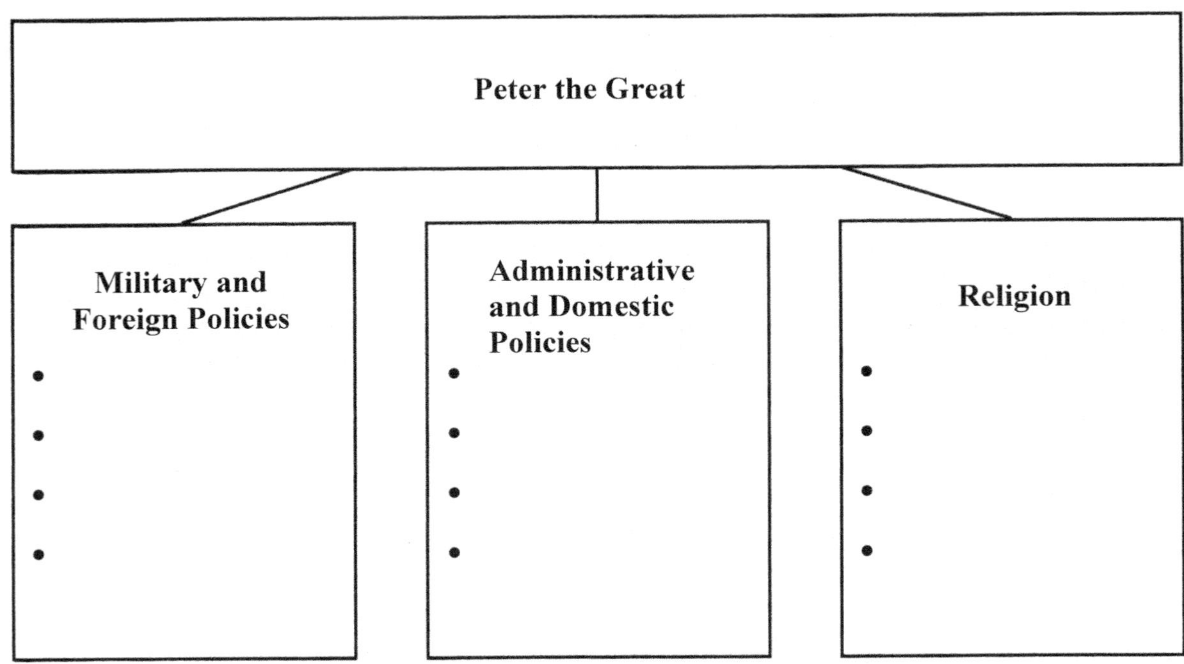

Using the information in your table, write a brief answer to the Focus Question.

OUTLINE

Read the section topic entitled "Russian Expansion in the Baltic: The Great Northern War" and create an outline of the section below. Note the key words that reflect the main ideas in each paragraph as well as the key words that inform those ideas.

I. Russian Expansion in the Baltic: The Great Northern War
   A. 1648 Sweden consolidates control of the Baltic
      1.
      2.
      3.
      4.
   B.
      1.
      2.
      3.
      4.
      5.
      6.
   C.
      1.
      2.

Review Questions

Write a brief answer to the following questions. Remember, each answer should highlight a primary idea using key words and supporting details.

1. How and why did Russia emerge as a great power but Poland did not?

2. How were Peter the Great's domestic reforms related to his military ambitions?

3. What were his methods of reform?

4. How did family conflict affect his later policies?

5. Was Peter a successful ruler? In what respects might one regard Peter as an imitator of Louis XIV?

REVIEW: KEY TERMS AND PEOPLE

Complete your review of the chapter by writing a brief definition of the following terms and people.

William III of Orange
Dutch East India Company
Parliamentary Monarchy
Political Absolutism
Divine Right of Kings
James I
Puritans
Charles I
Long Parliament
Oliver Cromwell
Restoration
Test Act
Glorious Revolution
Robert Walpole
Louis XIV
Parliaments
Triple Alliance
Jansenism
War of the Spanish Succession
Holy Roman Empire
Charles VI
Frederick William I
Streltsy
Peter the Great
Boyars
Table of Ranks
Holy synod

MY KEY TERMS

Write down terms that are unfamiliar. How are the words used? Do other words or examples reveal their meaning? Try to figure out meaning from the context.

CHAPTER 6
NEW DIRECTIONS IN THOUGHT AND CULTURE IN THE SIXTEENTH AND SEVENTEENTH CENTURIES

Complete the following exercises *as you read* this chapter.

SECTION 1 THE SCIENTIFIC REVOLUTION

FOCUS QUESTION

What was the scientific revolution?

Ideas of the Scientific Revolution	
Copernicus	
Brahe	
Kepler	
Galileo	
Newton	

Using the information in your chart, write a brief answer to the Focus Question.

OUTLINE

Read the section topic entitled "Nicolaus Copernicus Rejects an Earth-Centered Universe" and create an outline of the section below. Note the key words that reflect the main ideas in each paragraph as well as the key words that inform those ideas.

I. Nicolaus Copernicus Rejects an Earth-Centered Universe
   A. Copernicus
      1.
      2.
      3.
      4.
   B.
      1.
      2.
      3.
      4.
   C.
      1.
      2.
      3.
   D.
      1.
      2.
      3.
      4.
   E.
      1.
      2.
      3.

Review Questions

Write a brief answer to the following questions. Remember, each answer should highlight a primary idea using key words and supporting details.

1. How would you define the term *scientific revolution*? In what ways was it truly revolutionary?

2. Which is more enduring, a political revolution or an intellectual one?

3. What did Copernicus, Brahe, Kepler, Galileo, and Newton each contribute to the scientific revolution? Who do you think made the most important contributions and why?

SECTION 2 PHILOSOPHY RESPONDS TO CHANGING SCIENCE

FOCUS QUESTION

What impact did the new science have on philosophy?

New Science

1.

2.

3.

Philosophy

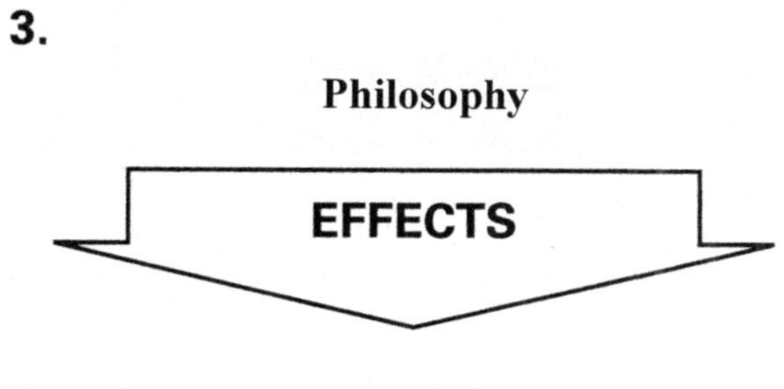

1.

2.

3.

Using the information in your chart, write a brief answer to the Focus Question.

OUTLINE

Read the section topic entitled "Nature as Mechanism" and create an outline of the section below. Note the key words that reflect the main ideas in each paragraph as well as the key words that inform those ideas.

I. Nature as Mechanism
   A. Shared Philosophical Outlook
      1.
      2.
      3.
      4.
   B.
      1.
      2.
   C.
      1.
      2.
      3.
      4.

READING SKILL: SUMMARIZE

Complete the chart below identifying the similarities and differences between the ideas of Thomas Hobbes and John Locke.

Thomas Hobbes	**John Locke**
•	•
•	•
•	•
•	•

Review Questions

Write a brief answer to the following questions. Remember, each answer should highlight a primary idea using key words and supporting details.

1. What were the differences between the political philosophies of Thomas Hobbes and John Locke? How did each view human nature?

2. Would you rather live under a government designed by Hobbes or by Locke? Why?

Section 3 The New Institutions of Expanding Knowledge

Focus Question

What were the social and political contexts for scientific inquiry in the seventeenth century?

Seventeenth Century Scientific Inquiry	
Social Context	**Political Context**

Using the information in your chart, write a brief answer to the Focus Question.

OUTLINE

Read the section topic entitled "The New Institutions of Expanding Natural Knowledge" and create an outline of the section below. Note the key words that reflect the main ideas in each paragraph as well as the key words that inform those ideas.

I. The New Institutions of Expanding Natural Knowledge
   A. Contrasting contemporary scholarship
      1.
      2.
      3.
   B.
      1.
      2.
      3.
   C.
      1.
      2.
      3.
      4.
   D.
      1.
      2.
      3.
   E.
      1.
      2.
      3.
      4.
   F.
      1.
      2.
   G.
      1.
      2.

Review Questions

Write a brief answer to the following questions. Remember, each answer should highlight a primary idea using key words and supporting details.

1 What made the knowledge amassed during the Scientific Revolution genuinely new?

2. What role did universities play in the Scientific Revolution?

SECTION 4 WOMEN IN THE WORLD OF THE SCIENTIFIC REVOLUTION

FOCUS QUESTION

What role did women play in the scientific revolution?

Women of the Scientific Revolution	
Queen Christina	
Margaret Cavendish	
Maria Cunitz	
Elisabetha Hevelius	
Maria Winkelmann	
Emilie du Châtelet	

Using the information in your table, write a brief answer to the Focus Question.

OUTLINE

Read the section topic entitled "Women in the World of the Scientific Revolution" and create an outline of the section below. Note the key words that reflect the main ideas in each paragraph as well as the key words that inform those ideas.

I. Women in the World of the Scientific Revolution

A. Monasteries, universities associated with celibate male clerical culture

1.

2.

3.

B.

1.

2.

3.

C.

1.

2.

3.

4.

D.

1.

2.

3.

E.

1.

2.

Review Questions

Write a brief answer to the following questions. Remember, each answer should highlight a primary idea using key words and supporting details.

1. Why were women unable to participate fully in the new science?

2. How did family relationships help some women become involved in the advance of natural philosophy?

SECTION 5 THE NEW SCIENCE AND RELIGIOUS FAITH

FOCUS QUESTION

What efforts were made to reconcile the new science and religion?

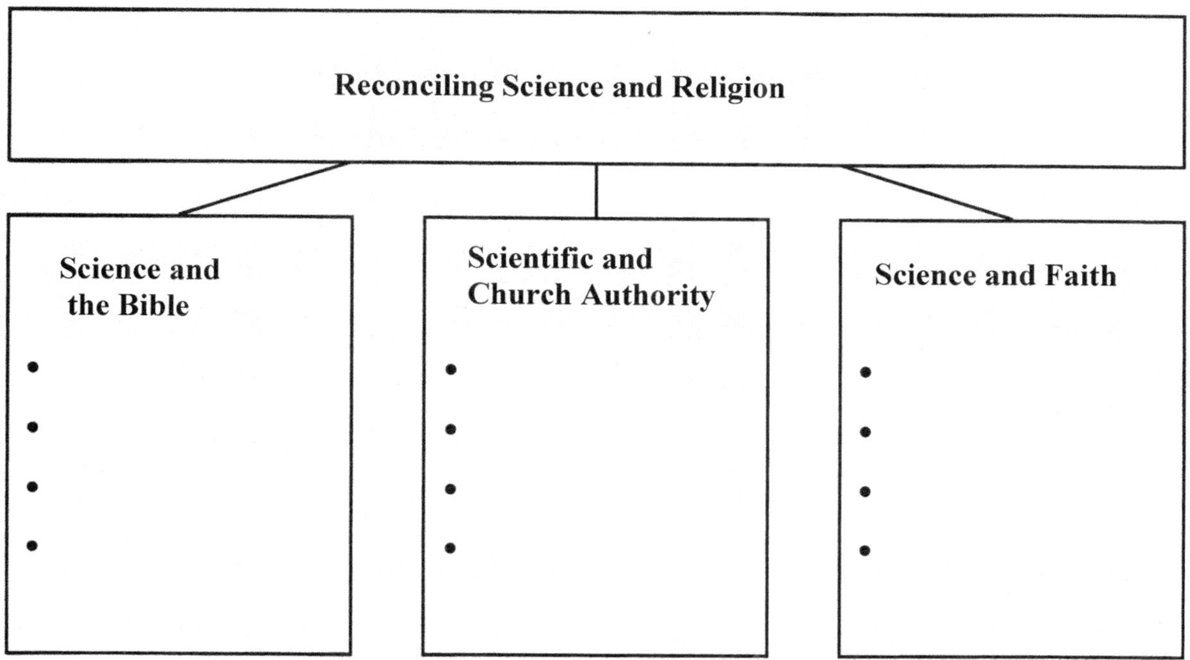

Using the information in your table, write a brief answer to the Focus Question.

OUTLINE

Read the section topic entitled "Blaise Pascal: Reason and Faith" and create an outline of the section below. Note the key words that reflect the main ideas in each paragraph as well as the key words that inform those ideas.

I. Blaise Pascal: Reason and Faith
   A. *Pensées*
      1.
      2.
      3.
   B.
      1.
      2.
      3.
      4.
      5.
   C.
      1.
      2.
   D.
      1.
      2.
      3.

Review Questions

Write a brief answer to the following questions. Remember, each answer should highlight a primary idea using key words and supporting details.

1. Why did the Catholic Church condemn Galileo?

2. How did Pascal seek to reconcile faith and reason?

3. How did English natural theology support economic expansion?

Section 6 Continuing Superstition

Focus Question

What explains the witch hunts and panics of the sixteenth and seventeenth centuries?

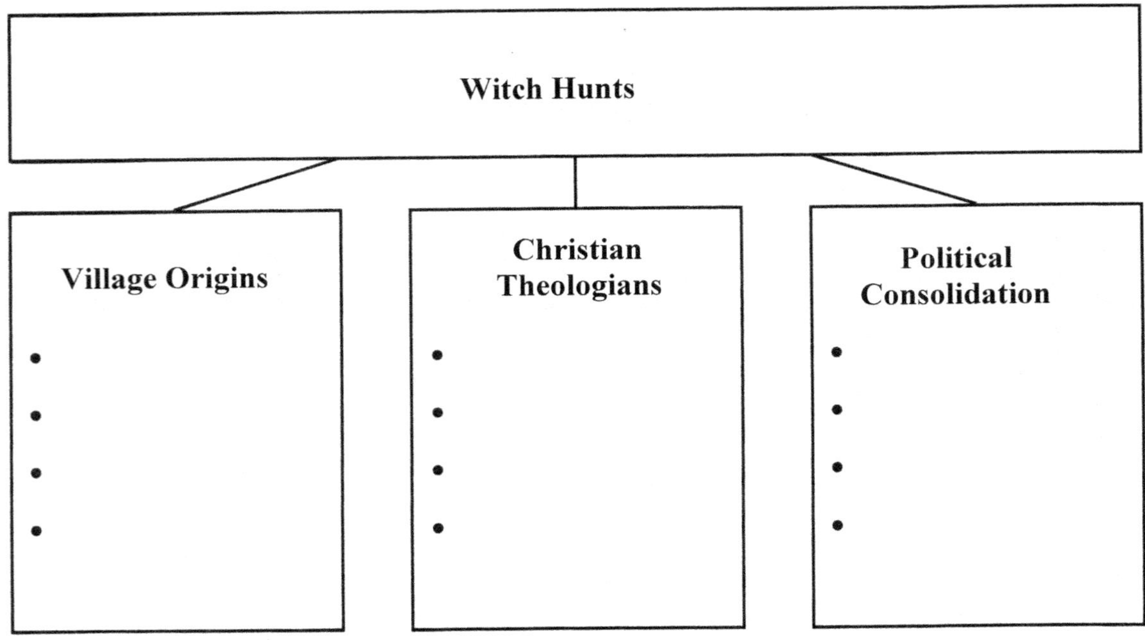

Using the information in your flowchart, write a brief answer to the Focus Question.

OUTLINE

Read the section topic entitled "Village Origins" and create an outline of the section below. Note the key words that reflect the main ideas in each paragraph as well as the key words that inform those ideas.

I. Village Origins

   A. "Cunning folk"

      1.

      2.

      3.

      4.

   B.

      1.

      2.

      3.

Review Questions

Write a brief answer to the following questions. Remember, each answer should highlight a primary idea using key words and supporting details.

1. How do you explain the phenomena of witchcraft and witch hunts in an age of scientific enlightenment?

2. Why did witch panics occur in the late sixteenth and early seventeenth centuries?

3. How might the Reformation have contributed to them?

Section 7 Baroque Art

Focus Question

How did Baroque art serve both religious and secular ends?

Baroque Art	
Religious Ends	**Secular Ends**

Using the information in your chart, write a brief answer to the Focus Question.

OUTLINE

Read the section topic entitled "Baroque Art" and create an outline of the section below. Note the key words that reflect the main ideas in each paragraph as well as the key words that inform those ideas.

I. Baroque Art
   A. Baroque
      1.
      2.
      3.
      4.
      5.
      6.
   B.
      1.
      2.
      3.
   C.
      1.
      2.
      3.
      4.
   D.
      1.
      2.
      3.
      4.
      5.

Review Questions

Write a brief answer to the following questions. Remember, each answer should highlight a primary idea using key words and supporting details.

1. How and why is the Baroque faithfulness to nature associated with both religious and secular ends?

2. Why did Baroque architecture dominate the capitals of small Germanic principalities and imperial Austria alike?

Review: Key Terms and People

Complete your review of the chapter by writing a brief definition of the following terms and people.

Scientific Revolution
Ptolemaic systems
Heliocentric
Epicycle
Empiricism
Mechanism
Francis Bacon
René Descartes
Scientific induction
Thomas Hobbes
John Locke
Royal Society of London
Projectors
Margaret Cavendish
Maria Cunitz
Maria Winkelmann
Emilie du Châtelet
Blaise Pascal
Physico-theology
Maleficium
Sabbats
Cunning folk
Baroque
Naturalism
Gian Lorenzo Bernini
Michelangelo
Caravaggio
Peter Paul Rubens

My Key Terms

Write down terms that are unfamiliar. How are the words used? Do other words or examples reveal their meaning? Try to figure out meaning from the context.

CHAPTER 7
SOCIETY AND ECONOMY UNDER THE OLD REGIME IN THE EIGHTEENTH CENTURY

Complete the following exercises *as you read* this chapter.

SECTION 1 MAJOR FEATURES OF LIFE IN THE OLD REGIME

FOCUS QUESTION

How did tradition, hierarchy, and privilege shape life in the Old Regime?

Tradition	Hierarchy	Privilege
• • •	• • •	• • •

Using the information in your table, write a brief answer to the Focus Question.

OUTLINE

Read the section topic entitled "Maintenance of Tradition" and create an outline of the section below. Note the key words that reflect the main ideas in each paragraph as well as the key words that inform those ideas.

I. Maintenance of Tradition
   A. Eighteenth century nobles
      1.
      2.
      3.
      4.
   B.
      1.
      2.
   C.
      1.
      2.
      3.
   D.

Section 2 The Aristocracy

Focus Question

What was the foundation for the wealth and power of the eighteenth-century aristocracy?

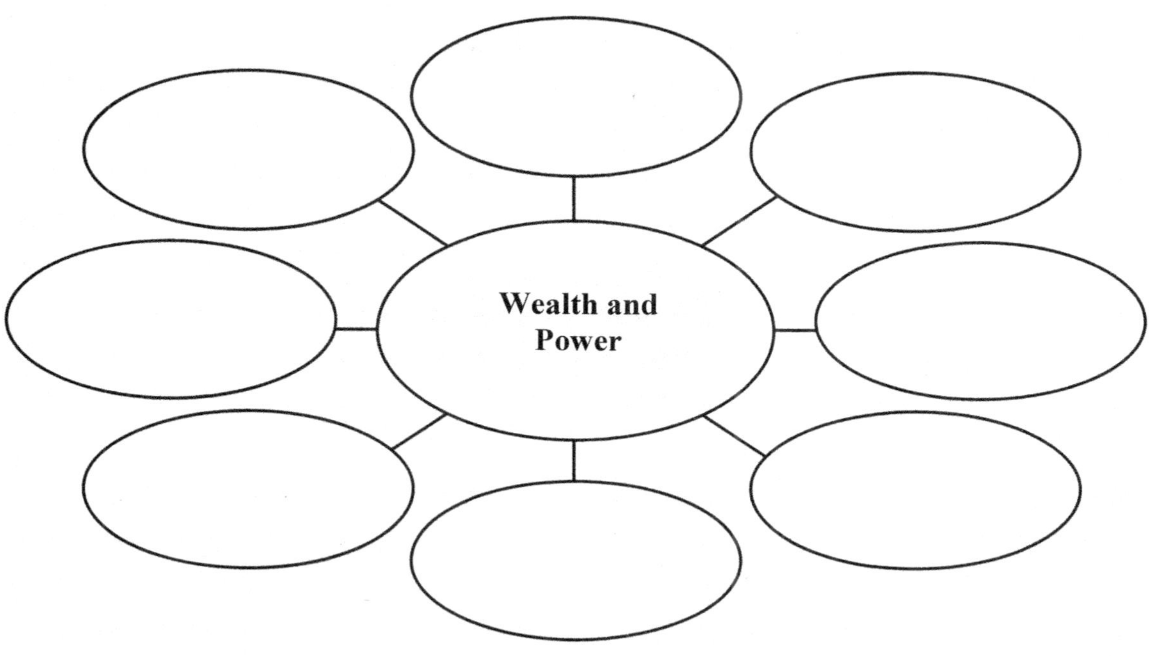

Using the information in your concept web, write a brief answer to the Focus Question.

Outline

Read the section topic entitled "Varieties of Aristocratic Privilege" and create an outline of the section below. Note the key words that reflect the main ideas in each paragraph as well as the key words that inform those ideas.

I. Varieties of Aristocratic Privilege

- A. Who is an Aristocrat?
  1.
  2.
  3.
  4.
- B.
  1.
  2.
  3.
  4.
  5.
- C.
  1.
  2.
  3.
  4.
  5.
     - a.
     - b.
  6.
  7.
- D.
  1.
  2.
  3.
  4.

Review Questions

Write a brief answer to the following questions. Remember, each answer should highlight a primary idea using key words and supporting details.

1. What kinds of privileges separated European aristocrats from other social groups?

2. How did their privileges and influence affect other people living in the countryside?

SECTION 3 THE LAND AND ITS TILLERS

FOCUS QUESTION

How were peasants and serfs tied to the land in eighteenth-century Europe?

Peasants	Serfs
•	•
•	•
•	•

Using the information in your table, write a brief answer to the Focus Question.

OUTLINE

Read the section topic entitled "Peasants and Serfs" and create an outline of the section below. Note the key words that reflect the main ideas in each paragraph as well as the key words that inform those ideas.

I. Peasants and Serfs
   A. Common experience: dependency on nobility
   B.
      1.
      2.
   C.
      1.
         a.
         b.
         c.
      2.
      3.
         a.
         b.
         c.
   D.
      1.
      2.
         a.
         b.

Section 4 Family Structures and the Family Economy

Focus Question

What role did the family play in the economy of preindustrial Europe?

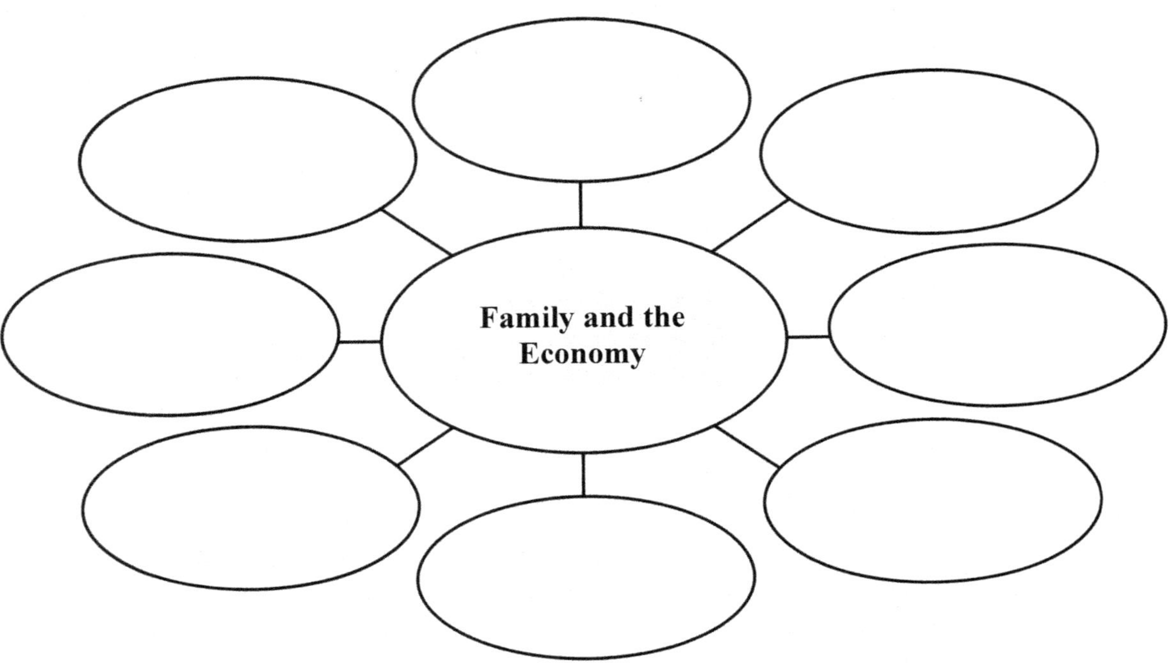

Using the information in your concept web, write a brief answer to the Focus Question.

OUTLINE

Read the section topic entitled "The Family Economy" and create an outline of the section below. Note the key words that reflect the main ideas in each paragraph as well as the key words that inform those ideas.

I. The Family Economy
  A. Household basic unit of production
    1.
    2.
  B.
    1.
    2.
    3.
    4.
  C.
    1.
  D.
  E.
    1.
    2.
    3.
  F.
    1.
    2.
    3.

REVIEW QUESTIONS

Write a brief answer to the following questions. Remember, each answer should highlight a primary idea using key words and supporting details.

1. How would you define the term *family economy*?

2. How did the family economy constrain the lives of women in preindustrial Europe?

SECTION 5 THE REVOLUTION IN AGRICULTURE

FOCUS QUESTION

What led to the agricultural revolution of the eighteenth century?

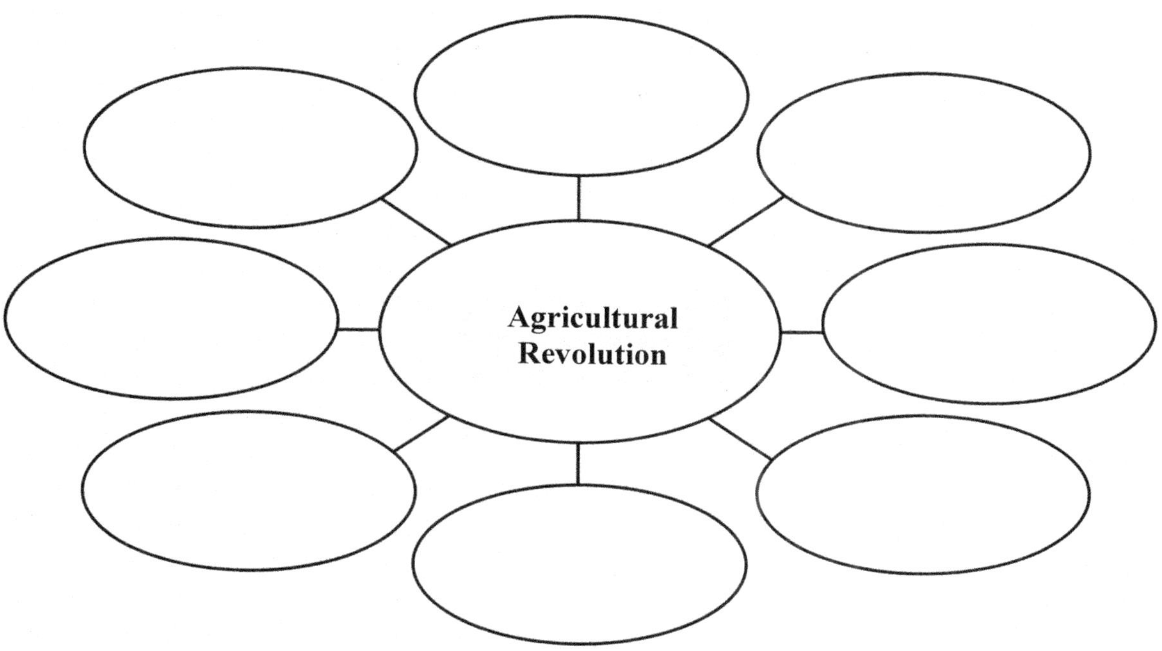

Using the information in your concept web, write a brief answer to the Focus Question.

OUTLINE

Read the section topic entitled "New Crops and New Methods" and create an outline of the section below. Note the key words that reflect the main ideas in each paragraph as well as the key words that inform those ideas.

I. New Crops and New Methods
    A. Early developments during sixteenth and seventeenth centuries
        1.
            a.
            b.
            c.
    B.
    C.
        1.
            a.
            b.
            c.
        2.
            a.
            b.
            c.
        3.
        4.
    D.
        1.
        2.
        3.
    E.
    F.
        1.
        2.

Review Questions

Write a brief answer to the following questions. Remember, each answer should highlight a primary idea using key words and supporting details.

1. What caused the Agricultural Revolution?

2. How did the English aristocracy contribute to the Agricultural Revolution?

3. Why did peasants revolt in the eighteenth century?

4. Why did Europe's population increase in the eighteenth century? How did population growth affect consumption?

SECTION 6 THE INDUSTRIAL REVOLUTION OF THE EIGHTEENTH CENTURY

FOCUS QUESTION

Why did the Industrial Revolution begin in Britain?

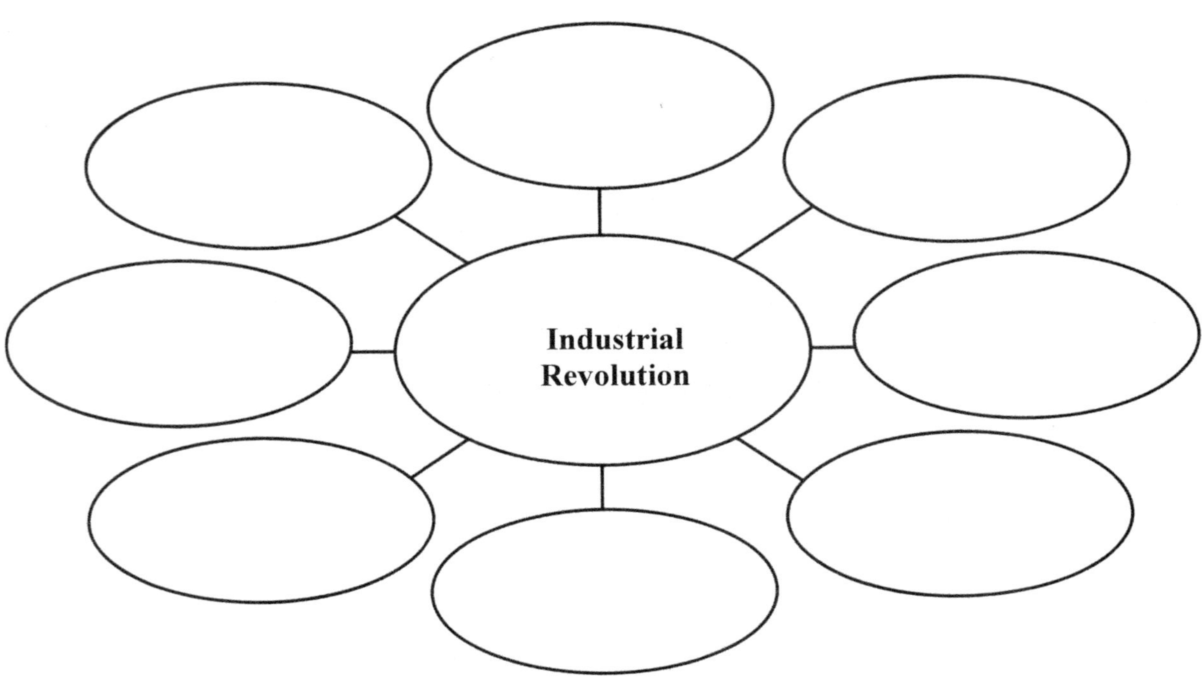

Using the information in your concept web, write a brief answer to the Focus Question.

OUTLINE

Read the section topic entitled "Industrial Leadership of Great Britain" and create an outline of the section below. Note the key words that reflect the main ideas in each paragraph as well as the key words that inform those ideas.

I. Industrial Leadership of Great Britain
   A. Home of the Industrial Revolution
      1.
         a.
         b.
         c.
         d.
         e.
      2.
         a.
         b.
         c.
         d.
         e.
         f.
      3.
         a.
         b.
   B.

READING SKILL: SUMMARIZE

Complete the chart below identifying the key innovations of the Industrial Revolution.

Innovations of the Industrial Revolution
• • •

Review Questions

Write a brief answer to the following questions. Remember, each answer should highlight a primary idea using key words and supporting details.

1. What was the Industrial Revolution and what caused it?

2. Why did Great Britain take the lead in the Industrial Revolution?

3. How did consumers contribute to the Industrial Revolution?

SECTION 7 THE GROWTH OF CITIES

FOCUS QUESTION

What problems arose as the result of the growth of cities?

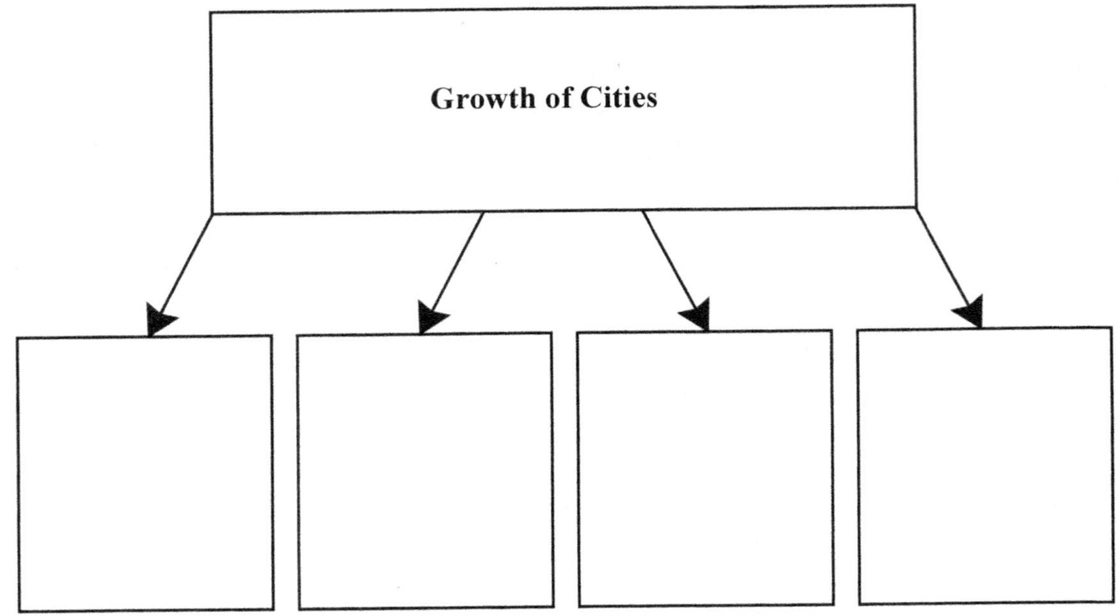

Using the information in your chart, write a brief answer to the Focus Question.

OUTLINE

Read the section topic entitled "Urban Classes" and create an outline of the section below. Note the key words that reflect the main ideas in each paragraph as well as the key words that inform those ideas.

I. Urban Classes
  A. Classes segregated; the impoverished more visible than in rural settings
    1.
    2.
    3.
    4.
  B.
    1.
    2.
    3.
    4.
  C.
    1.
    2.
    3.
    4.
    5.
    6.
  D.
    1.
    2.
    3.
    4.

Review Questions

Write a brief answer to the following questions. Remember, each answer should highlight a primary idea using key words and supporting details.

1. How did the distribution of population in cities and towns change?

2. How did the lifestyle of the upper class compare to that of the middle and lower classes?

3. What were some of the causes of urban riots?

SECTION 8 THE JEWISH POPULATION: THE AGE OF THE GHETTO

FOCUS QUESTION

How did the suppression of Jews in European cities lead to the formation of ghettos?

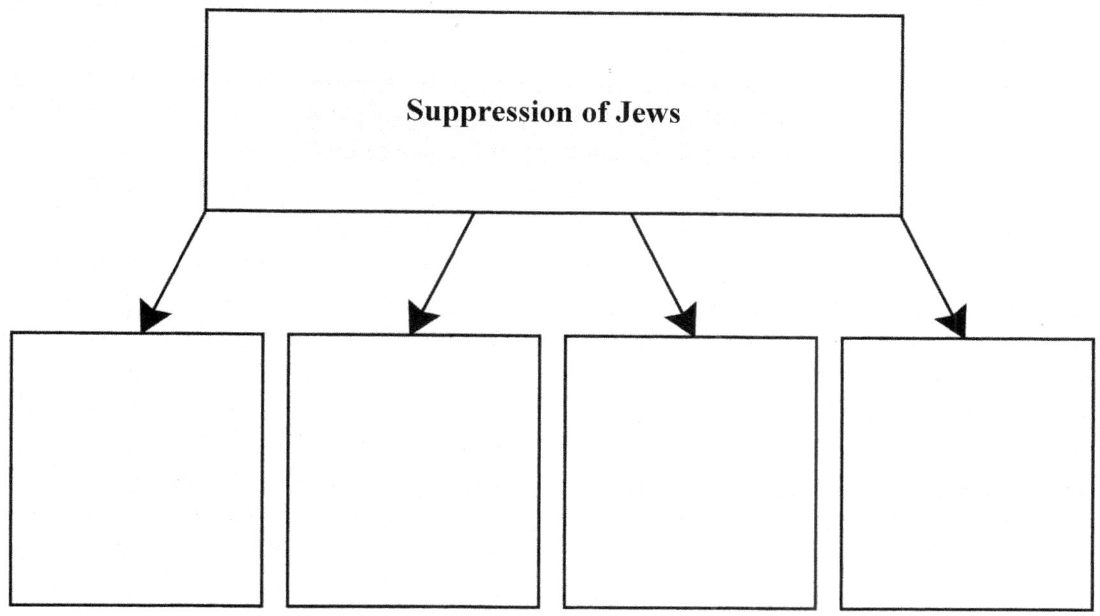

Using the information in your chart, write a brief answer to the Focus Question.

Outline

Read the section topic entitled "The Jewish Population: the Age of the Ghetto" and create an outline of the section below. Note the key words that reflect the main ideas in each paragraph as well as the key words that inform those ideas.

I. The Jewish Population: The Age of the Ghetto
   A. Eighteenth century onwards, Jewish life concentrated in Eastern Europe:
      1.
      2.
   B.
      1.
      2.
   C.
   D.
   E.
   F.
      1.
         a.
         b.
   G.
   H.
      1.
      2.
   I.
      1.
      2.
      3.
      4.
      5.
      6.
      7.

Review Questions

Write a brief answer to the following questions. Remember, each answer should highlight a primary idea using key words and supporting details.

1. Where were the largest Jewish populations in eighteenth-century Europe?

2. What was their social and legal position?

3. What were the sources of prejudices against Jews?

REVIEW: KEY TERMS AND PEOPLE

Complete your review of the chapter by writing a brief definition of the following terms and people.

Old Regime
Customary rights
Sumptuary Laws
Hobereaux
Corvée
Banalities
Barshchina
Pugachev's Rebellion
Family economy
Servants
"Economy of expedients"
Agricultural Revolution
Cornelius Vermuyden
Crop rotation
Industrial Revolution
Consumer revolution
James Watt
Henry Cort
Priscilla Wakefield
Guild
Ghetto
Samuel Oppenheimer

MY KEY TERMS

Write down terms that are unfamiliar. How are the words used? Do other words or examples reveal their meaning? Try to figure out meaning from the context.

Chapter 8
The Transatlantic Economy, Trade Wars, and Colonial Rebellion

Complete the following exercises *as you read* this chapter.

Section 1 Periods of European Overseas Empires

Focus Question

How did European contact with the rest of the world evolve in the centuries since the Renaissance?

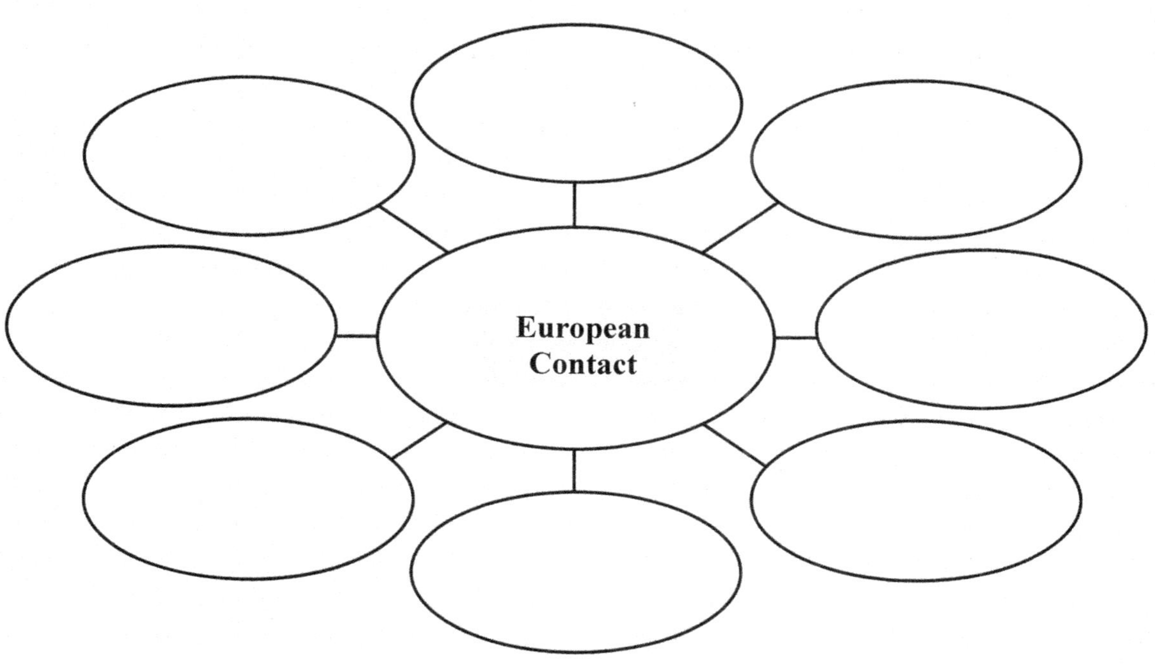

Using the information in your concept web, write a brief answer to the Focus Question.

OUTLINE

Read the section topic entitled "Periods of European Overseas Empires" and create an outline of the section below. Note the key words that reflect the main ideas in each paragraph as well as the key words that inform those ideas.

I. Periods of European Overseas Empires

A. First phase

1.

2.

3.

4.

B.

1.

2.

3.

4.

C.

1.

2.

3.

4.

5.

6.

D.

E.

F.

G.

1.

2.

H.

I.

SECTION 2 MERCANTILE EMPIRES

FOCUS QUESTION

What were the characteristics of European mercantile empires?

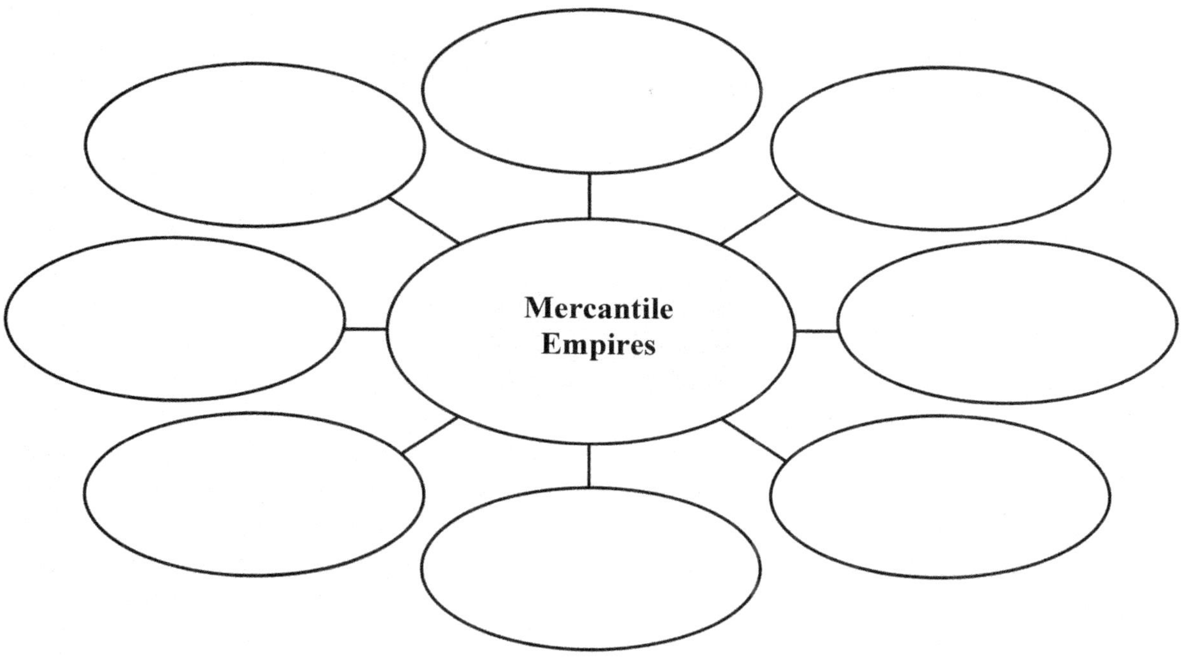

Using the information in your concept web, write a brief answer to the Focus Question.

OUTLINE

Read the section topic entitled "Mercantilist Goals" and create an outline of the section below. Note the key words that reflect the main ideas in each paragraph as well as the key words that inform those ideas.

I. Mercantilist Goals

   A. Mercantilism

      1.

      2.

      3.

      4.

   B.

      1.

      2.

   C.

   D.

      1.

REVIEW QUESTIONS

Write a brief answer to the following questions. Remember, each answer should highlight a primary idea using key words and supporting details.

1. What were the fundamental ideas associated with mercantile theory? Did they work?

2. Which European country was most successful in establishing a mercantile empire? Who was least successful? Why?

3. What were the main points of conflict between Britain and France in North America, the West Indies, and India?

4. How did the triangles of trade function among the Americas, Europe, and Africa?

SECTION 3 THE SPANISH COLONIAL SYSTEM

FOCUS QUESTION

How did the Spanish colonial organization reflect its imperial goals?

Spanish Colonial Organization
• • • •

Using the information in your chart, write a brief answer to the Focus Question.

OUTLINE

Read the section topic entitled "Trade Regulation" and create an outline of the section below. Note the key words that reflect the main ideas in each paragraph as well as the key words that inform those ideas.

I. Trade Regulation
   A. House of Trade
      1.
      2.
      3.
   B.
      1.
      2.
   C.
      1.
      2.
   D.

READING SKILL: SUMMARIZE

Complete the concept web below identifying the colonial reforms of Charles III.

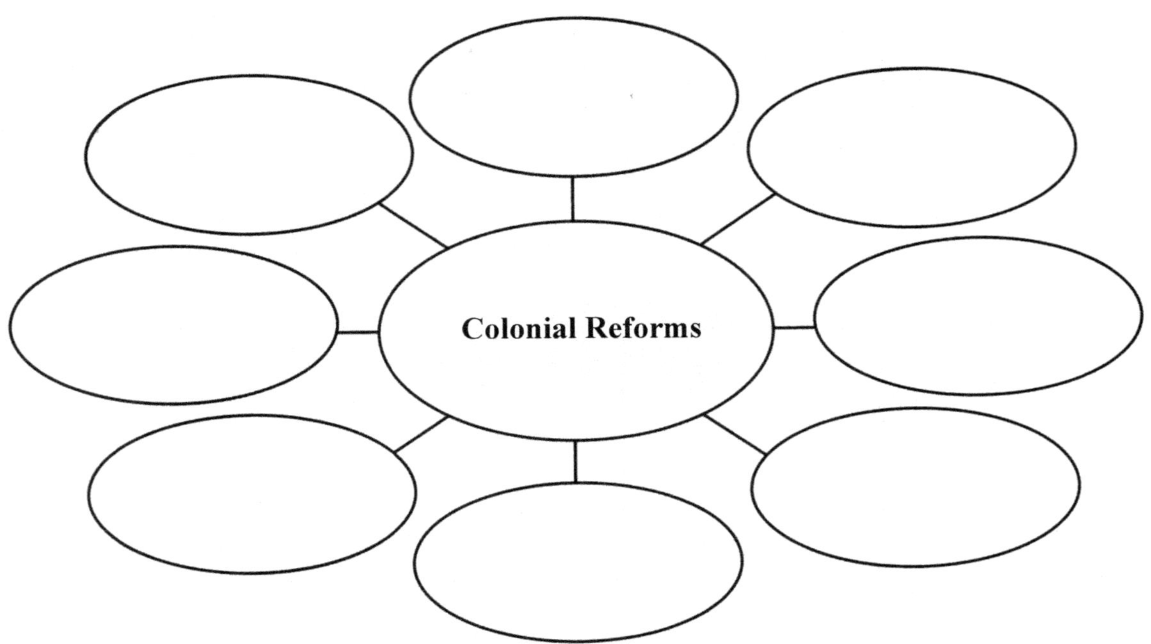

Review Questions

Write a brief answer to the following questions. Remember, each answer should highlight a primary idea using key words and supporting details.

1. How was the Spanish colonial empire in the Americas organized and managed?

2. What changes did the Bourbon monarchs institute in the Spanish Empire?

SECTION 4 BLACK AFRICAN SLAVERY, THE PLANTATION SYSTEM, AND THE ATLANTIC ECONOMY

FOCUS QUESTION

What were the origins of slavery in the Americas?

Origins of Slavery
•   •   •

Using the information in your chart, write a brief answer to the Focus Question.

OUTLINE

Read the section topic entitled "The African Presence in the Americas" and create an outline of the section below. Note the key words that reflect the main ideas in each paragraph as well as the key words that inform those ideas.

I. The African Presence in the Americas
    A. Shortage of labor
        1.
        2.
        3.
    B.
        1.
    C.
        1.
        2.
        3.
        4.
        5.
        6.
        7.
            a.
            b.
            c.

Review Questions

Write a brief answer to the following questions. Remember, each answer should highlight a primary idea using key words and supporting details.

1. What was the nature of slavery in the Americas?

2. How was it linked to the economies of the Americas, Europe, and Africa??

3. Why was the plantation system unprecedented? How did the plantation system contribute to the inhumane treatment of slaves?

SECTION 5 MID-EIGHTEENTH-CENTURY WARS

FOCUS QUESTION

Why did mid-eighteenth-century European wars often involve both continental and global conflicts?

Continental Conflicts	Global Conflicts
• • •	• • •

Using the information in your table, write a brief answer to the Focus Question.

OUTLINE

Read the section topic entitled "The Seven Years' War (1756–1763)" and create an outline of the section below. Note the key words that reflect the main ideas in each paragraph as well as the key words that inform those ideas.

I. The Seven Years' War (1756–1763)

A. Frederick the Great of Prussia opened hostilities

1.

2.

3.

4.

B.

1.

2.

a.

b.

3.

4.

5.

C.

1.

2.

D.

1.

2.

3.

4.

5.

6.

7.

REVIEW QUESTIONS

Write a brief answer to the following questions. Remember, each answer should highlight a primary idea using key words and supporting details.

1. What were the results of the Seven Years' War?

2. Which countries emerged in a stronger position , and why?

SECTION 6 THE AMERICAN REVOLUTION AND EUROPE

FOCUS QUESTION

What were the causes of the American Revolution?

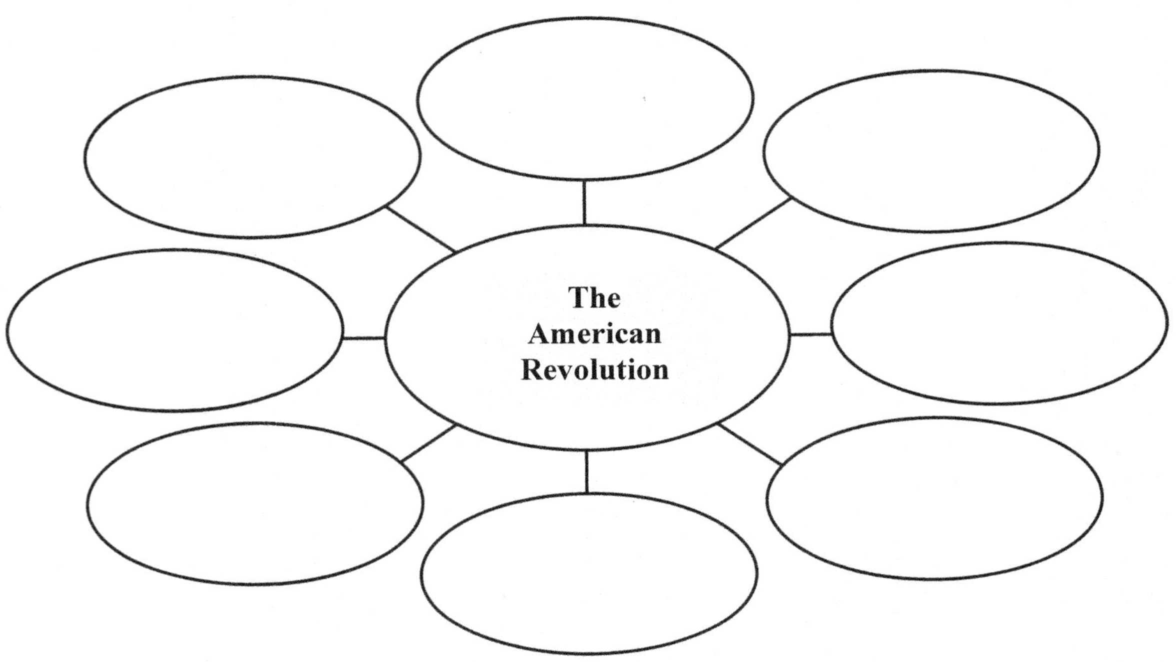

Using the information in your concept web, write a brief answer to the Focus Question.

OUTLINE

Read the section topic entitled "Resistance to the Imperial Search for Revenue" and create an outline of the section below. Note the key words that reflect the main ideas in each paragraph as well as the key words that inform those ideas.

I. Resistance to the Imperial Search for Revenue
  A. Need for revenue
    1.
      a.
      b.
      c.
    2.
  B.
    1.
      a.
      b.
    2.
      a.
    3.
      a.
      b.
      c.
      d.
      e.
      f.
    4.
    5.
  C.
  D.

Review Questions

Write a brief answer to the following questions. Remember, each answer should highlight a primary idea using key words and supporting details.

1. How did European ideas and political developments influence the American colonists? How did their actions, in turn, influence Europe?

2. What was the relationship between American colonial radicals and contemporary political radicals in Great Britain?

Review: Key Terms and People

Complete your review of the chapter by writing a brief definition of the following terms and people.

Mercantilism
Monopoly
Bullion
Flota system
Charles III
Intendant
Peninsulares
West Indies
Seasoning
Atlantic Passage
War of the Austrian Succession
Diplomatic Revolution
Seven Years' War
Treaty of Paris
William Pitt
British East India Company
Stamp Act
Boston Massacre
Intolerable Acts
Continental Congress
Whigs
John Wilkes
Yorkshire Association Movement
Plantation economies
Decolonization

My Key Terms

Write down terms that are unfamiliar. How are the words used? Do other words or examples reveal their meaning? Try to figure out meaning from the context.

CHAPTER 9
THE AGE OF ENLIGHTENMENT: EIGHTEENTH-CENTURY THOUGHT

Complete the following exercises *as you read* this chapter.

SECTION 1 FORMATIVE INFLUENCES ON THE ENLIGHTENMENT

FOCUS QUESTION

What was the intellectual and social background of the Enlightenment?

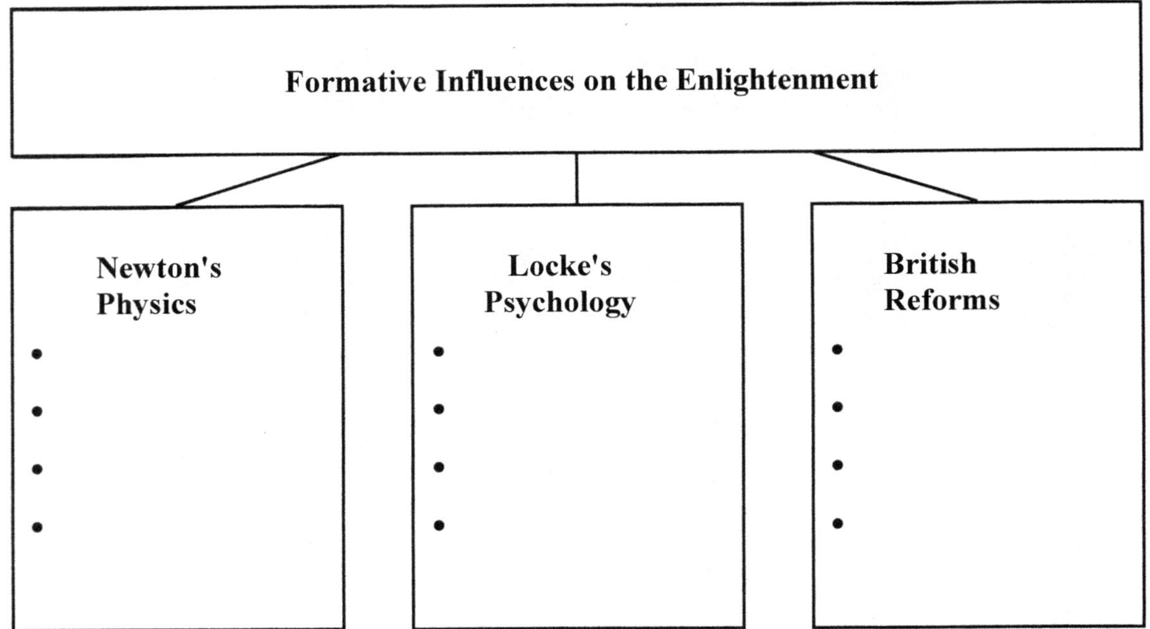

Using the information in your chart, write a brief answer to the Focus Question.

OUTLINE

Read the section topic entitled "The Emergence of a Print Culture" and create an outline of the section below. Note the key words that reflect the main ideas in each paragraph as well as the key words that inform those ideas.

I. The Emergence of a Print Culture

  A. Driving forces behind expansion of printed materials

    1.

    2.

    3.

    4.

    5.

  B.

    1.

    2.

    3.

    4.

  C.

    1.

    2.

    3.

    4.

  D.

    1.

    2.

    3.

REVIEW QUESTIONS

Write a brief answer to the following questions. Remember, each answer should highlight a primary idea using key words and supporting details.

1. What did Newton's and Locke's conception of Natural Law share? How did the convergence of physics and human psychology become manifest in English law?

2. How did print culture come about? How did it challenge traditional intellectual, social, and political authorities?

SECTION 2 THE *PHILOSOPHES*

FOCUS QUESTION

Who were the philosophes?

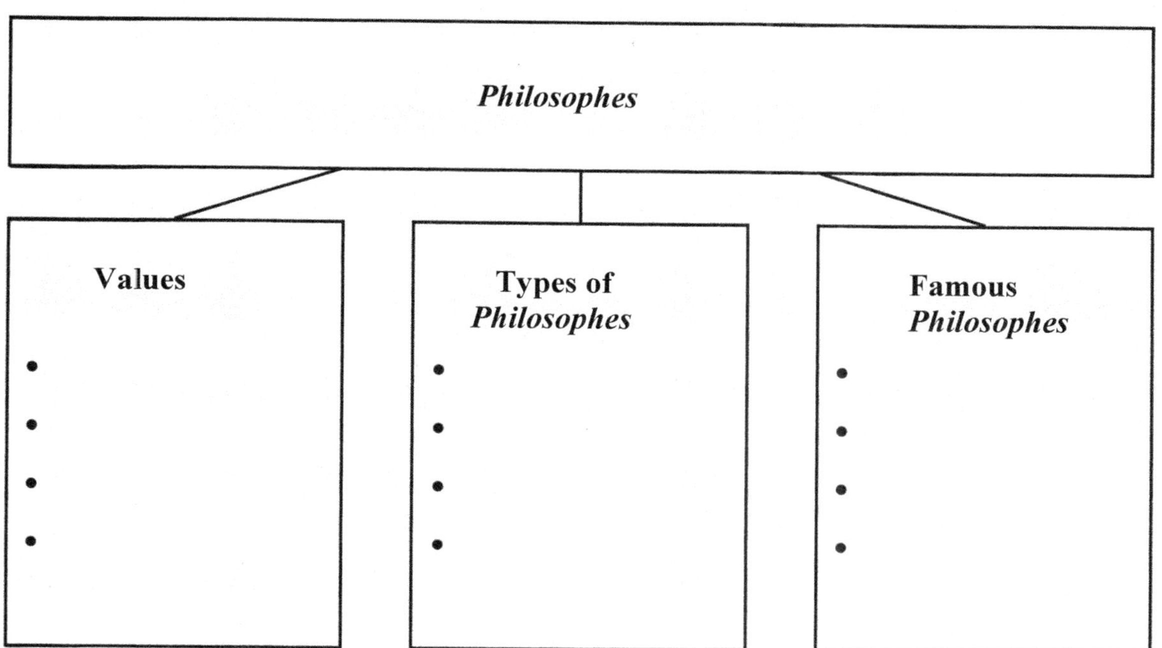

Using the information in your chart, write a brief answer to the Focus Question.

OUTLINE

Read the section topic entitled "Voltaire and Kant" and create an outline of the section below. Note the key words that reflect the main ideas in each paragraph as well as the key words that inform those ideas.

I. Voltaire—most influential of the *Philosophes*

   A. Popularizes British tolerance and Newtonian thought

      1.

      2.

      3.

      4.

   B.

      1.

      2.

      3.

      4.

II.

   A.

      1.

      2.

   B.

      1.

      2.

Review Questions

Write a brief answer to the following questions. Remember, each answer should highlight a primary idea using key words and supporting details.

1. What aspects of Voltaire's work made him both a celebrated and censored figure?

2. Why can Voltaire be characterized as both an optimist and pessimistic philosopher?

SECTION 3 THE ENLIGHTENMENT AND RELIGION

FOCUS QUESTION

How did the philosophes *challenge traditional religious ideas and institutions?*

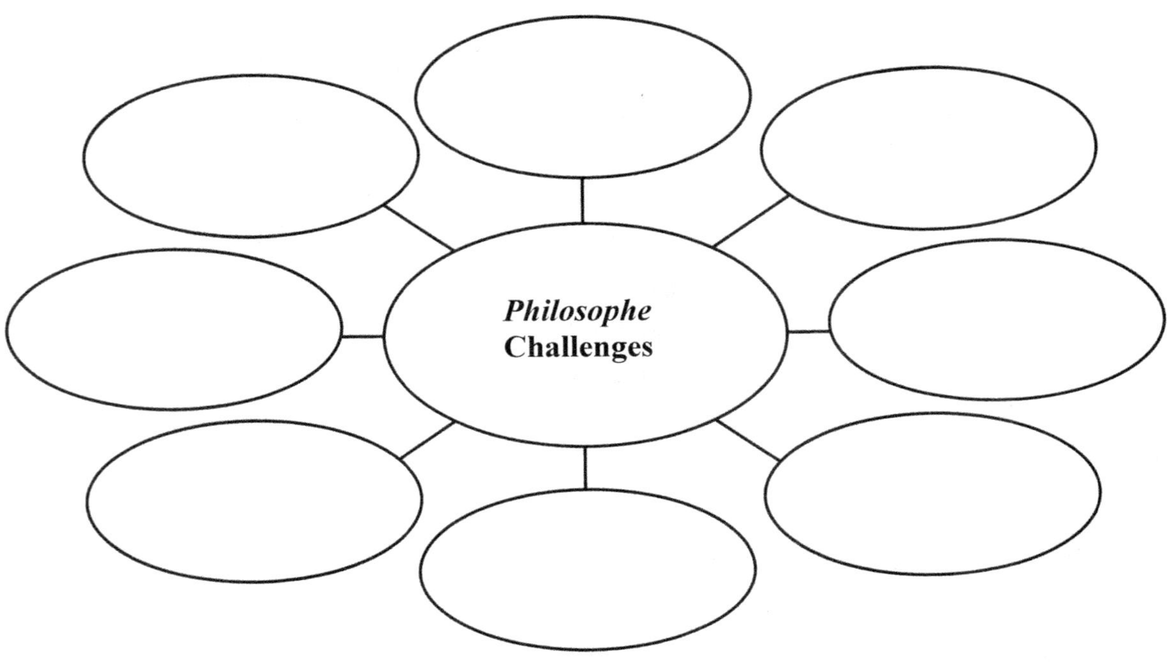

Using the information in your concept web, write a brief answer to the Focus Question.

OUTLINE

Read the section topic entitled "Deism" and create an outline of the section below. Note the key words that reflect the main ideas in each paragraph as well as the key words that inform those ideas.

I. Deism

A. *Philosophes* and a rational God

1.

2.

3.

4.

B.

1.

2.

3.

C.

1.

2.

3.

4.

5.

Review Questions

Write a brief answer to the following questions. Remember, each answer should highlight a primary idea using key words and supporting details.

1. Why did some *philosophe*s consider organized religion to be their greatest enemy?

2. What were the basic tenets of deism?

3. How did Jewish writers contribute to Enlightenment thinking about religion?

4. What are the similarities and differences between the Enlightenment evaluation of Islam and its evaluations of Christianity and Judaism?

SECTION 4 THE ENLIGHTENMENT AND SOCIETY

FOCUS QUESTION

How did the philosophes apply Enlightenment ideas to social and economic problems?

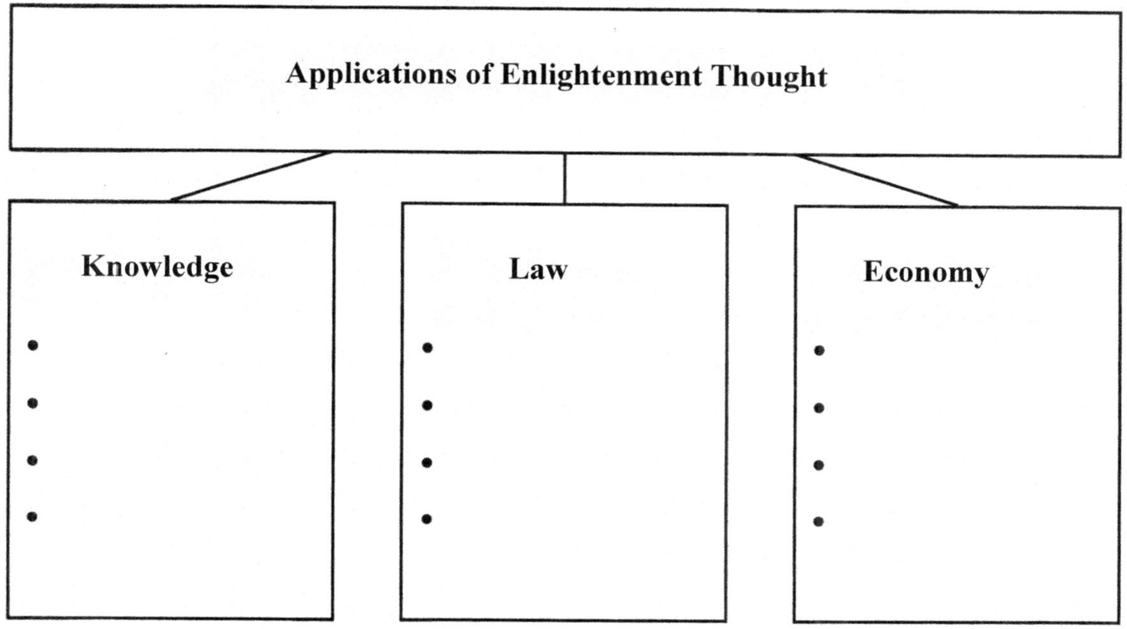

Using the information in your chart, write a brief answer to the Focus Question.

OUTLINE

Read the section topic entitled "Adam Smith on Economic Growth and Social Progress" and create an outline of the section below. Note the key words that reflect the main ideas in each paragraph as well as the key words that inform those ideas.

I. Adam Smith on Economic Growth and Social Progress
   A. 1776 Inquiry into the Nature and Causes of *the Wealth of Nations*
      1.
      2.
   B.
      1.
      2.
      3.
      4.
   C.
      1.
      2.
      3.
   D.
      1.
      2.
   E.
      1.
      2.
      3.
      4.
      5.

Review Questions

Write a brief answer to the following questions. Remember, each answer should highlight a primary idea using key words and supporting details.

1. How did the views of the mercantilists about the earth's resources differ from those of Adam Smith in his book *The Wealth of Nations*?

2. Why might Smith be regarded as an advocate of the consumer?

3. How did his theory of history work to the detriment of less economically advanced non-European peoples?

SECTION 5 POLITICAL THOUGHT OF THE *PHILOSOPHES*

FOCUS QUESTION

How did the philosophes apply Enlightenment ideas to political issues?

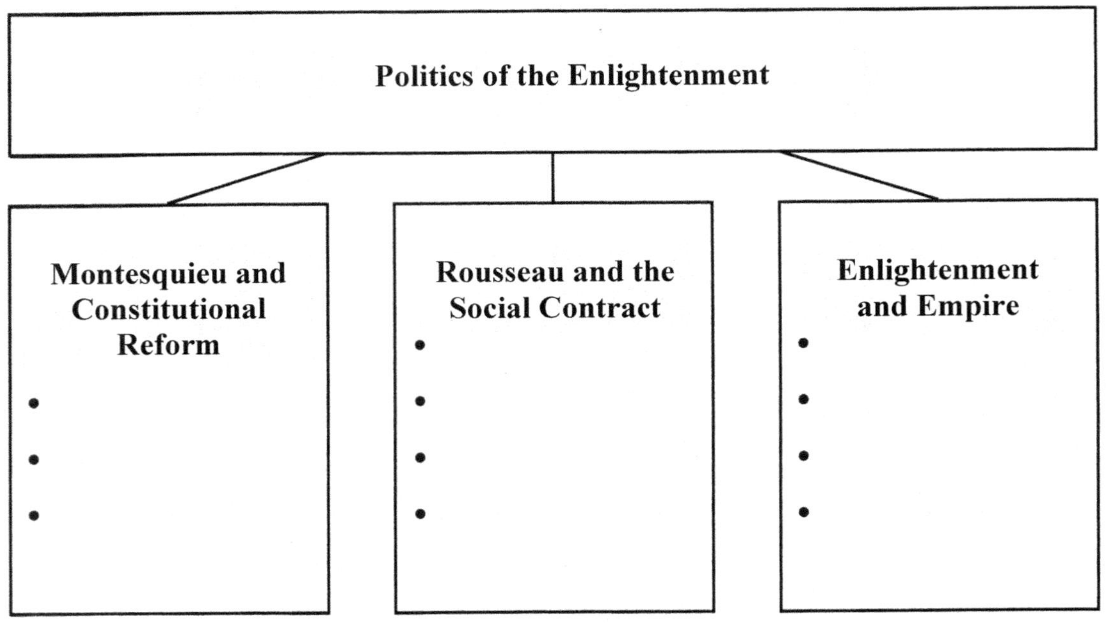

Using the information in your chart, write a brief answer to the Focus Question.

Outline

Read the section topic entitled "Montesquieu and *Spirit of the Laws*" and create an outline of the section below. Note the key words that reflect the main ideas in each paragraph as well as the key words that inform those ideas.

I. Montesquieu and *Spirit of the Laws*

  A. Montesquieu

    1.

    2.

    3.

    4.

    5.

    6.

  B.

    1.

    2.

    3.

  C.

    1.

    2.

    3.

  D.

    1.

    2.

READING SKILL: SUMMARIZE

Complete the concept web below identifying the primary philosophical principles associated with Rousseau.

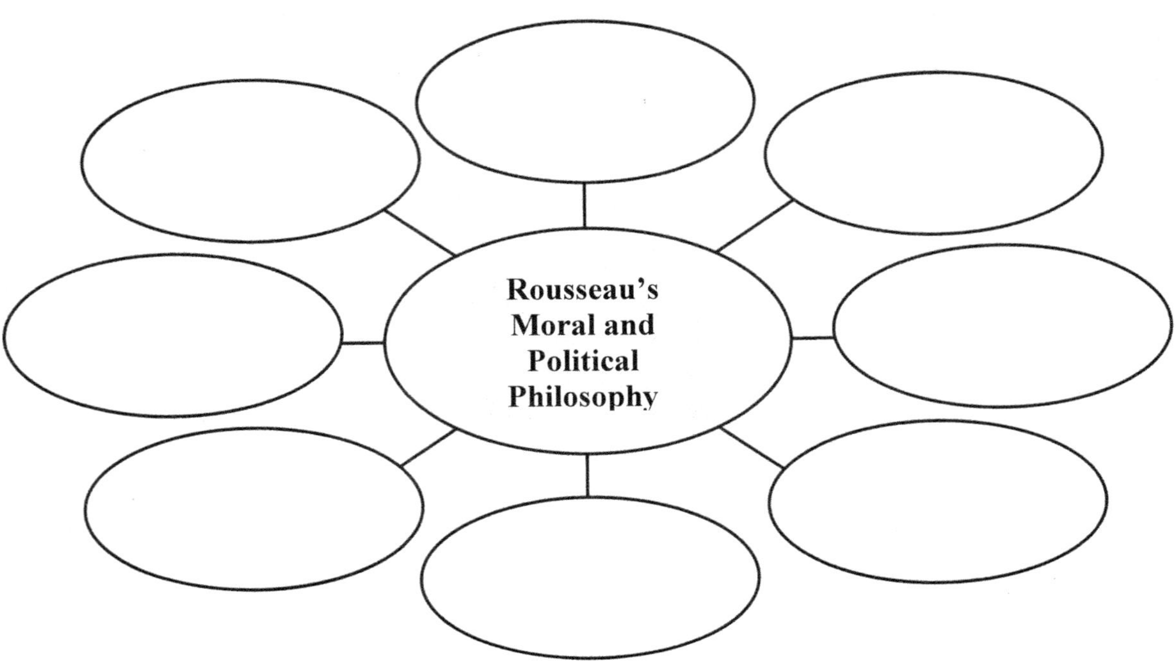

Review Questions

Write a brief answer to the following questions. Remember, each answer should highlight a primary idea using key words and supporting details.

1. How did the political views of Montesquieu differ from those of Rousseau?

2. Was Montesquieu's view of England accurate?

3. Was Rousseau a child of the Enlightenment or its enemy?

4. Which did Rousseau value more, the individual or society?

SECTION 6 WOMEN IN THE THOUGHT AND PRACTICE OF THE ENLIGHTENMENT

FOCUS QUESTION

What role did women play in the Enlightenment?

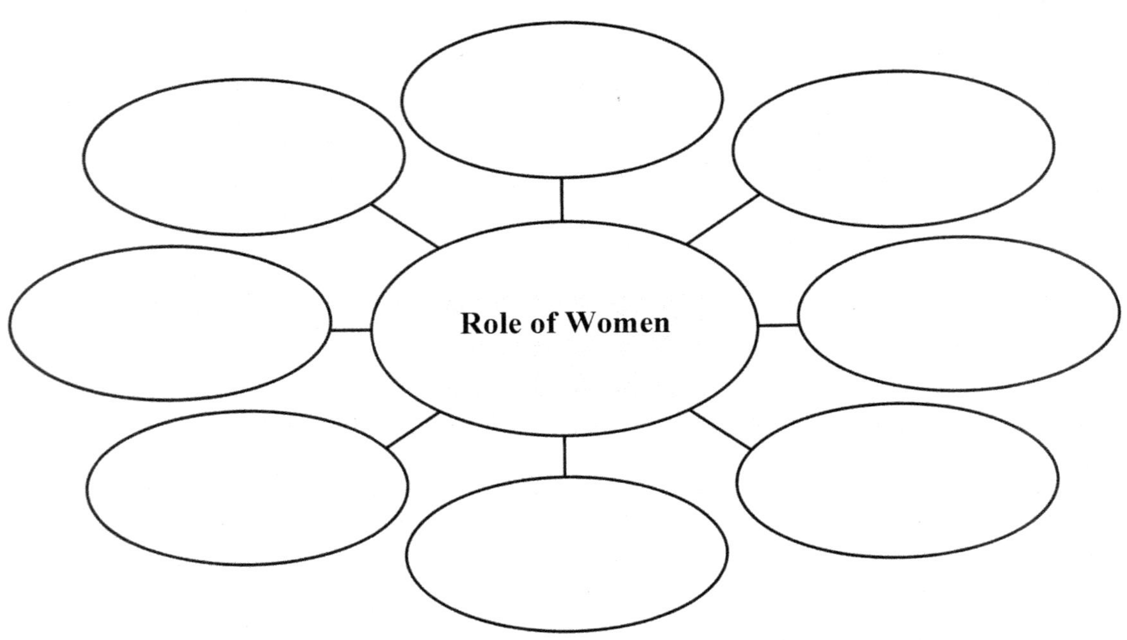

Using the information in your concept web, write a brief answer to the Focus Question.

OUTLINE

Read the section topic entitled "Women in the Thought and Practice of the Enlightenment" and create an outline of the section below. Note the key words that reflect the main ideas in each paragraph as well as the key words that inform those ideas.

I. Women in the Thought and Practice of the Enlightenment
   A. Common Enlightenment view regarding women
      1.
      2.
      3.
      4.
      5.
      6.
   B.
      1.
      2.
      3.
      4.

Review Questions

Write a brief answer to the following questions. Remember, each answer should highlight a primary idea using key words and supporting details.

1. What were the attitudes of the *philosophes* toward women?

2. What was Rousseau's view of women? What were the separate spheres he imagined men and women occupying?

3. What were Mary Wollstonecraft's criticisms of Rousseau's view?

SECTION 7 ROCOCO AND NEOCLASSICAL STYLES IN EIGHTEENTH-CENTURY ART

FOCUS QUESTION

How did rococo and neoclassical styles reflect and contribute to the prevailing trends of the age?

Art and Society	
Artistic Style	**Reflection in Society**
•	•
•	•
•	•

Using the information in your chart, write a brief answer to the Focus Question.

OUTLINE

Read the section topic entitled "Rococo and Neoclassical Styles in Eighteenth-Century Art" and create an outline of the section below. Note the key words that reflect the main ideas in each paragraph as well as the key words that inform those ideas.

I. Rococo and Neoclassical Styles in Eighteenth-Century Art

    A. Rococo

        1.

        2.

        3.

        4.

        5.

        6.

        7.

    B.

        1.

        2.

        3.

        4.

        5.

        6.

        7.

        8.

        9.

        10.

        11.

        12.

Review Questions

Write a brief answer to the following questions. Remember, each answer should highlight a primary idea using key words and supporting details.

1. How did the art and architecture of intimate home settings become associated with aristocratic decadence?

2. How and why did portrayals of the ancient world come to represent criticism of the Old Regime?

SECTION 8 ENLIGHTENED ABSOLUTISM

FOCUS QUESTION

What was enlightened absolutism?

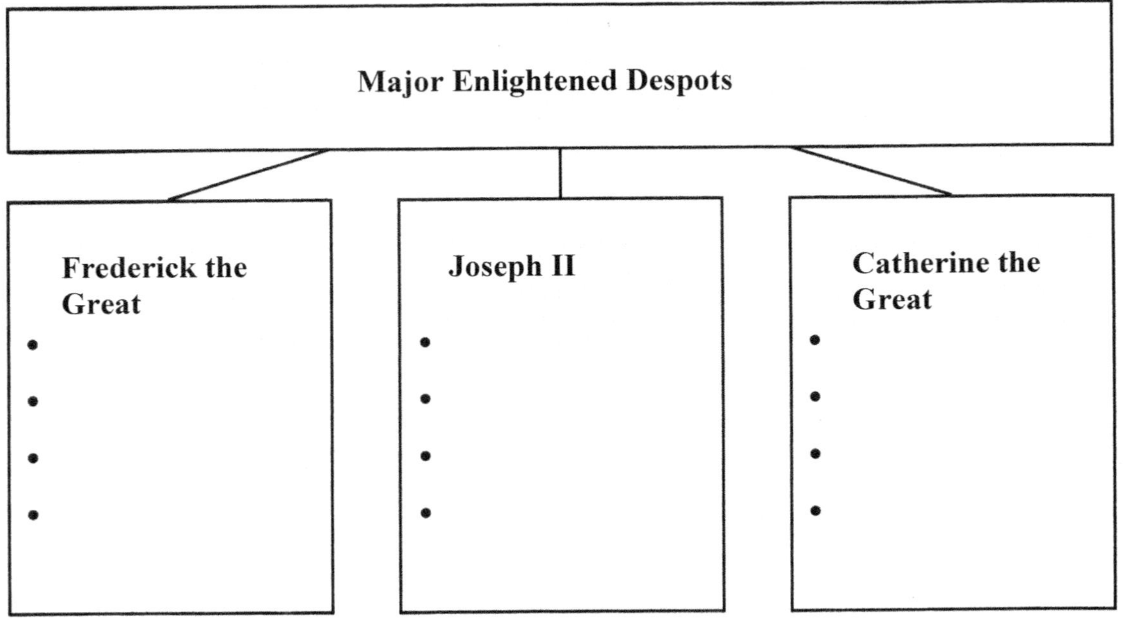

Using the information in your concept web, write a brief answer to the Focus Question.

OUTLINE

Read the section topic entitled "Catherine the Great of Russia" and create an outline of the section below. Note the key words that reflect the main ideas in each paragraph as well as the key words that inform those ideas.

I. Catherine the Great of Russia

  A. Russia 1725–1765

    1.

    2.

    3.

    4.

    5.

    6.

    7.

    8.

  B.

    1.

    2.

  C.

    1.

    2.

    3.

  D.

    1.

    2.

  E.

    1.

    2.

    3.

    4.

REVIEW QUESTIONS

Write a brief answer to the following questions. Remember, each answer should highlight a primary idea using key words and supporting details.

1. Were the enlightened monarchs true believers in the ideals of the *philosophes*, or was their enlightenment just a veneer?

2. Was their power really absolute? What motivated their reforms?

3. What does the partition of Poland indicate about the spirit of enlightened absolutism?

REVIEW: KEY TERMS AND PEOPLE

Complete your review of the chapter by writing a brief definition of the following terms and people.

Isaac Newton
Tabula rasa
*Philosophe*s
Voltaire
Candide
Deism
David Hume
Gotthold Lessing
Baruch Spinoza
Moses Mendelssohn
Edward Gibbon
Mary Wortley Montagu
Laissez-faire
Adam Smith
Denis Diderot
Physiocrats
Charles Louis de Secondat, baron de Montesquieu
Jean Jacques Rousseau
Social Contract
Marquise de Pompadour
Émile
Mary Wollstonecraft
Rococo
Neoclassical
Louis XV
Jean-Louis David
Enlightened Absolutism
Frederick the Great
Joseph II of Austria
Josephinism
Catherine the Great

MY KEY TERMS

Write down terms that are unfamiliar. How are the words used? Do other words or examples reveal their meaning? Try to figure out meaning from the context.

CHAPTER 10
THE FRENCH REVOLUTION

Complete the following exercises *as you read* this chapter.

SECTION 1 THE CRISIS OF THE FRENCH MONARCHY

FOCUS QUESTION

How did the financial weakness of the French monarchy lay the foundations of revolution in 1789?

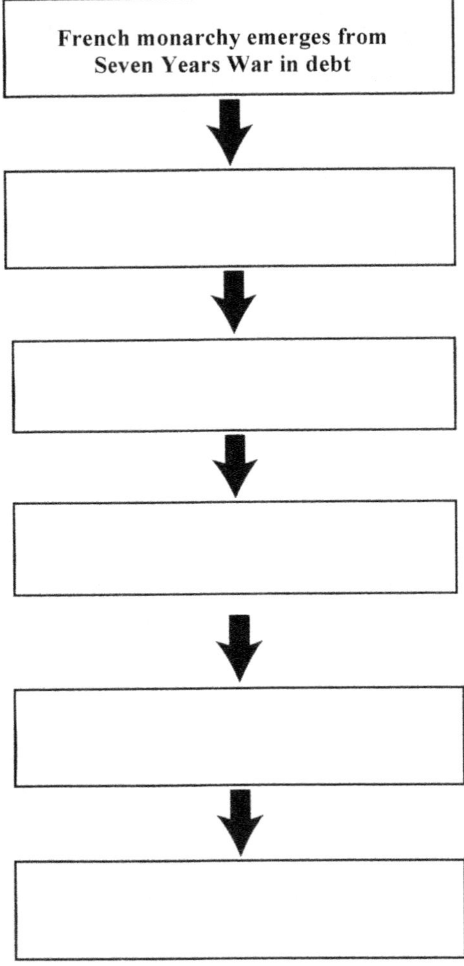

Using the information in your flowchart, write a brief answer to the Focus Question.

OUTLINE

Read the section topic entitled "Calonne's Reform Plan and the Assembly of Notables" and create an outline of the section below. Note the key words that reflect the main ideas in each paragraph as well as the key words that inform those ideas.

I. Calonne's Reform Plan and the Assembly of Notables
    A. French Minster of Finance Calonne's tax reform plan
        1.
        2.
        3.
        4.
        5.
        6.
    B.
        1.
        2.
        3.
    C.
        1.
        2.
    D.
        1.
        2.
        3.
    E.
        1.
        2.
        3.
        4.
        5.
    F.
        1.
        2.

REVIEW QUESTIONS

Write a brief answer to the following questions. Remember, each answer should highlight a primary idea using key words and supporting details.

1. Why has France been called a rich nation with an impoverished government?

2. How did the financial weaknesses of the French monarchy lay the foundations of the revolution of 1789?

SECTION 2 THE REVOLUTION OF 1789

FOCUS QUESTION

How did the calling of the Estates General lead to revolution?

Cause

- Louis XVI agrees to convoke the Estates General
- Reconvened Assembly of Notables demands that each estate have an equal number of representatives.
-
-
-

Event
Revolution

Using the information in your chart, write a brief answer to the Focus Question.

OUTLINE

Read the section topic entitled "The 'Great Fear' and the Night of August 4th" and create an outline of the section below. Note the key words that reflect the main ideas in each paragraph as well as the key words that inform those ideas.

I. The "Great Fear" and the Night of August 4th
   A. The "Great Fear" French peasant disturbance: summer 1789
      1.
      2.
      3.
      4.
      5.
      6.
      7.
   B.
      1.
      2.
      3.
      4.
      5.
      6.
   C.
      1.
      2.
      3.
      4.
      5.

READING SKILL: SUMMARIZE

Complete the chart below identifying key rights enumerated in the Declaration of the Rights of Man and Citizen promoting the two ideals of civic equality and popular sovereignty.

Declaration of the Rights of Man and Citizen	
Civic Equality	**Popular Sovereignty**

Review Questions

Write a brief answer to the following questions. Remember, each answer should highlight a primary idea using key words and supporting details.

1. What were Louis XVI's most serious mistakes during the French Revolution?

2. Had he been a more able ruler, could the French Revolution have been avoided or a constitutional monarchy have succeeded? Did the revolution ultimately have little to do with the competence of the monarch?

SECTION 3 THE RECONSTRUCTION OF FRANCE

FOCUS QUESTION

How did the National Constituent Assembly reorganize France?

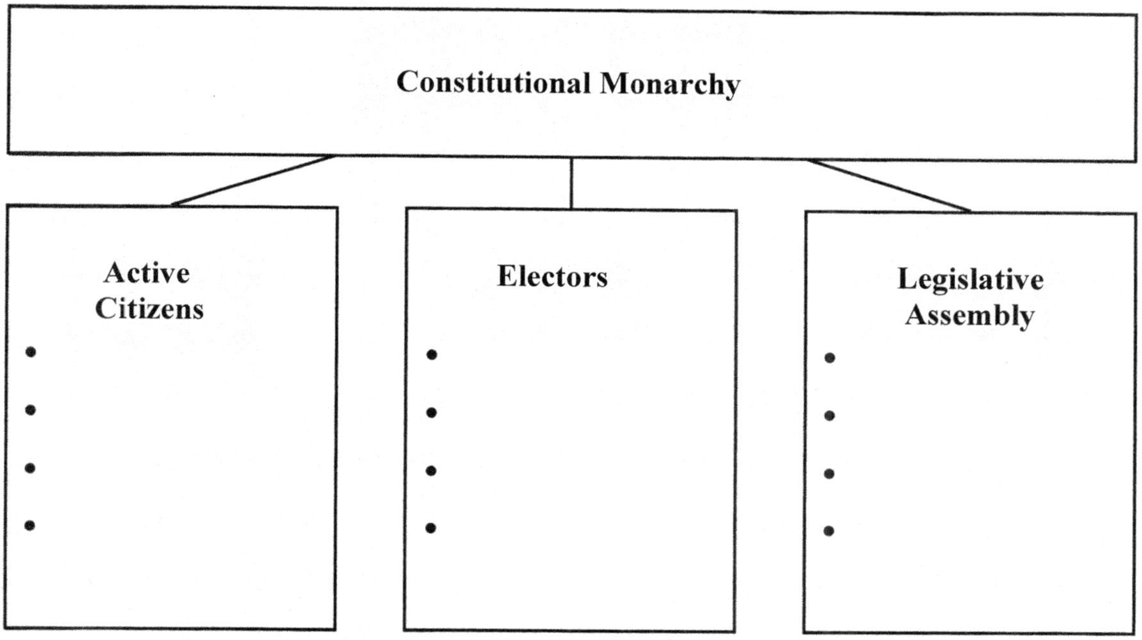

Using the information in your flowchart, write a brief answer to the Focus Question.

OUTLINE

Read the section topic entitled "The Civil Constitution of the Clergy" and create an outline of the section below. Note the key words that reflect the main ideas in each paragraph as well as the key words that inform those ideas.

I. The Civil Constitution of the Clergy
    A. National Constituent Assembly intends to confiscate church lands
        1.
        2.
        3.
    B.
        1.
        2.
        3.
    C.
        1.
        2.
        3.
        4.
    D.
        1.
        2.
        3.
        4.
        5.
        6.

REVIEW QUESTIONS

Write a brief answer to the following questions. Remember, each answer should highlight a primary idea using key words and supporting details.

1. How was the Estates General transformed into the National Assembly?

2. How did the Declaration of the Rights of Man and Citizen reflect the social and political values of the eighteenth-century Enlightenment?

3. How were France and its government reorganized in the early years of the revolution?

4. Why has the Civil Constitution of the Clergy been called the greatest blunder of the National Assembly?

SECTION 4 THE END OF THE MONARCHY: A SECOND REVOLUTION

FOCUS QUESTION

What led to the radicalization of the French Revolution?

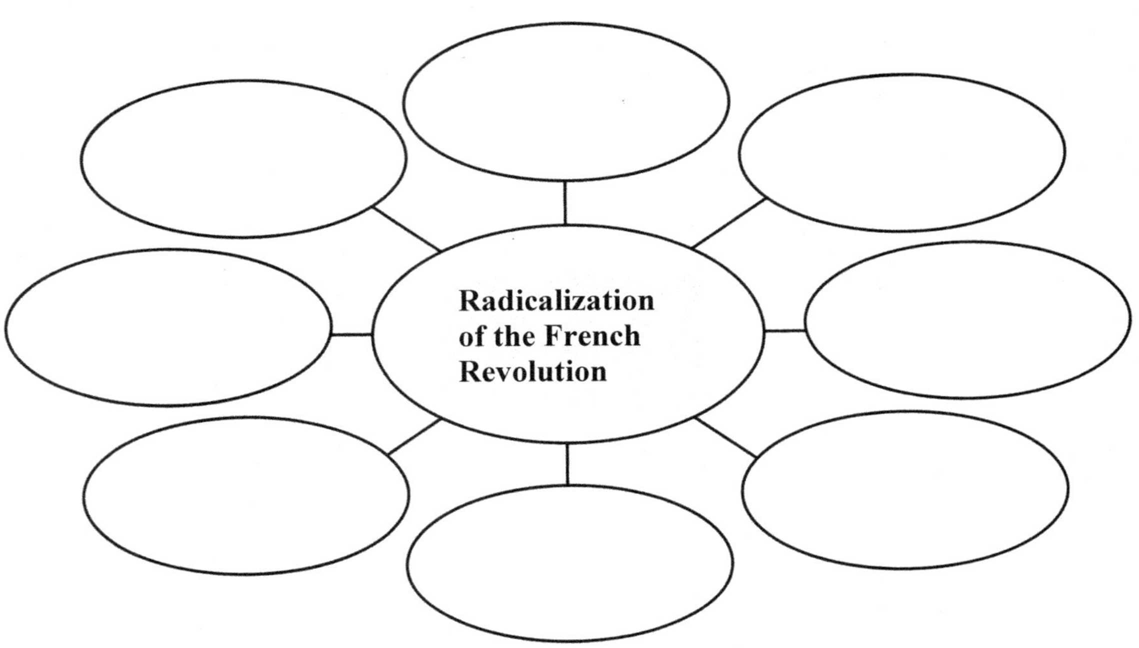

Using the information in your concept web, write a brief answer to the Focus Question.

OUTLINE

Read the section topic entitled "Emergence of the Jacobins" and create an outline of the section below. Note the key words that reflect the main ideas in each paragraph as well as the key words that inform those ideas.

I. Emergence of the Jacobins

  A. Jacobins (named after priory of St. James where club met in Paris)

    1.

    2.

    3.

    4.

    5.

  B.

    1.

    2.

    3.

    4.

  C.

    1.

    2.

    3.

    4.

    5.

  D.

    1.

    2.

  E.

    1.

    2.

  F.

    1.

    2.

    3.

    4.

    5.

READING SKILL: SUMMARIZE

Complete the chart below identifying the distinguishing characteristics differentiating Jacobins, Girondists, the Mountain, and *sans-culottes*.

Revolutionaries	
Faction	**Characteristics**

REVIEW QUESTIONS

Write a brief answer to the following questions. Remember, each answer should highlight a primary idea using key words and supporting details.

1. Why were some political factions dissatisfied with the constitutional settlement of 1791?

2. What was the revolution of 1792 and why did it occur?

3. Who were the *sans-culottes,* and how did they become a factor in the politics of the period? How influential were they during the Terror in particular?

4. Why did the *sans-culottes* and the Jacobins cooperate at first? Why did that cooperation end?

5. Why did France go to war with Austria in 1792?

SECTION 5 EUROPE AT WAR WITH THE REVOLUTION

FOCUS QUESTION

How did Europe respond to the French Revolution?

European Response to French Revolution		
Type	**Political Philosophy**	**Government Actions**
Conservative	•	• • • • •
Liberal	•	• • •

Using the information in your table, write a brief answer to the Focus Question.

Outline

Read the section topic entitled "Edmund Burke Attacks the Revolution" and create an outline of the section below. Note the key words that reflect the main ideas in each paragraph as well as the key words that inform those ideas.

I. Edmund Burke Attacks the Revolution
  A. Edmund Burke
    1.
    2.
  B.
    1.
    2.
    3.
  C.
    1.
    2.
    3.
    4.
  D.
    1.
    2.
  E.
    1.
    2.

READING SKILL: SUMMARIZE

Complete the chart below identifying the principal actors and motivations for the partitions of Poland.

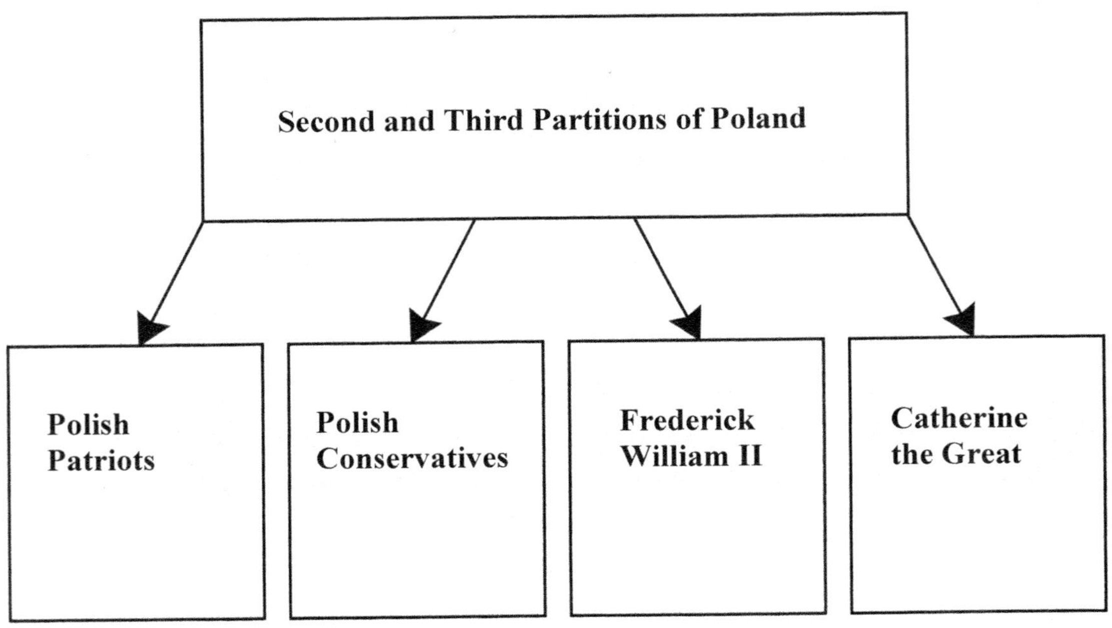

Review Questions

Write a brief answer to the following questions. Remember, each answer should highlight a primary idea using key words and supporting details.

1. How did events in France influence the last two partitions of Poland?

2. Why in the long run did the political philosophy of Edmund Burke gain more influence than that of Thomas Paine?

3. How did the rest of Europe react to the French Revolution and the Terror?

SECTION 6 THE REIGN OF TERROR

FOCUS QUESTION

How did war and ideology combine to create the Reign of Terror?

Using the information in your chart, write a brief answer to the Focus Question.

OUTLINE

Read the section topic entitled "Revolutionary Tribunals" and create an outline of the section below. Note the key words that reflect the main ideas in each paragraph as well as the key words that inform those ideas.

I. Revolutionary Tribunals

   A. 1793 Convention established tribunals to try the enemies of the republic

      1.

      2.

      3.

      4.

      5.

      6.

   B.

      1.

      2.

   C.

      1.

      2.

      3.

      4.

      5.

READING SKILL: SUMMARIZE

Complete the concept web below identifying the primary values of Robespierre's "Republic of Virtue."

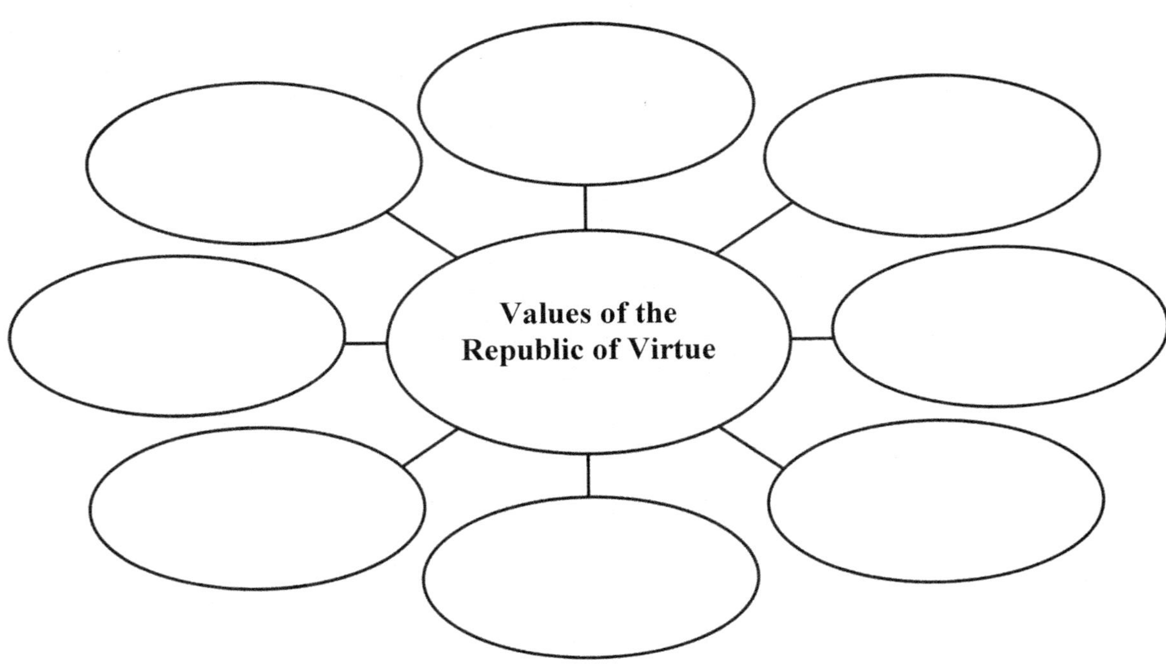

Review Questions

Write a brief answer to the following questions. Remember, each answer should highlight a primary idea using key words and supporting details.

1. What were the benefits and drawbacks for France of fighting an external war in the midst of a domestic political revolution?

2. What were the causes of the Terror?

3. Why did the revolutionaries turn on themselves?

Section 7 The Thermidorian Reaction

Focus Question

What course did the French Revolution take after 1794?

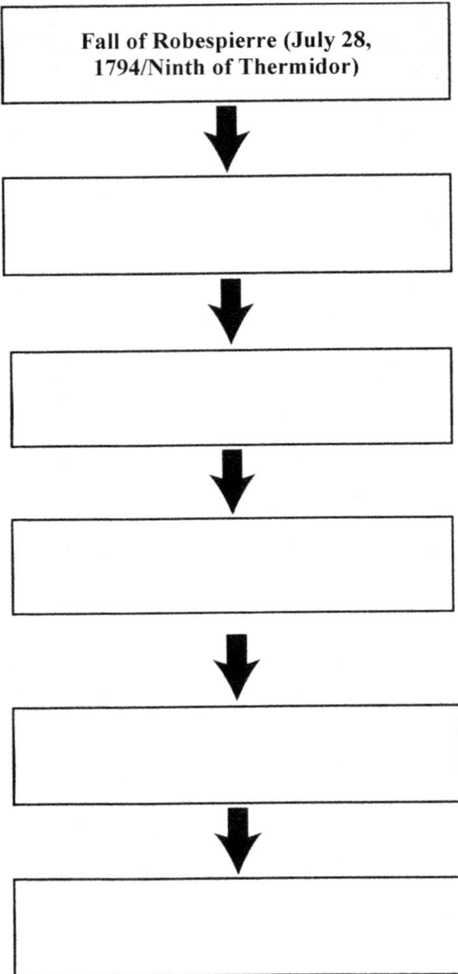

Using the information in your flowchart, write a brief answer to the Focus Question.

OUTLINE

Read the section topic entitled "Establishment of the Directory" and create an outline of the section below. Note the key words that reflect the main ideas in each paragraph as well as the key words that inform those ideas.

I. Establishment of the Directory
   A. Constitution of the Year III
      1.
      2.
      3.
   B.
      1.
      2.
   C.
      1.
      2.
   D.
      1.
      2.
   E.
      1.
      2.
      3.
      4.
      5.
   F.
      1.
      2.
   G.
      1.
      2.

Review Questions

Write a brief answer to the following questions. Remember, each answer should highlight a primary idea using key words and supporting details.

1. A motto of the French Revolution was "equality, liberty, and fraternity." How did the revolution both support and violate this motto?

2. Did French women benefit from the revolution?

3. Did French peasants benefit from it?

REVIEW: KEY TERMS AND PEOPLE

Complete your review of the chapter by writing a brief definition of the following terms and people.

Louis XVI
Parlements
Assembly of Notables
Third Estate
Abbé Siéyès
Tennis Court Oath
National Constituent Assembly
Declaration of the Rights of Man and Citizen
Jacobins
Girondists
September Massacres
Citizen Capet
Edmund Burke
William Pitt the Younger
Frederick William II
Reign of Terror
Committee of Public Safety
Levée en Masse
Maximilien de Robespierre
Pauline Léon
Cult of the Supreme Being
Olympe de Gouges
Chapelier Law
Civil Constitution of the Clergy
Declaration of Pillnitz
Thermidorian Reaction
Council of Five Hundred
"The white terror"
Treaties of Basel
Two-Thirds Law
Conspiracy of Equals

MY KEY TERMS

Write down terms that are unfamiliar. How are the words used? Do other words or examples reveal their meaning? Try to figure out meaning from the context.

CHAPTER 11
THE AGE OF NAPOLEON AND THE TRIUMPH OF ROMANTICISM

Complete the following exercises *as you read* this chapter.

SECTION 1 THE RISE OF NAPOLEON BONAPARTE

FOCUS QUESTION

How did Napoleon come to power in France?

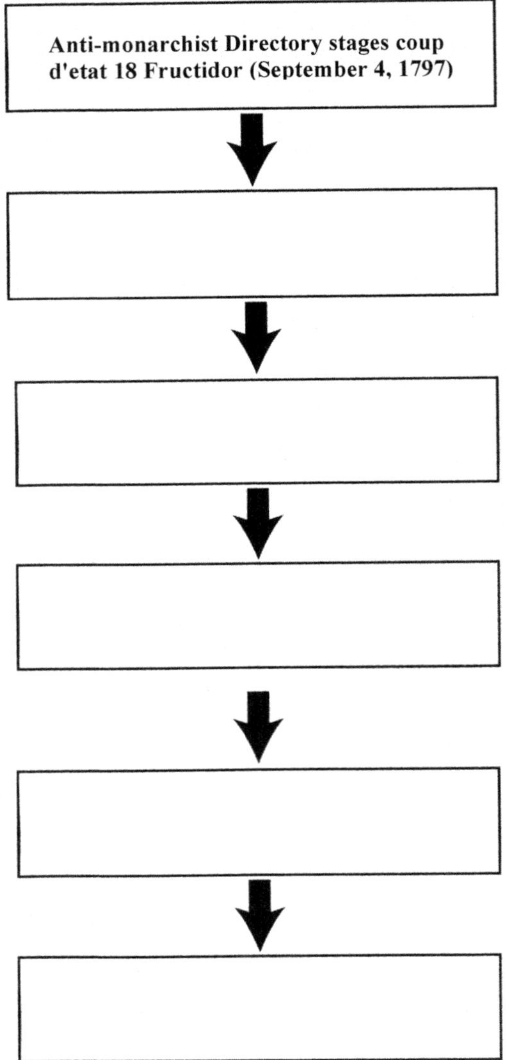

Using the information in your flowchart, write a brief answer to the Focus Question.

OUTLINE

Read the section topic entitled "The Constitution of the Year VIII" and create an outline of the section below. Note the key words that reflect the main ideas in each paragraph as well as the key words that inform those ideas.

I. The Constitution of the Year VIII
   A. Director Abbé Siéyès calls for a new constitution
      1.
      2.
      3.
      4.
      5.
      6.
      7.
      8.
   B.
      1.
      2.
      3.
      4.
      5.
      6.
      7.
   C.
      1.
      2.
      3.
   D.
      1.
      2.
      3.

REVIEW QUESTIONS

Write a brief answer to the following questions. Remember, each answer should highlight a primary idea using key words and supporting details.

1. How did Napoleon rise to power?

2. What was Napoleon's strategy regarding Britain? Why didn't it work?

Section 2 The Consulate in France (1799–1804)

Focus Question

How did the Consulate end the revolution in France?

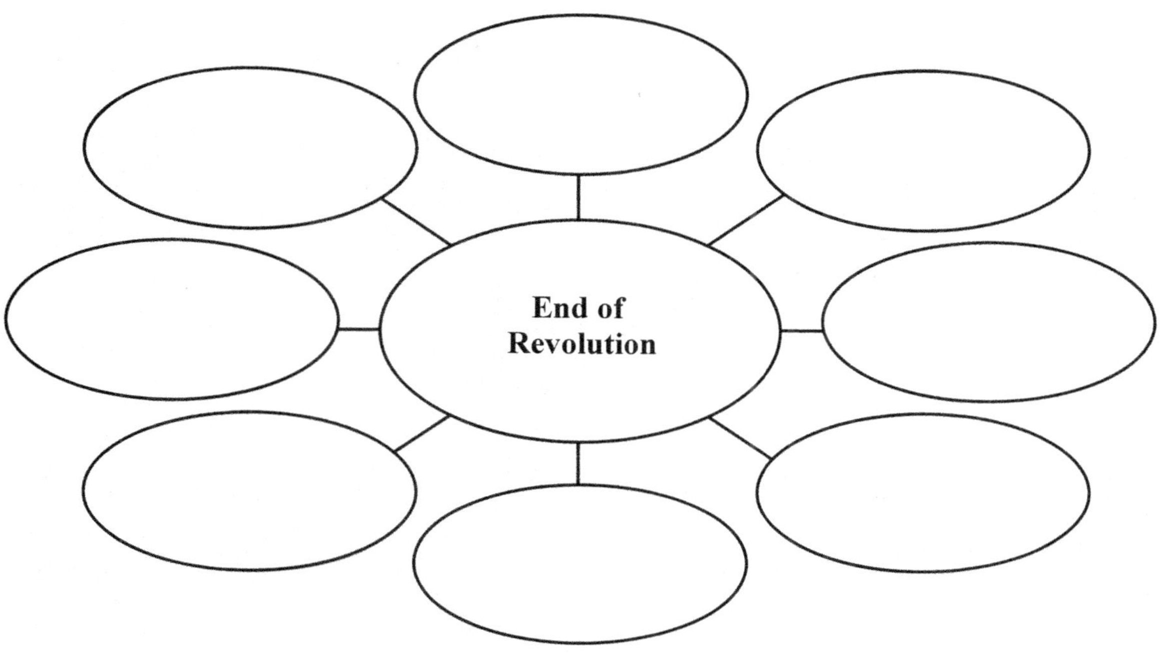

Using the information in your concept web, write a brief answer to the Focus Question.

Outline

Read the section topic entitled "Concordat with the Roman Catholic Church" and create an outline of the section below. Note the key words that reflect the main ideas in each paragraph as well as the key words that inform those ideas.

I. Concordat with the Roman Catholic Church
   A. France and Pope Pius VII
      1.
      2.
   B.
      1.
      2.
   C.
      1.
      2.
      3.
      4.
      5.
      6.
   D.
      1.
      2.

Review Questions

Write a brief answer to the following questions. Remember, each answer should highlight a primary idea using key words and supporting details.

1. What were Napoleon's major domestic achievements?

2. What groups supported him?

3. Did his rule fulfill or betray the French Revolution?

SECTION 3 NAPOLEON'S EMPIRE (1804–1814)

FOCUS QUESTION

How did Napoleon build an empire?

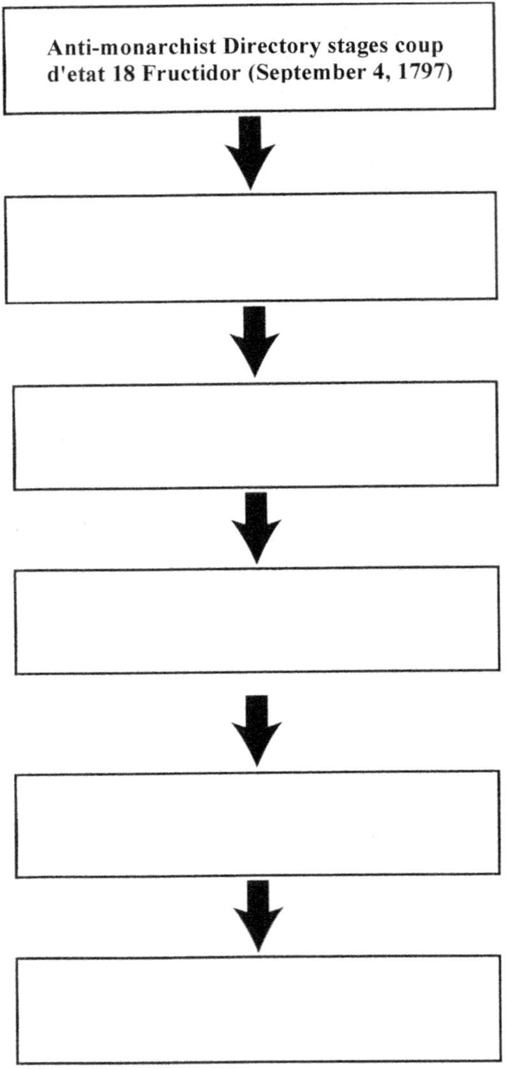

Using the information in your flowchart, write a brief answer to the Focus Question.

Outline

Read the section topic entitled "The Continental System" and create an outline of the section below. Note the key words that reflect the main ideas in each paragraph as well as the key words that inform those ideas.

I. The Continental System
    A. Strategy to defeat the British
        1.
        2.
        3.
        4.
        5.
        6.
    B.
        1.
        2.
        3.
    C.
        1.
        2.
        3.
    D.
        1.
        2.
    E.
        1.
        2.

Review Questions

Write a brief answer to the following questions. Remember, each answer should highlight a primary idea using key words and supporting details.

1. What regions made up Napoleon's realm and what was the status of each region within it?

2. Did his administration show foresight, or was the empire a burden he could not afford?

SECTION 4 EUROPEAN RESPONSE TO THE EMPIRE

FOCUS QUESTION

Why did Napoleonic rule breed resentment in Europe?

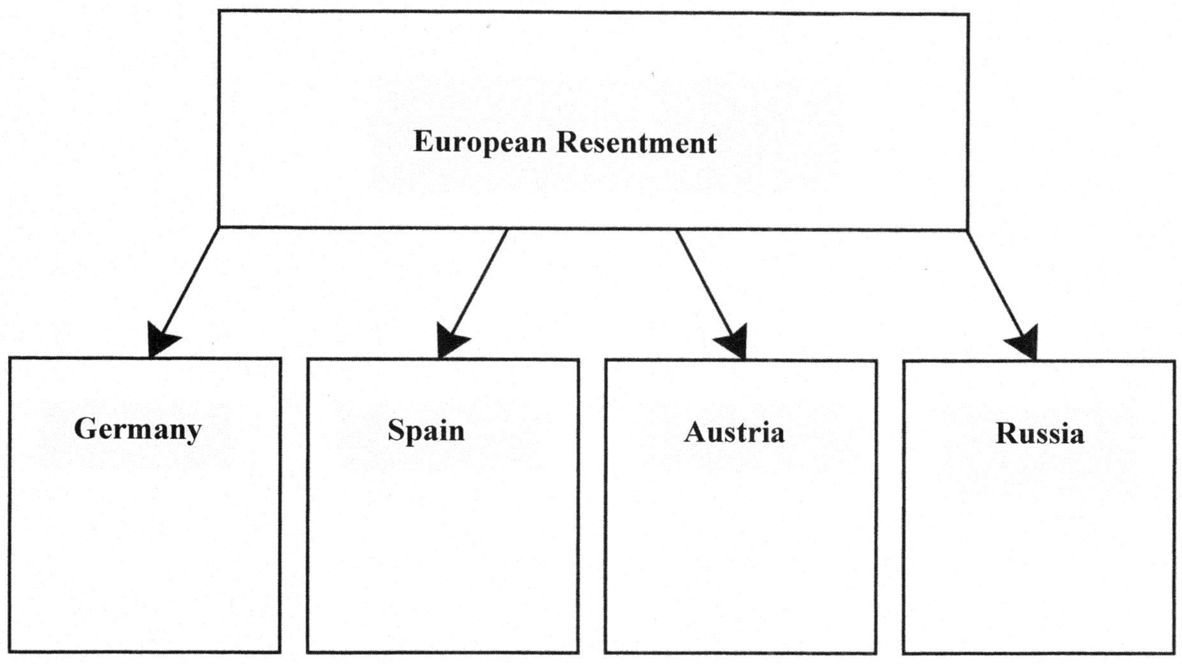

Using the information in your chart, write a brief answer to the Focus Question.

OUTLINE

Read the section topic entitled "German Nationalism and Prussian Reform" and create an outline of the section below. Note the key words that reflect the main ideas in each paragraph as well as the key words that inform those ideas.

I. German Nationalism and Prussian Reform
   A. Two phases of German nationalism pursued by intellectuals
      1.
      2.
      3.
   B.
      1.
      2.
      3.
      4.
      5.
   C.
      1.
      2.
      3.
   D.
      1.
      2.
      3.
      4.
      5.
   E.
      1.
      2.
      3.
      4.
      5.
   F.
      1.
      2.

READING SKILL: SUMMARIZE

Complete the chart below identifying the steps that led Napoleon into war with Russia and his subsequent defeat there.

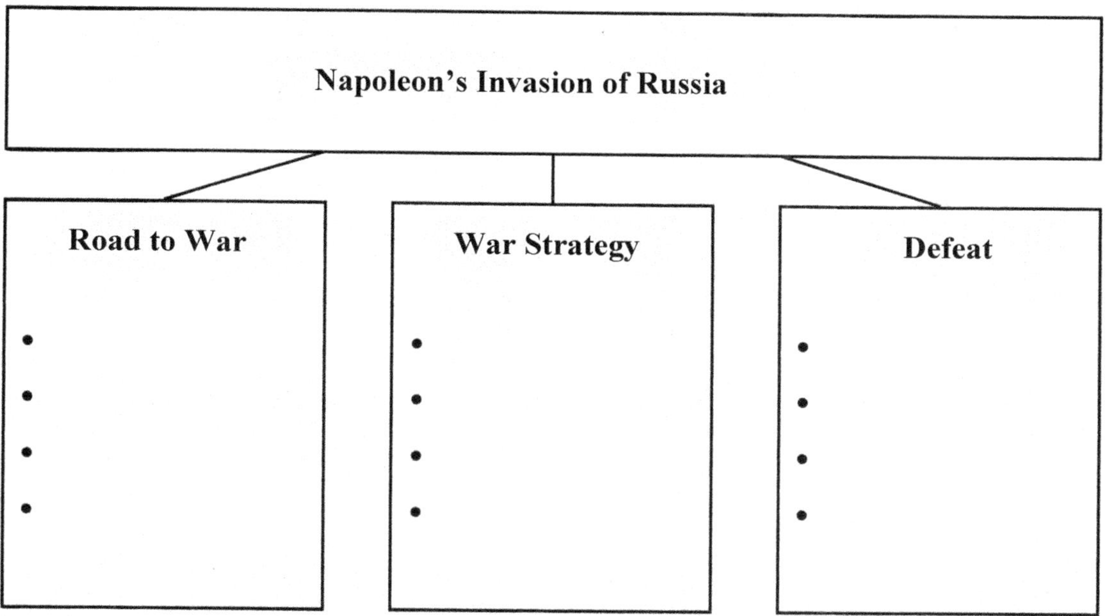

Review Questions

Write a brief answer to the following questions. Remember, each answer should highlight a primary idea using key words and supporting details.

1. Why did Napoleon decide to invade Russia?

2. Why did the operation fail?

SECTION 5 THE CONGRESS OF VIENNA AND THE EUROPEAN SETTLEMENT

FOCUS QUESTION

What were the consequences of the Congress of Vienna?

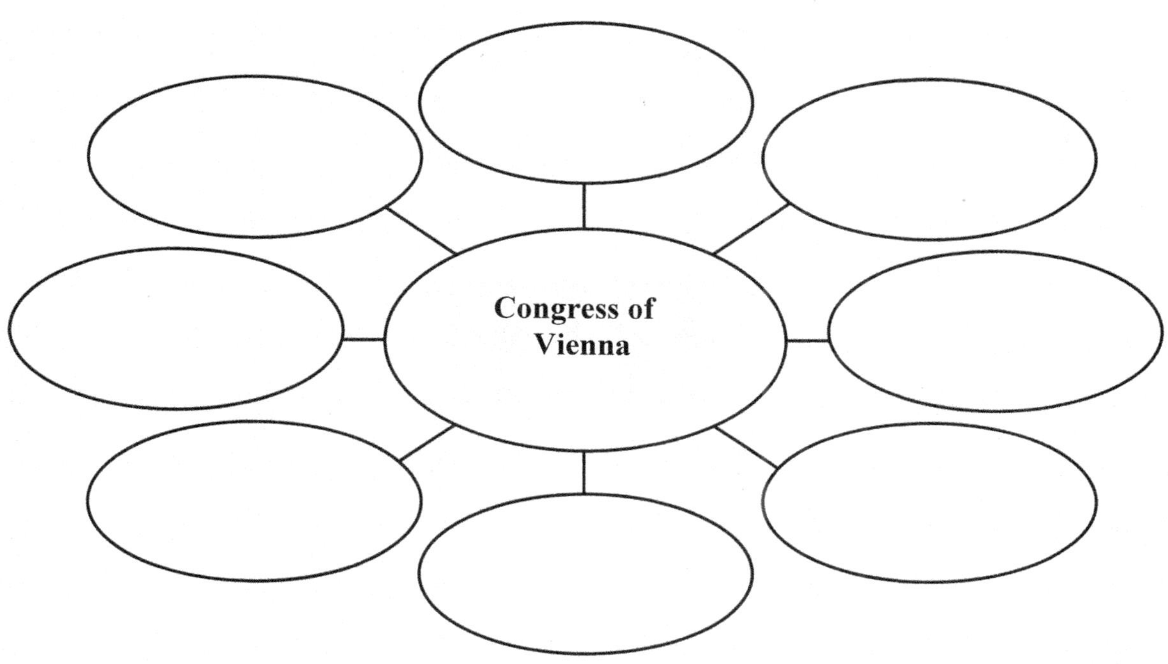

Using the information in your concept web, write a brief answer to the Focus Question.

Outline

Read the section topic entitled "Territorial Adjustments" and create an outline of the section below. Note the key words that reflect the main ideas in each paragraph as well as the key words that inform those ideas.

I. Territorial Adjustments
    A. The big four at the Congress of Vienna (1814–1815)
        1.
        2.
    B.
        1.
        2.
    C.
        1.
        2.
        3.
        4.
    D.
        1.
        2.
    E.
        1.
        2.
        3.
    F.
        1.
        2.
        3.

REVIEW QUESTIONS

Write a brief answer to the following questions. Remember, each answer should highlight a primary idea using key words and supporting details.

1. What were the results of the Congress of Vienna?

2. Was the Vienna settlement a success?

Section 6 Romantic Questioning of the Supremacy of Reason

Focus Question

How did Rousseau and Kant contribute to the development of romanticism?

Development of Romanticism	
Kant	**Rousseau**
•	•
•	•
•	•

Using the information in your chart, write a brief answer to the Focus Question.

OUTLINE

Read the section topic entitled "Kant and Reason" and create an outline of the section below. Note the key words that reflect the main ideas in each paragraph as well as the key words that inform those ideas.

I. Kant and Reason
   A. Immanuel Kant
      1.
      2.
   B.
      1.
      2.
      3.
      4.
   C.
      1.
      2.
   D.
      1.
      2.
   E.
      1.
      2.
      3.
      4.
   F.
      1.
      2.
      3.

Review Questions

Write a brief answer to the following questions. Remember, each answer should highlight a primary idea using key words and supporting details.

1. Why did romantic writers champion feelings over reason?

2. What questions did Rousseau and Kant raise about reason?

Section 7 Romantic Literature

Focus Question

How were the ideals of romanticism reflected in English and German literature?

English and German Romantic Literature	
English Literature	**German Literature**
•	•
•	•
•	•

Using the information in your table, write a brief answer to the Focus Question.

Outline

Read the section topic entitled "English Romantic Writers" and create an outline of the section below. Note the key words that reflect the main ideas in each paragraph as well as the key words that inform those ideas.

I. English Romantic Writers
   A. English romantic backlash
      1.
      2.
      3.
      4.
   B.
      1.
      2.
      3.
      4.
      5.
   C.
      1.
      2.
      3.
      4.
      5.
      6.
      7.
      8.
      9.
      10.
   D.
      1.
      2.
      3.
      4.
      5.

Review Questions

Write a brief answer to the following questions. Remember, each answer should highlight a primary idea using key words and supporting details.

1. Why was poetry important to romantic writers?

2. Why were Wordsworth and Coleridge's conceptions of childhood indicative of romanticism?

Section 8 Romantic Art

Focus Question

How were the ideals of romanticism reflected in English and German art?

English and German Romantic Art	
English Art	**German Art**
• • •	• • •

Using the information in your table, write a brief answer to the Focus Question.

OUTLINE

Read the section topic entitled "Nature and the Sublime" and create an outline of the section below. Note the key words that reflect the main ideas in each paragraph as well as the key words that inform those ideas.

I. Nature and the Sublime
   A. The sublime
      1.
      2.
      3.
   B.
      1.
      2.
      3.
      4.
      5.
   C.
      1.
      2.
      3.
      4.
   D.
      1.
      2.

REVIEW QUESTIONS

Write a brief answer to the following questions. Remember, each answer should highlight a primary idea using key words and supporting details.

1. Why did romantic artists look to the Middle Ages for inspiration?

2. In what way did art of the period often symbolize contradictory forces affecting romantic artists?

Section 9 Religion in the Romantic Period

Focus Question

How did romantic religious thinkers view the religious experience?

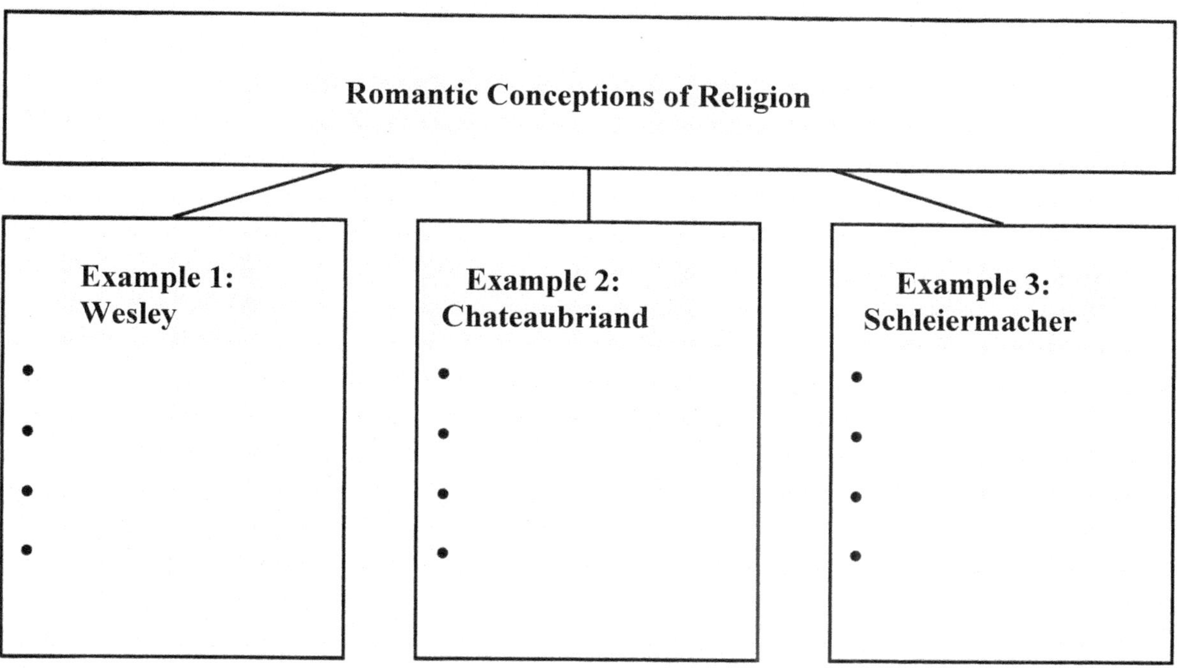

Using the information in your chart, write a brief answer to the Focus Question.

Outline

Read the section topic entitled "Methodism" and create an outline of the section below. Note the key words that reflect the main ideas in each paragraph as well as the key words that inform those ideas.

I. Methodism
   A. John Wesley
      1.
      2.
      3.
      4.
      5.
      6.
   B.
      1.
      2.
      3.
   C.
      1.
      2.
      3.
      4.
   D.
      1.
      2.
      3.
      4.

Review Questions

Write a brief answer to the following questions. Remember, each answer should highlight a primary idea using key words and supporting details.

1. How did the romantic concept of religion differ from Reformation Protestantism and Enlightenment Deism?

2. What was the turning point for John Wesley's faith? How was it significant for the development of Methodism?

SECTION 10 ROMANTIC VIEWS OF NATIONALISM AND HISTORY

FOCUS QUESTION

What were the romantic views of history and national identity?

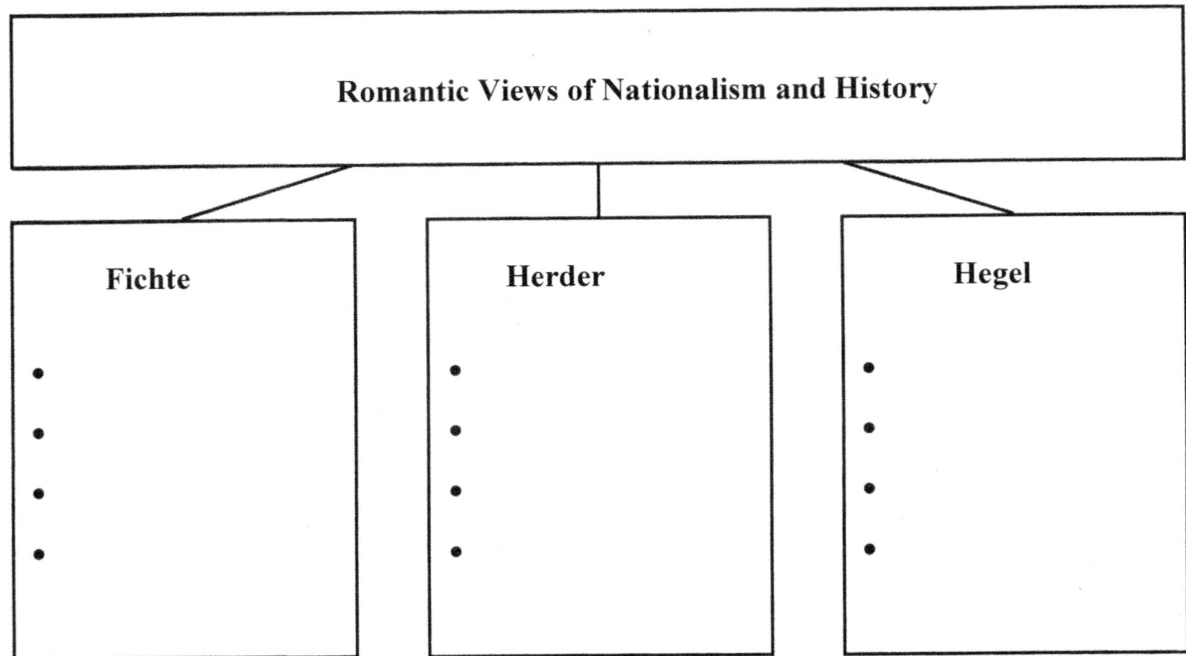

Using the information in your chart, write a brief answer to the Focus Question.

OUTLINE

Read the section topic entitled "Herder and Culture" and create an outline of the section below. Note the key words that reflect the main ideas in each paragraph as well as the key words that inform those ideas.

I. Herder and Culture
   A. German romantic writers
      1.
      2.
      3.
      4.
      5.
      6.
   B.
      1.
      2.
   C.
      1.
      2.
      3.
   D.
      1.
      2.
   E.
      1.
      2.
      3.
      4.

Review Questions

Write a brief answer to the following questions. Remember, each answer should highlight a primary idea using key words and supporting details.

1. How did romantic ideas and sensibilities modify European ideas of Islam and the Middle East?

2. What were the cultural results of Napoleon's invasion of Egypt?

Review: Key Terms and People

Complete your review of the chapter by writing a brief definition of the following terms and people.

Napoleon Bonaparte
Admiral Horatio Nelson
Treaty of Amiens
Napoleonic Code
Third Coalition
Battle of Trafalgar
Berlin Decrees
Treaty of Tilsit
Peace of Schönbrunn
Marie Louise
Congress of Vienna
Treaty of Chaumont
Waterloo
The Hundred Days
Quadruple Alliance
Romanticism
Sturm und Drang
Immanuel Kant
Samuel Coleridge
Friedrich Schlegel
Neo-Gothicism
Methodism
John Wesley
François René de Chateaubriand
Friedrich Schleiermacher
Johann Gottfried Herder
Georg Wilhelm Friedrich Hegel
Grimm brothers
Thomas Carlyle
Sir Walter Scott
Rosetta Stone

My Key Terms

Write down terms that are unfamiliar. How are the words used? Do other words or examples reveal their meaning? Try to figure out meaning from the context.

CHAPTER 12
THE CONSERVATIVE ORDER AND THE CHALLENGES OF REFORM (1815–1832)

Complete the following exercises *as you read* this chapter.

SECTION 1 THE CONSERVATIVE ORDER

FOCUS QUESTION

How did early-nineteenth-century nationalists define the nation?

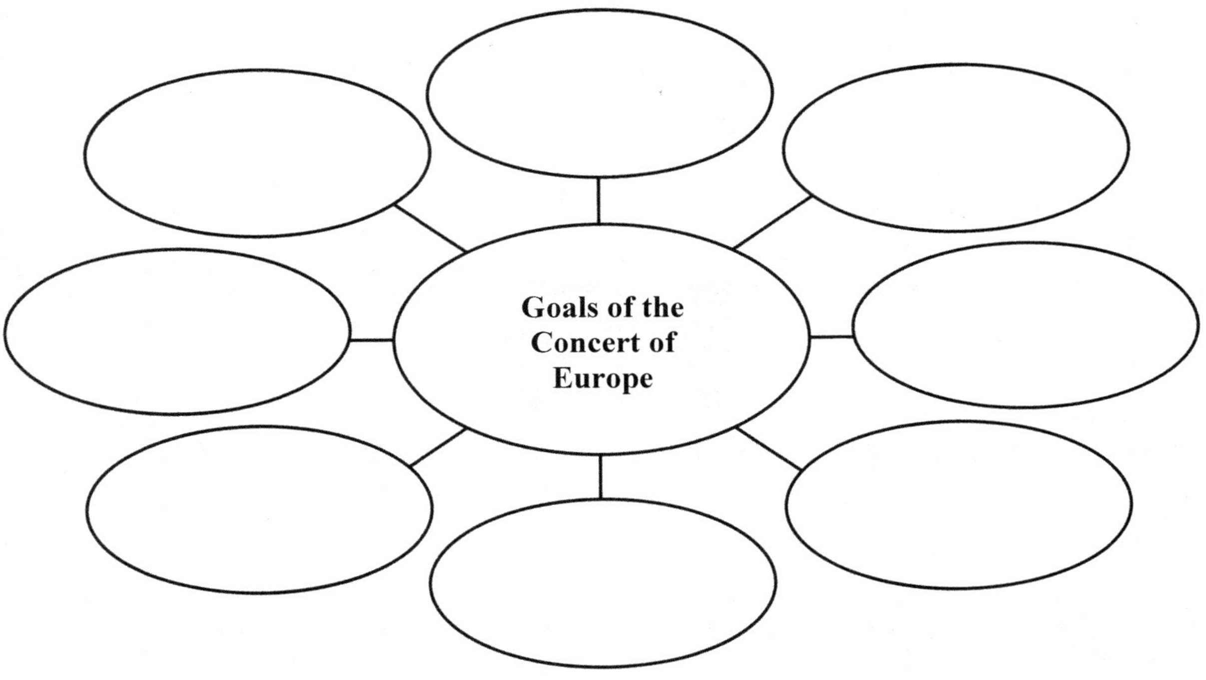

Using the information in your concept web, write a brief answer to the Focus Question.

Reading Skill: Cause and Effect

Complete the chart below to explain the strength of conservatism in the early nineteenth century.

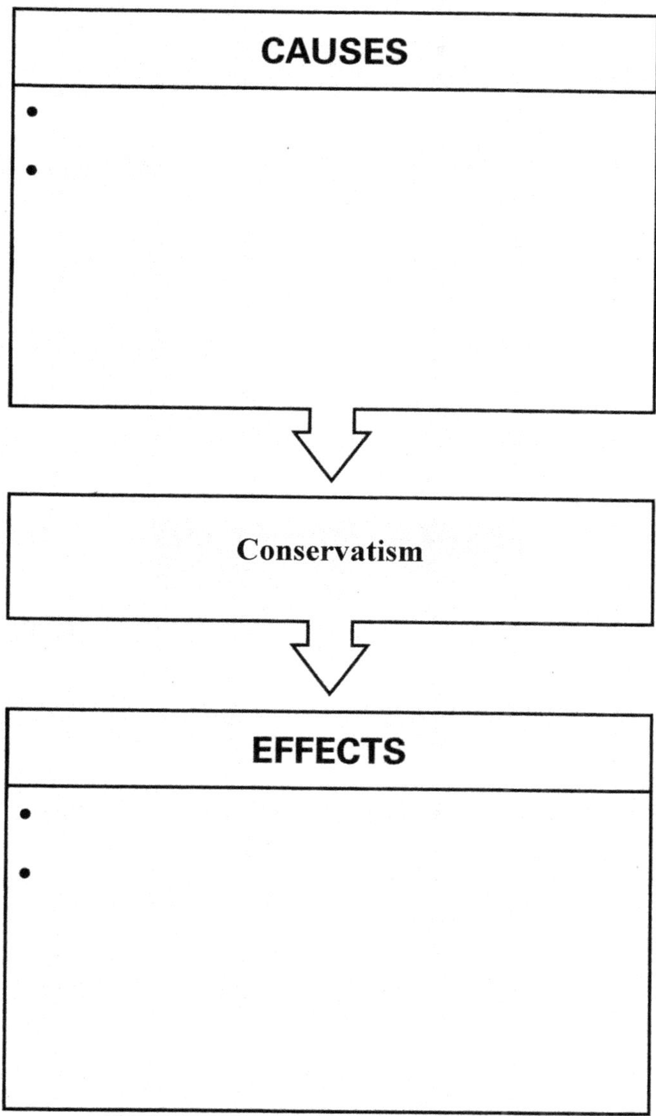

Review Questions

Write a brief answer to the following questions. Remember, each answer should highlight a primary idea using key words and supporting details.

1. What were the aims of the Concert of Europe?

2. How did the Congress of Vienna change international relations?

SECTION 2 THE EMERGENCE OF NATIONALISM AND LIBERALISM

FOCUS QUESTION

What explains the strength of conservatism in the early nineteenth century?

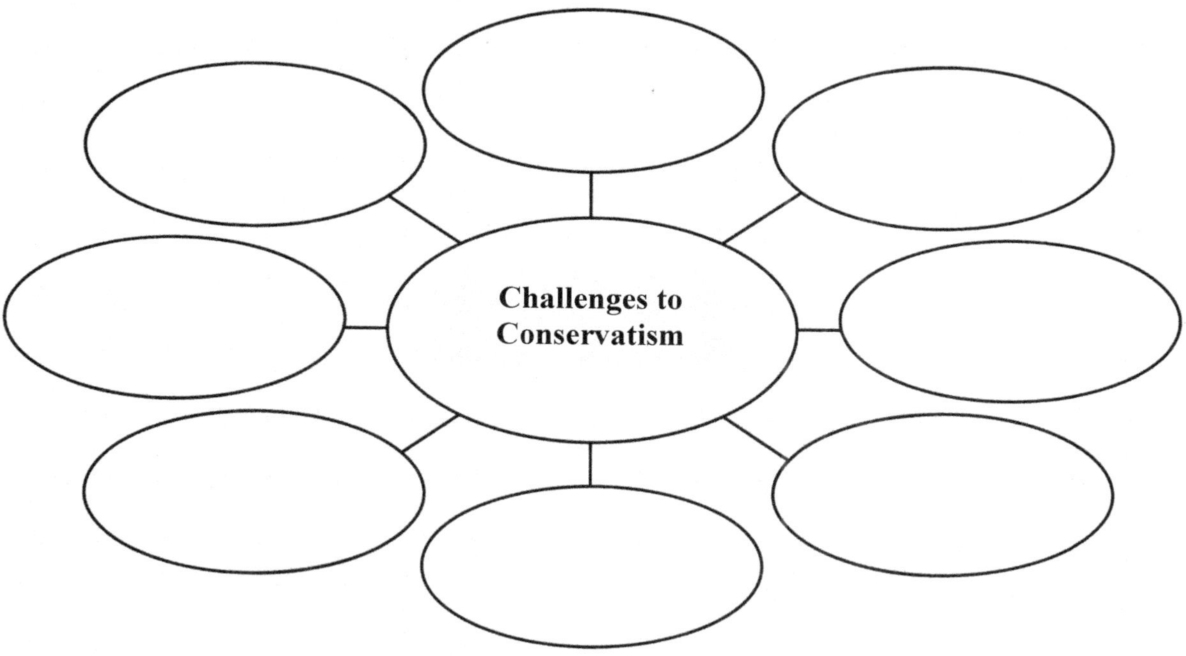

Using the information in your concept web, write a brief answer to the Focus Question.

FOCUS QUESTION

What were the key assumptions of classical economic theory?

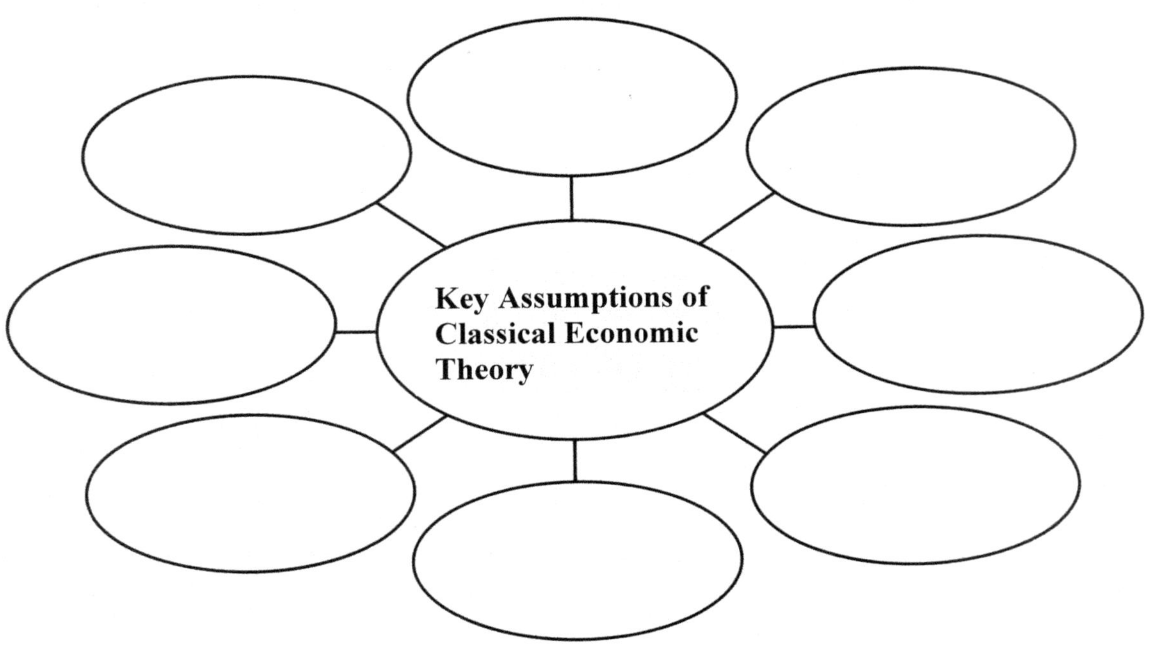

Using the information in your concept web, write a brief answer to the Focus Question.

OUTLINE

Read the section topic entitled "Nationalism" and create an outline of the section below. Note the key words that reflect the main ideas in each paragraph as well as the key words that inform those ideas.

I. The Emergence of Nationalism

   A. Nationalism

      1.

      2.

      3.

      4.

   B.

      1.

      2.

      3.

      4.

   C.

      1.

      2.

      3.

   D.

      1.

      2.

      3.

   E.

      1.

      2.

   F.

      1.

      2.

      3.

   G.

      1.

      2.

   H.

      1.

      2.

      3.

Review Questions

Write a brief answer to the following questions. Remember, each answer should highlight a primary idea using key words and supporting details.

1. What is nationalism?

2. What were the tenets of liberalism?

3. What was the relationship of liberalism to nationalism?

SECTION 3 CONSERVATIVE RESTORATION IN EUROPE

OUTLINE

Read the section topic entitled "Liberalism and Nationalism Resisted in Austria and the Germanies" and create an outline of the section below. Note the key words that reflect the main ideas in each paragraph as well as the key words that inform those ideas.

I. Liberalism and Nationalism Resisted in Austria and the Germanies
   A. Prince Klemens von Metternich of Austria
      1.
      2.
      3.
   B.
      1.
      2.
      3.
      4.
      5.
      6.
   C.
      1.
      2.
      3.
      4.
      5.
      6.
      7.
   D.
      1.
      2.
   E.
      1.
      2.
      3.
      4.

REVIEW QUESTIONS

Write a brief answer to the following questions. Remember, each answer should highlight a primary idea using key words and supporting details.

1. What were the goals of nationalists in the Germanies? What difficulties did nationalists confront in realizing those goals?

2. Why was nationalism a special threat to the Austrian Empire?

3. Who were the liberals, and how did liberalism affect the political developments of the early nineteenth century?

FOCUS QUESTION

How did Russia, France, and Britain respond to the challenges to the conservative order?

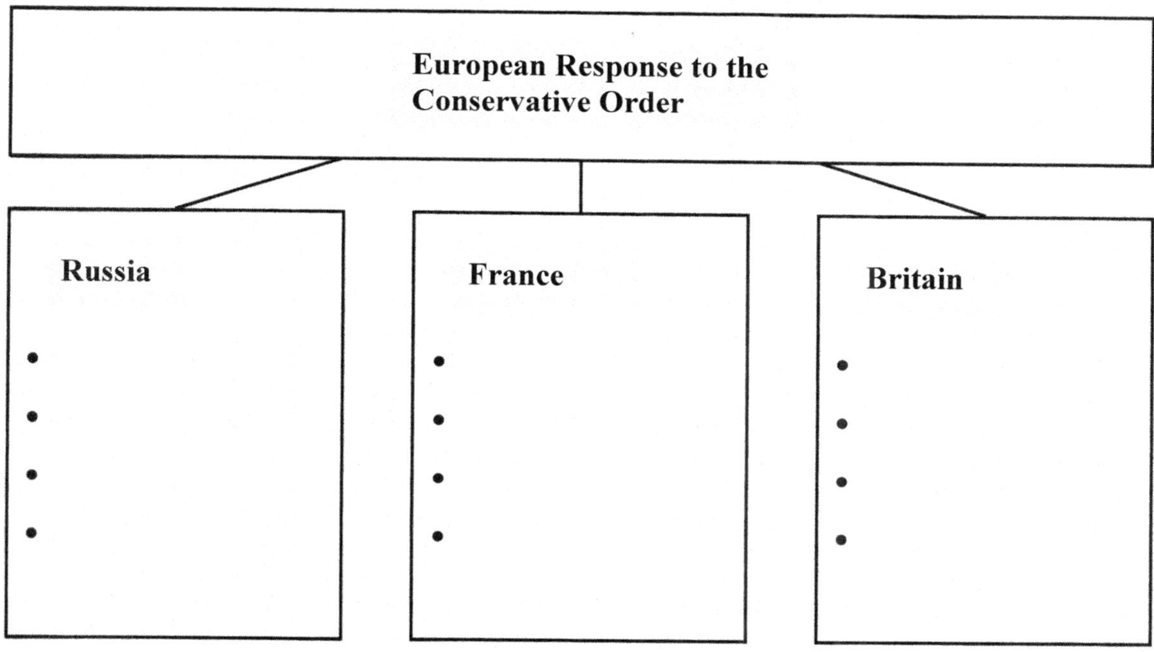

Using the information in your chart, write a brief answer to the Focus Question.

OUTLINE

Read the section topic entitled "Revolt against Ottoman Rule in the Balkans" and create an outline of the section below. Note the key words that reflect the main ideas in each paragraph as well as the key words that inform those ideas.

I. Revolt against Ottoman Rule in the Balkans

  A. Western liberals respond to Greek revolt

    1.

    2.

    3.

    4.

  B.

    1.

    2.

    3.

    4.

    5.

    6.

    7.

  C.

    1.

    2.

    3.

    4.

    5.

    6.

    7.

  D.

    1.

    2.

    3.

    4.

    5.

OUTLINE

Read the section topic entitled "The Great Reform Bill in Britain (1832)" and create an outline of the section below. Note the key words that reflect the main ideas in each paragraph as well as the key words that inform those ideas.

I. The Great Reform Bill in Britain (1832)

  A. Great Reform Bill as the result of events/conditions unique to Britain

    1.

    2.

    3.

    4.

    5.

  B.

    1.

    2.

  C.

    1.

    2.

    3.

    4.

    5.

    6.

    7.

    8.

    9.

  D.

    1.

    2.

    3.

    4.

    5.

REVIEW QUESTIONS

Write a brief answer to the following questions. Remember, each answer should highlight a primary idea using key words and supporting details.

1. What were the main provisions of the constitution of the restored monarchy in France?

2. What did Charles X hope to accomplish? Why did revolution break out in France in 1830? What did this revolution achieve and what problems did it fail to resolve?

3. Why did Britain avoid a revolution in the early 1830s? What was the purpose of the Great Reform Bill? What did it achieve? Would you call it a "revolutionary" document?

4. What areas saw significant nationalist movements between 1815 and 1830? Which were successful and which unsuccessful?

Section 5 The Wars of Independence in Latin America

Focus Question

What sparked the wars of independence in Latin America?

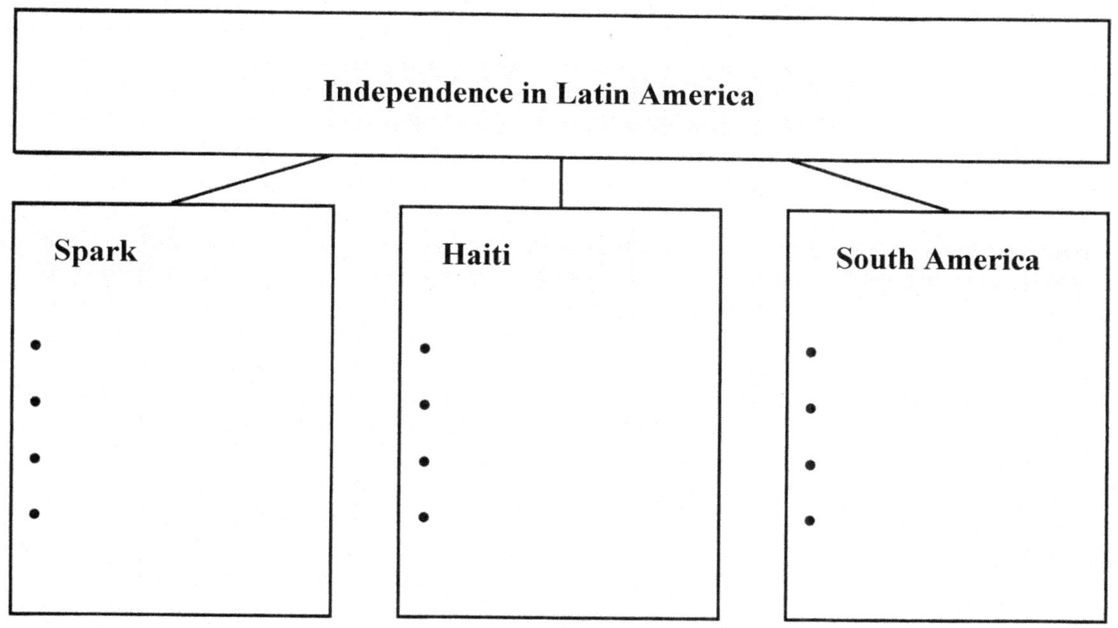

Using the information in your table, write a brief answer to the Focus Question.

OUTLINE

Read the section topic entitled "Independence in New Spain" and create an outline of the section below. Note the key words that reflect the main ideas in each paragraph as well as the key words that inform those ideas.

I. Independence in New Spain

A.

1.

2.

B.

1.

2.

3.

4.

5.

6.

7.

C.

1.

2.

3.

4.

D.

1.

2.

3.

4.

5.

6.

READING SKILL: SUMMARIZE

Complete the chart below identifying the key figures and interests that determined colonial independence in Latin America.

Colonial Independence in Latin America			
Region	**Key Figures**	**Interests**	**Actions**

REVIEW QUESTIONS

Write a brief answer to the following questions. Remember, each answer should highlight a primary idea using key words and supporting details.

1. What were the main reasons for Creole discontent with Spanish rule, and to what extent did Enlightenment political philosophy influence the Creole leaders?

2. Who were some of the primary leaders of Latin American independence?

3. Why was Brazil's path to independence different from that of Spanish America?

Review: Key Terms and People

Complete your review of the chapter by writing a brief definition of the following terms and people.

Nationalism
Liberal
Magyars
Conservatism
Klemens von Metternich
Burschenschaft
Corn Law
Peterloo Massacre
Louis XVIII
The Charter
Concert of Europe
Congress system
Protocol of Troppau
George Canning
Ferdinand VII of Spain
Treaty of Adrianople
François-Dominique Toussaint L'Ouverture
Peninsulares
Junta
José de San Martín
Simón Bolívar
Miguel Hidalgo y Costilla
Dom Pedro II
Decembrist Revolt
Nicholas I
Charles X
July Monarchy
The Convention of 1839
Daniel O'Connell
Great Reform Bill

My Key Terms

Write down terms that are unfamiliar. How are the words used? Do other words or examples reveal their meaning? Try to figure out meaning from the context.

CHAPTER 13
ECONOMIC ADVANCE AND SOCIAL UNREST (1830–1850)

Complete the following exercises in order *as you read* this chapter.

SECTION 1 TOWARD AN INDUSTRIAL SOCIETY

FOCUS QUESTION

How did industrialization spread across Europe?

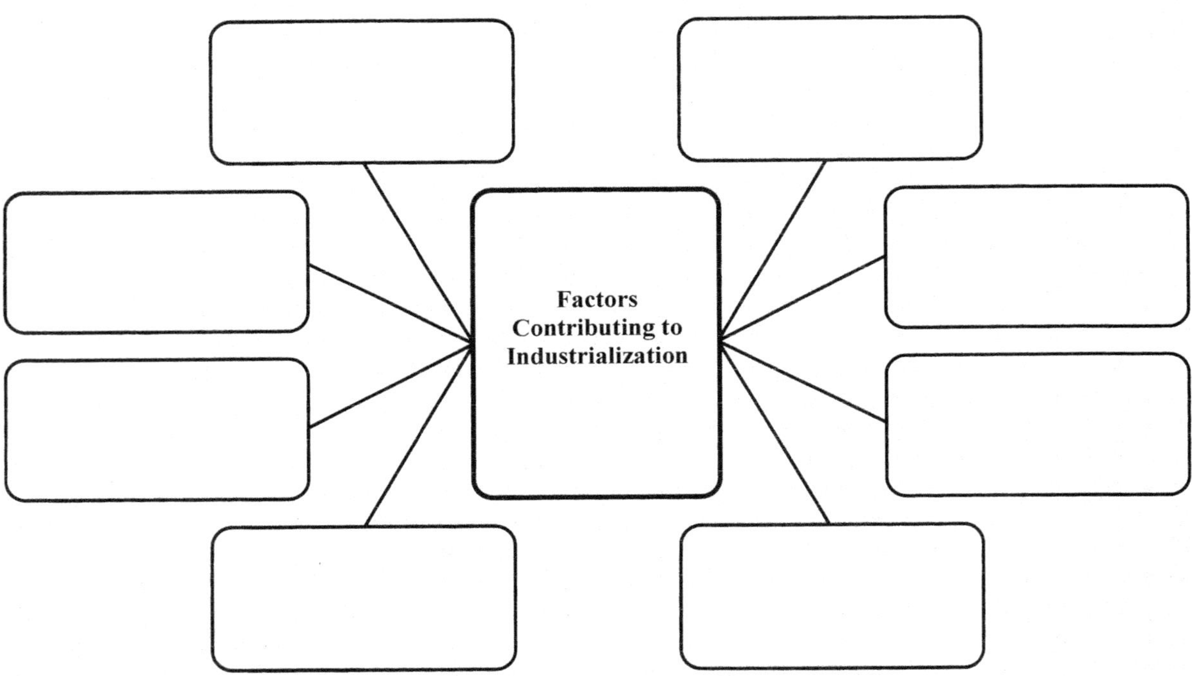

Using the information in your concept web, write a brief answer to the Focus Question.

OUTLINE

Read the section topic entitled "Population and Migration" and create an outline of the section below. Note the key words that reflect the main ideas in each paragraph as well as the key words that inform those ideas.

I. Population and Migration
   A. Spread of industrialization, population explosion 1831–1851
      1.
      2.
      3.
   B.
      1.
      2.
      3.
   C.
      1.
      2.
   D.
      1.
      2.
      3.
   E.
      1.
      2.
      3.
      4.
   F.
      1.
      2.
      3.
   G.
      1.
      2.

REVIEW QUESTIONS

Write a brief answer to the following questions. Remember, each answer should highlight a primary idea using key words and supporting details.

1. What natural resources and inventions were particularly important in the development of industrialism?

2. How did the British textile industry become a worldwide economic network?

3. Why are the different dates of rural emancipation across Europe significant?

4. How did the railway epitomize the character of the industrial economy during the second quarter of the century?

SECTION 2 THE LABOR FORCE

FOCUS QUESTION

How did industrialization change the European labor force?

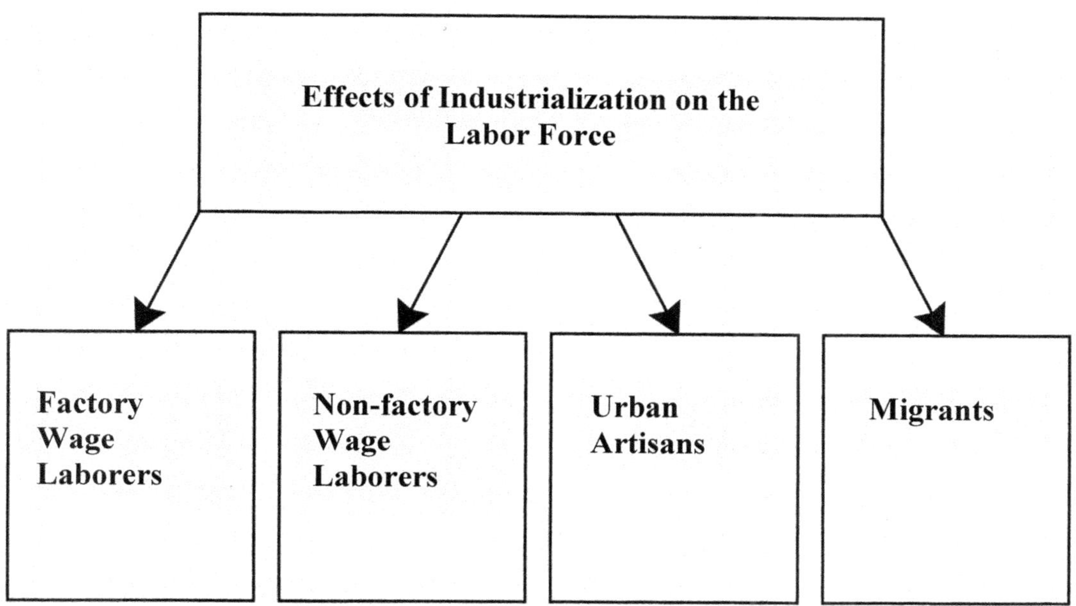

Using the information in your chart, write a brief answer to the Focus Question.

OUTLINE

Read the section topic entitled "Working-Class Political Action: The Example of British Chartism" and create an outline of the section below. Note the key words that reflect the main ideas in each paragraph as well as the key words that inform those ideas.

I. Working-Class Political Action: The Example of British Chartism
   A. By mid-century, European artisans radicalized
      1.
      2.
   B.
      1.
      2.
      3.
      4.
      5.
      6.
      7.
      8.
   C.
      1.
      2.
      3.
      4.
      5.
      6.
      7.
   D.
      1.
      2.
   E.
      1.
      2.

REVIEW QUESTIONS

Write a brief answer to the following questions. Remember, each answer should highlight a primary idea using key words and supporting details.

1. What difficulties due to industrialization did artisans, in particular, have to contend with?

2. How was the European labor force transformed into a wage-labor workforce?

Section 3 Family Structures and the Industrial Revolution

Focus Question

How did industrialization affect European families?

Industrialization's Effect on Family Structure		
Period	**Mode of Production**	**Family Structure**
Pre-late eighteenth century revolution in textile production		
Early factory production		
Shift from mid-1820s to 1830		
By mid-1840s		

Using the information in your table, write a brief answer to the Focus Question.

OUTLINE

Read the section topic entitled "The Family in the Early Factory System" and create an outline of the section below. Note the key words that reflect the main ideas in each paragraph as well as the key words that inform those ideas.

I. The Family in the Early Factory System
   A. Family work structure in textile industry before the late eighteenth century
      1.
      2.
      3.
   B.
      1.
      2.
      3.
      4.
      5.
   C.
      1.
      2.
      3.
      4.
      5.
      6.
      7.
   D.
      1.
      2.
      3.
      4.
      5.
   E.
      1.
      2.

Review Questions

Write a brief answer to the following questions. Remember, each answer should highlight a primary idea using key words and supporting details.

1. How did the industrial economy change the working-class family?

2. What roles and duties did various family members assume?

Section 4 Women in the Early Industrial Revolution

Focus Question

What role did women play in the Industrial Revolution?

Women and their Work in the Industrial Revolution	
The Factory	
Cottage Industries	
On the Land	
In the Home	
Supplementing Wages	

Using the information in your table, write a brief answer to the Focus Question.

OUTLINE

Read the section topic entitled "Changing Expectations in the Working-Class Marriage" and create an outline of the section below. Note the key words that reflect the main ideas in each paragraph as well as the key words that inform those ideas.

I. Changing Expectations in the Working-Class Marriage
   A. Wage-economy in cities, wider opportunities for marriage
      1.
      2.
   B.
      1.
      2.
      3.
      4.
   C.
      1.
      2.
      3.
   D.
      1.
      2.
   E.
      1.
      2.
      3.
   F.
      1.
      2.
      3.

Review Questions

Write a brief answer to the following questions. Remember, each answer should highlight a primary idea using key words and supporting details.

1. How did the role of women change in the new industrial era?

2. In what ways did working-class women come to imitate the family patterns of the middle and upper classes?

SECTION 5 PROBLEMS OF CRIME, ORDER, AND POVERTY

FOCUS QUESTION

How did the establishment of police forces and the reform of prisons change society?

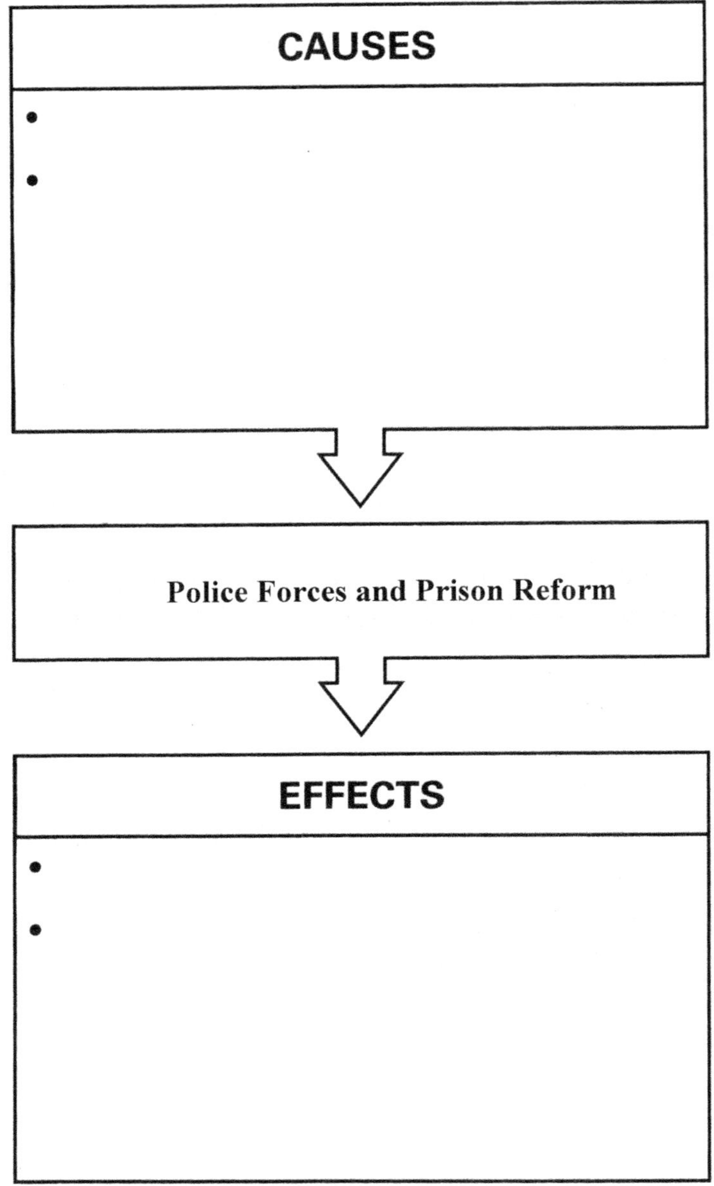

Using the information in your chart, write a brief answer to the Focus Question.

OUTLINE

Read the section topic entitled "New Police Forces" and create an outline of the section below. Note the key words that reflect the main ideas in each paragraph as well as the key words that inform those ideas.

I. New Police Forces
   A. Purpose of the police
      1.
      2.
      3.
      4.
      5.
   B.
      1.
      2.
      3.
      4.
      5.
   C.
      1.
      2.
      3.
      4.
      5.
   D.
      1.
      2.
      3.

OUTLINE

Read the section topic entitled "Government Policies Based on Classical Economics" and create an outline of the section below. Note the key words that reflect the main ideas in each paragraph as well as the key words that inform those ideas.

I. Government Policies Based on Classical Economics

A. France

1.

2.

3.

B.

1.

2.

3.

4.

C.

1.

2.

3.

4.

D.

1.

2.

3.

4.

5.

E.

1.

2.

3.

F.

1.

2.

Review Questions

Write a brief answer to the following questions. Remember, each answer should highlight a primary idea using key words and supporting details.

1. Why did European states create police forces in the nineteenth century?

2. How and why did prisons change during this era? Were the reforms successful? Why? Why not?

3. How did the Poor Law represent utilitarian policy?

Section 6 Early Socialism

Focus Question

How did socialism challenge classical economics?

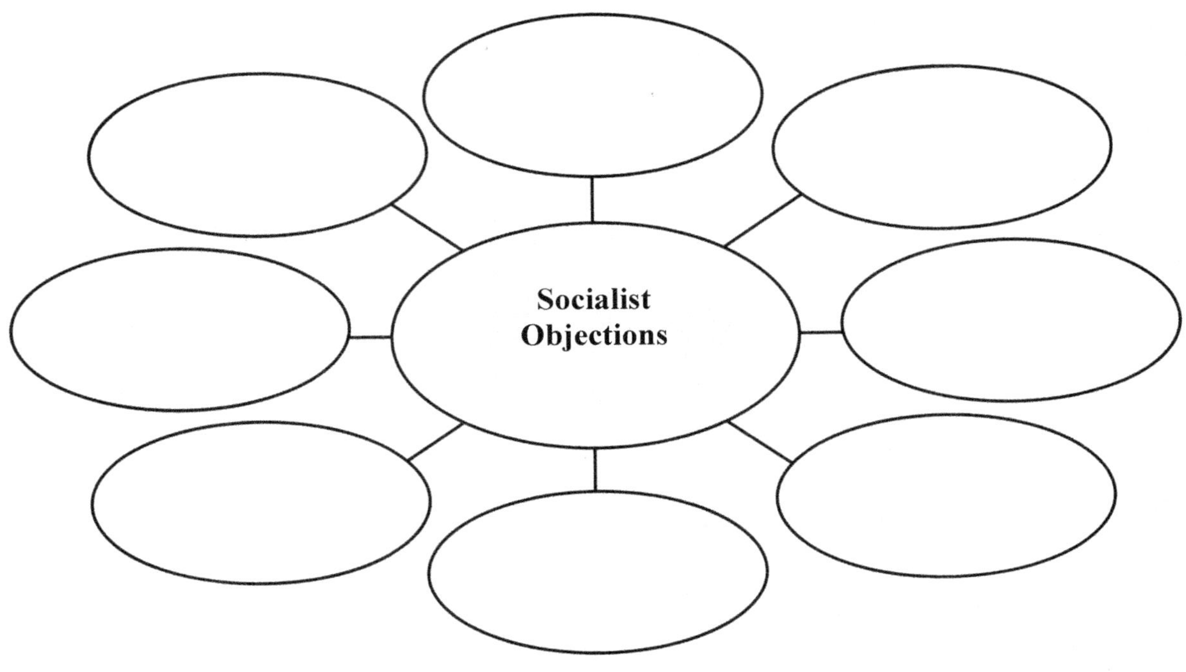

Using the information in your concept web, write a brief answer to the Focus Question.

Outline

Read the section topic entitled "Utopian Socialism" and create an outline of the section below. Note the key words that reflect the main ideas in each paragraph as well as the key words that inform those ideas.

I. Utopian Socialism
   A. Utopian socialism
      1.
      2.
      3.
      4.
   B.
      1.
      2.
      3.
      4.
      5.
      6.
   C.
      1.
      2.
      3.
      4.
      5.
      6.
   D.
      1.
      2.
      3.
      4.
   E.
      1.
      2.
   F.
      1.
      2.

Review Questions

Write a brief answer to the following questions. Remember, each answer should highlight a primary idea using key words and supporting details.

1. How would you define Socialism?

2. What were the chief ideas of the early Socialists?

3. How did the ideas of Karl Marx differ from those of the Socialists? What historical role did Marx assign to the proletariat?

Section 7 1848: Year of Revolutions

Focus Question

Why did a series of revolutions erupt across Europe in 1848?

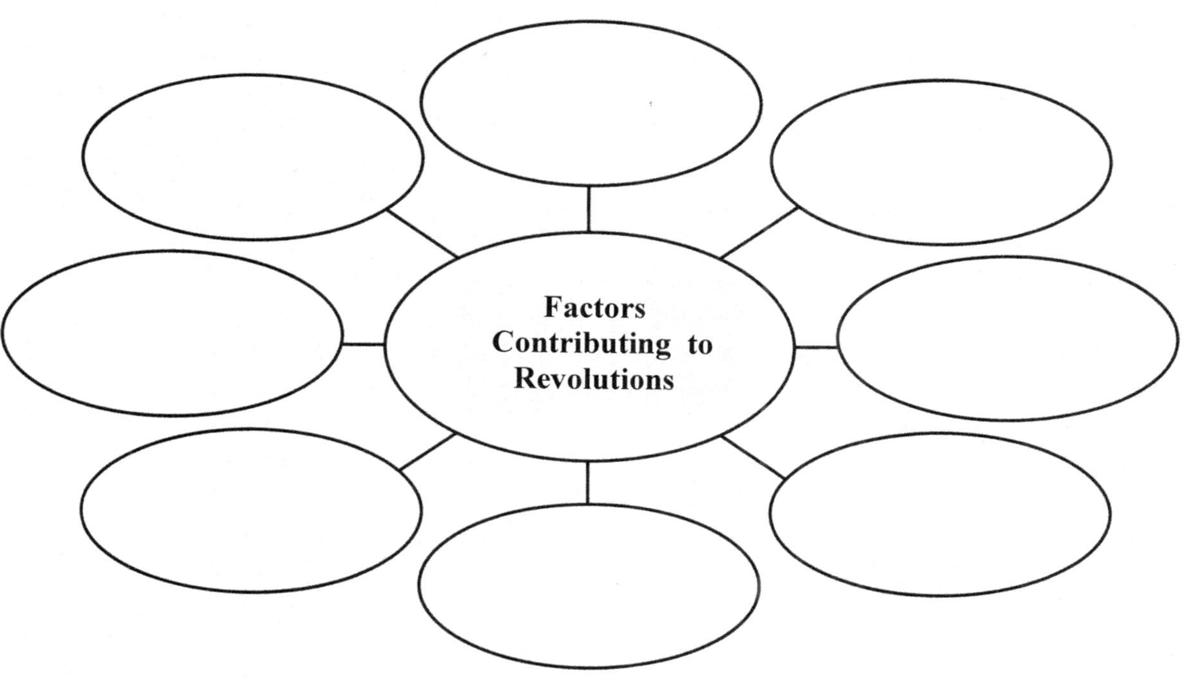

Using the information in your concept web, write a brief answer to the Focus Question.

OUTLINE

Read the section topic entitled "Italy: Republicanism Defeated" and create an outline of the section below. Note the key words that reflect the main ideas in each paragraph as well as the key words that inform those ideas.

I. Italy: Republicanism Defeated

   A. Preparing for Italian unification

      1.

      2.

      3.

   B.

      1.

      2.

   C.

      1.

      2.

      3.

      4.

      5.

      6.

      7.

   D.

      1.

      2.

      3.

   E.

      1.

      2.

      3.

      4.

      5.

READING SKILL: SUMMARIZE

Complete the table below identifying key events of the Second Republic of Louis Napoleon.

Second Republic of Louis Napoleon	
Event	**Description**
•	•
•	•
•	•

Review Questions

Write a brief answer to the following questions. Remember, each answer should highlight a primary idea using key words and supporting details.

1. What factors, old and new, led to the widespread outbreak of the revolutions in 1848?

2. Were the causes in the various countries essentially the same, or did each have its own particular set of circumstances?

3. Why did these revolutions fail throughout Europe?

4. What roles did liberals and nationalists play in the revolutions? Why did they sometimes clash?

REVIEW: KEY TERMS AND PEOPLE

Complete your review of the chapter by writing a brief definition of the following terms and people.

Irish famine
Capital industries
Wage-labor
Proletarianization
Chartism
Production unit
English Factory Act
Family wage economy
Transportation policy
Auburn system
Philadelphia system
Zollverein
Utilitarianism
Corn Laws
Utopian socialism
Anarchism
Marxism
Communist
Capitalist
Class conflict
Louis Blanc
Louis Napoleon Bonaparte
Louis Kossuth
Pan-Slavism
Grossdeutsch

MY KEY TERMS

Write down terms that are unfamiliar. How are the words used? Do other words or examples reveal their meaning? Try to figure out meaning from the context.

CHAPTER 14
THE AGE OF NATION-STATES

Complete the following exercises *as you read* this chapter.

SECTION 1 THE CRIMEAN WAR (1853–1856)

FOCUS QUESTION

Why was the Crimean War fought?

Reasons for Crimean War	
Country	**Interests**
•	•
•	•
•	•

Using the information in your table, write a brief answer to the Focus Question.

Outline

Read the section topic entitled "The Crimean War (1853–1856)" and create an outline of the section below. Note the key words that reflect the main ideas in each paragraph as well as the key words that inform those ideas.

I. The Crimean War (1853–1856)

   A. Rooted in Russian interest in extending influence in Ottoman territory

      1.

      2.

      3.

      4.

      5.

      6.

      7.

      8.

   B.

      1.

      2.

      3.

      4.

   C.

      1.

      2.

      3.

      4.

      5.

Review Questions

Write a brief answer to the following questions. Remember, each answer should highlight a primary idea using key words and supporting details.

1. Why did Britain and France object to Russian expansion into the Ottoman Empire?

2. What shattered the Concert of Europe? Why was this significant?

SECTION 2 REFORMS IN THE OTTOMAN EMPIRE

FOCUS QUESTION

How did the Ottoman Empire attempt to reform itself?

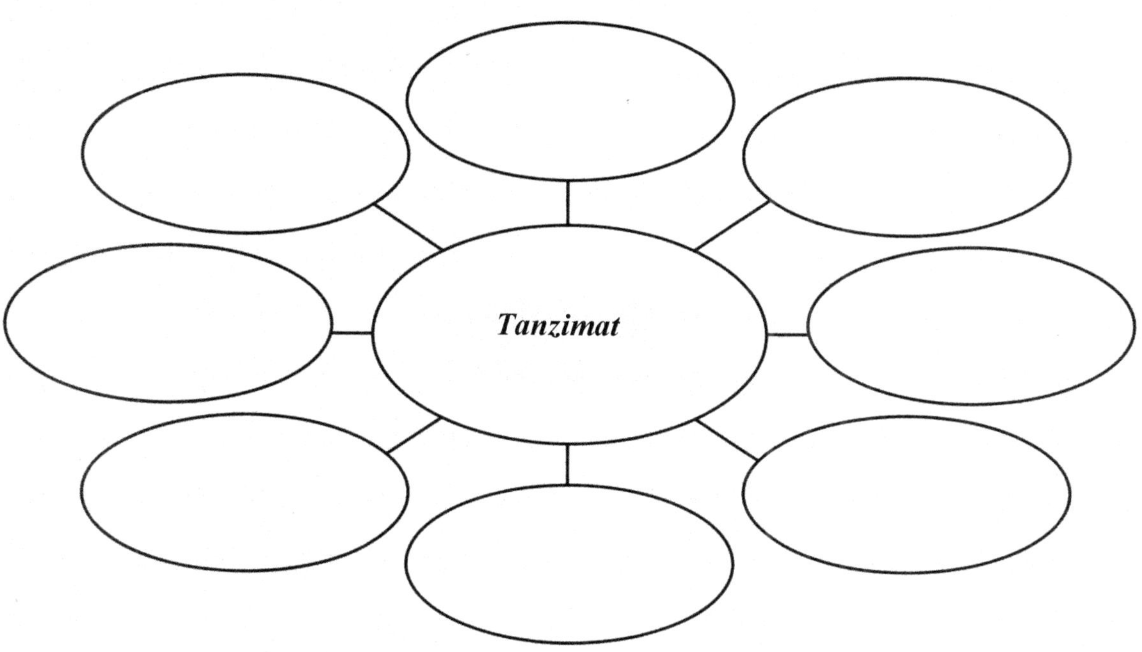

Using the information in your concept web, write a brief answer to the Focus Question.

OUTLINE

Read the section topic entitled "Reforms in the Ottoman Empire" and create an outline of the section below. Note the key words that reflect the main ideas in each paragraph as well as the key words that inform those ideas.

I. Reforms in the Ottoman Empire
   A. *Tanzimat* (reform) in the Ottoman Empire (1839–1876)
      1.
      2.
      3.
      4.
      5.
      6.
      7.
   B.
      1.
      2.
   C.
      1.
      2.
      3.
      4.
      5.
   D.
      1.
      2.
      3.
   E.
      1.
      2.
      3.

Review Questions

Write a brief answer to the following questions. Remember, each answer should highlight a primary idea using key words and supporting details.

1. Why did the Ottoman Empire attempt to reform itself between 1839 and 1914?

2. What was the result of these efforts?

SECTION 3 ITALIAN UNIFICATION

FOCUS QUESTION

How did Italy achieve unification?

Cavour and Italian Unification	
Force of Arms	**Secret Diplomacy**
• • •	• • •

Using the information in your table, write a brief answer to the Focus Question.

OUTLINE

Read the section topic entitled "The New Italian State" and create an outline of the section below. Note the key words that reflect the main ideas in each paragraph as well as the key words that inform those ideas.

I. The New Italian State

   A. 1861 Victor Emmanuel II, new king of a unified Italy, confronts problems

      1.

      2.

      3.

      4.

      5.

   B.

      1.

      2.

      3.

      4.

   C.

      1.

      2.

      3.

      4.

      5.

   D.

      1.

      2.

REVIEW QUESTIONS

Write a brief answer to the following questions. Remember, each answer should highlight a primary idea using key words and supporting details.

1. Why was it so difficult to unify Italy?

2. What groups wanted unification?

3. Why did Cavour succeed?

4. What did Garibaldi contribute to Italian unification?

SECTION 4 GERMAN UNIFICATION

FOCUS QUESTION

How did Otto von Bismarck use war as a tool for achieving German unification?

Bismarck's War Strategy	
Danish War (1864)	**Austro-Prussian War (1866)**
•	•
•	•
•	•

Using the information in your table, write a brief answer to the Focus Question.

Outline

Read the section topic entitled "The Franco-Prussian War and the German Empire (1870–1871)" and create an outline of the section below. Note the key words that reflect the main ideas in each paragraph as well as the key words that inform those ideas.

I. The Franco-Prussian War and the German Empire (1870–1871)
    A. German unification and the Spanish excuse, June 1870
        1.
        2.
        3.
        4.
        5.
        6.
    B.
        1.
        2.
        3.
    C.
        1.
        2.
        3.
        4.
    D.
        1.
        2.
    E.
        1.
        2.
    F.
        1.
        2.
        3.

Review Questions

Write a brief answer to the following questions. Remember, each answer should highlight a primary idea using key words and supporting details.

1. How and why did Bismarck unify Germany?

2. Why had earlier attempts failed?

3. How did German unification affect the rest of Europe?

Section 5 France: From Liberal Empire to the Third Republic

Focus Question

What event led to the establishment of a Third Republic in France?

Second Empire ends at Battle of Sedan 1870

Using the information in your flowchart, write a brief answer to the Focus Question.

OUTLINE

Read the section topic entitled "The Paris Commune" and create an outline of the section below. Note the key words that reflect the main ideas in each paragraph as well as the key words that inform those ideas.

I. The Paris Commune
  A. Division between Paris and the provinces
    1.
    2.
    3.
  B.
    1.
    2.
    3.
    4.
  C.
    1.
    2.
    3.
    4.
  D.
    1.
    2.

READING SKILL: SUMMARIZE

Complete the chart below identifying the key events and participants in the Dreyfus Affair.

Military court finds Dreyfus guilty of passing secrets to the German army	
Events	**Participants**
•	•
•	•
•	•

Review Questions

Write a brief answer to the following questions. Remember, each answer should highlight a primary idea using key words and supporting details.

1. What events led to the establishment of the Third Republic in France?

2. What were the objectives of the Paris Commune?

3. How did the Dreyfus affair affect the Third Republic?

Section 6 The Habsburg Empire

Focus Question

Why was nationalism such a threat to the Habsburg Empire?

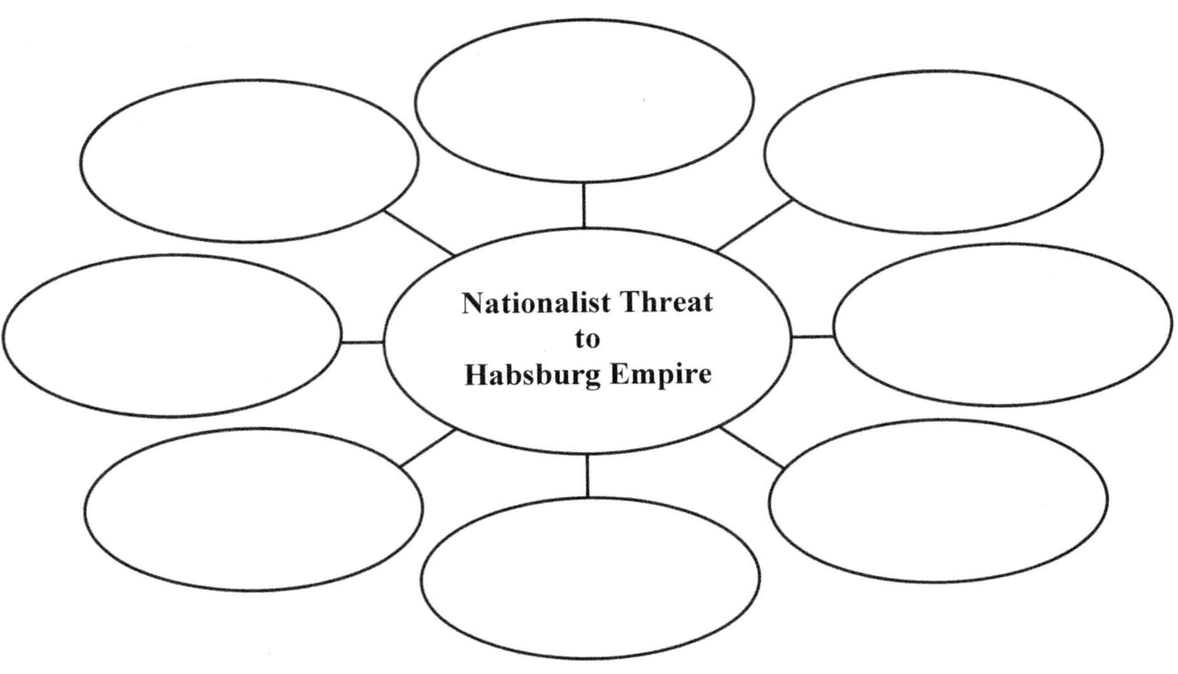

Using the information in your concept web, write a brief answer to the Focus Question.

OUTLINE

Read the section topic entitled "Unrest of Nationalities" and create an outline of the section below. Note the key words that reflect the main ideas in each paragraph as well as the key words that inform those ideas.

I. Unrest of Nationalities
   A. The Compromise of 1867 and two principles of political legitimacy
      1.
      2.
   B.
      1.
      2.
      3.
   C.
      1.
      2.
      3.
   D.
      1.
      2.
      3.
      4.
   E.
      1.
      2.
   F.
      1.
      2.
      3.
      4.
   G.
      1.
      2.
      3.
      4.
      5.

Review Questions

Write a brief answer to the following questions. Remember, each answer should highlight a primary idea using key words and supporting details.

1. What problems did Austria share with other eastern European empires? Were they solved?

2. Why did the Habsburgs agree to the Compromise of 1867? Was it a success?

Section 7 Russia: Emancipation and Revolutionary Stirrings

Focus Question

Why did reform in Russia fail to produce political stability?

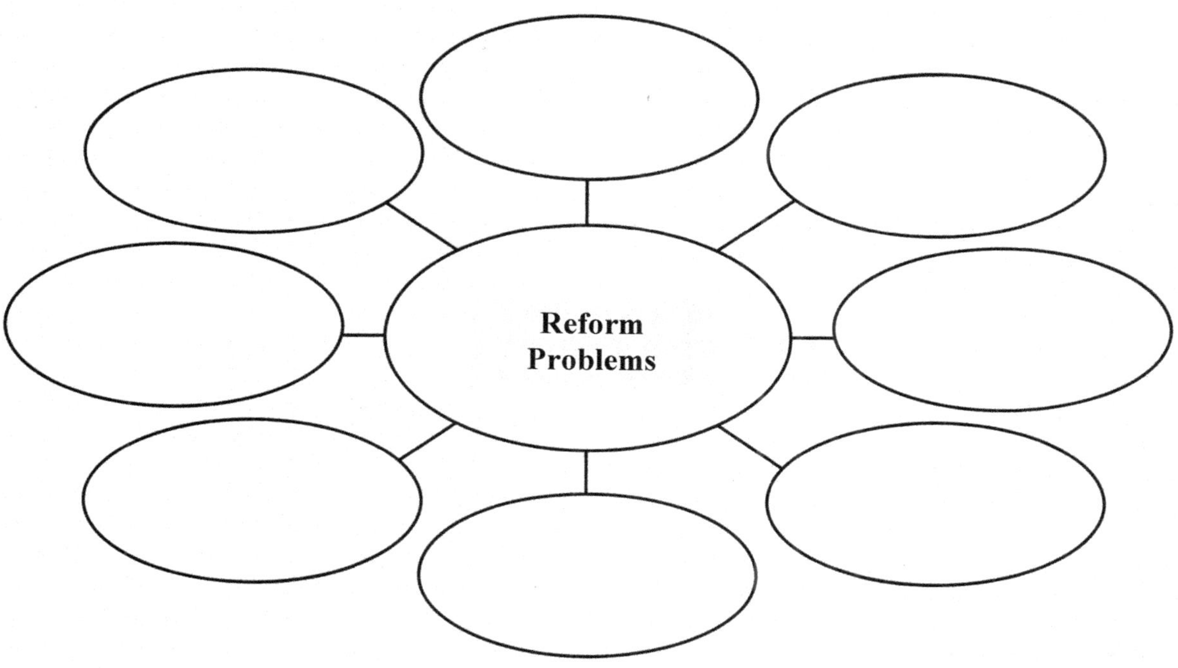

Using the information in your concept web, write a brief answer to the Focus Question.

OUTLINE

Read the section topic entitled "Reforms of Alexander II" and create an outline of the section below. Note the key words that reflect the main ideas in each paragraph as well as the key words that inform those ideas.

I. Reforms of Alexander II
   A. Abolition of Serfdom
      1.
      2.
      3.
      4.
      5.
   B.
      1.
      2.
      3.
      4.
      5.
   C.
      1.
      2.
      3.
      4.
      5.
      6.
   D.
      1.
      2.
   E.
      1.
      2.
   F.
      1.
      2.
   G.
      1.
      2.
      3.

REVIEW QUESTIONS

Write a brief answer to the following questions. Remember, each answer should highlight a primary idea using key words and supporting details.

1. What reforms did Alexander II institute in Russia?

2. Why did the abolition of serfdom not satisfy the peasants?

3. What were the goals of The People's Will?

SECTION 8 GREAT BRITAIN: TOWARD DEMOCRACY

FOCUS QUESTION

What forces led to the expansion of democracy in Great Britain?

Expanding Democracy in Great Britain	
Factor	**Description**
Culture	
Institutions	
Politics	
Education Policy	
Social Reform	

Using the information in your table, write a brief answer to the Focus Question.

OUTLINE

Read the section topic entitled "Gladstone's Great Ministry (1868–1874)" and create an outline of the section below. Note the key words that reflect the main ideas in each paragraph as well as the key words that inform those ideas.

I. Gladstone's Great Ministry (1868–1874)

   A. Culmination of classical British liberalism

      1.

      2.

      3.

      4.

   B.

      1.

      2.

   C.

      1.

      2.

      3.

      4.

Review Questions

Write a brief answer to the following questions. Remember, each answer should highlight a primary idea using key words and supporting details.

1. How did the policies of the British Liberal and Conservative parties differ between 1860 and 1890?

2. Why was Irish home rule such a divisive issue in British politics?

Review: Key Terms and People

Complete your review of the chapter by writing a brief definition of the following terms and people.

The Crimean War
Napoleon III
Tanzimat
Hatt-i Hümayun
Giuseppe Mazzini
Giuseppe Garibaldi
Count Camillo Cavour
William I
Otto von Bismarck
Franco-Prussian war
Treaty of Prague
Reichstag
Indemnity
Battle of Sedan
Paris Commune
Third Republic
Patrice MacMahon
Dreyfus Affair
Émile Zola
Francis Joseph
Compromise of 1867
Trialism
Alexander II
Populism
The People's Will
Second Reform Act
Benjamin Disraeli
William Gladstone
Public Health Act of 1875
Artisan Dwelling Act of 1875
Home rule

My Key Terms

Write down terms that are unfamiliar. How are the words used? Do other words or examples reveal their meaning? Try to figure out meaning from the context.

CHAPTER 15
THE BUILDING OF EUROPEAN SUPREMACY: SOCIETY AND POLITICS TO WORLD WAR I

Complete the following exercises in order *as you read* this chapter.

SECTION 1 POPULATION TRENDS AND MIGRATION

FOCUS QUESTION

Why were so many Europeans on the move in the late nineteenth century?

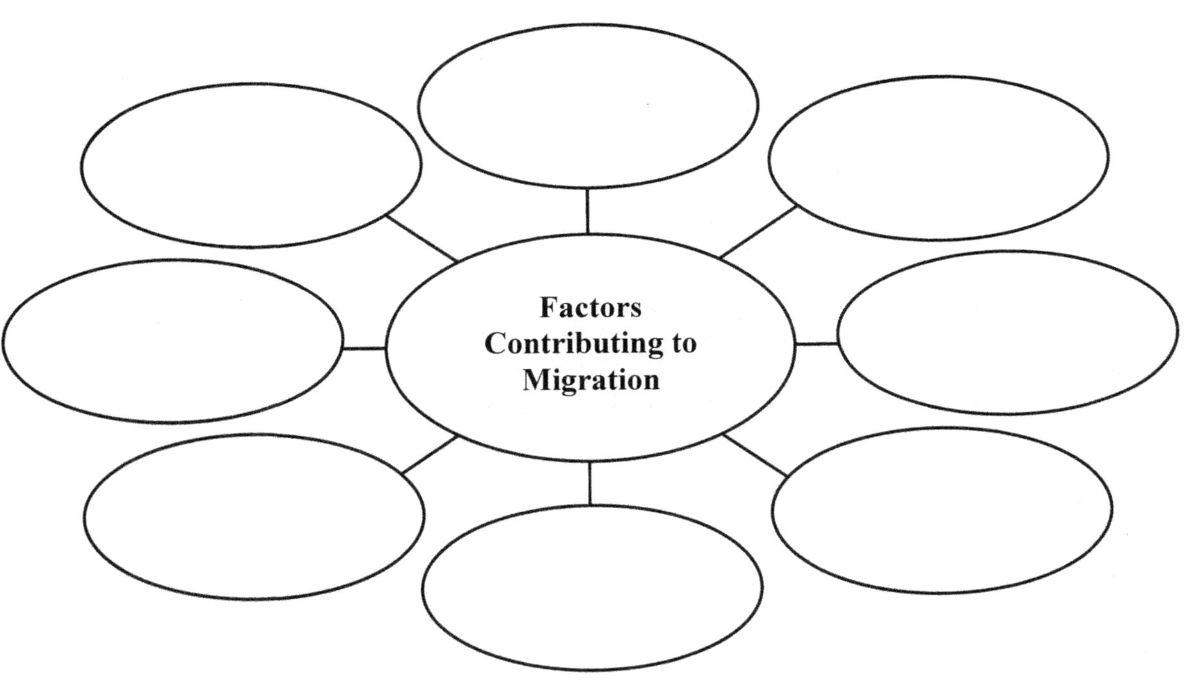

Using the information in your concept web, write a brief answer to the Focus Question.

OUTLINE

Read the section topic entitled "Population Trends and Migration" and create an outline of the section below. Note the key words that reflect the main ideas in each paragraph as well as the key words that inform those ideas.

I. Population Trends and Migration
  A. Proportion of Europeans in world's population greatest in 1900
    1.
    2.
    3.
    4.
    5.
  B.
    1.
    2.
    3.
    4.
    5.
    6.
    7.
    8.
    9.
  C.
    1.
    2.

Review Questions

Write a brief answer to the following questions. Remember, each answer should highlight a primary idea using key words and supporting details.

1. Why was emancipating European serfs significant to world Europeanization?

2. What was one reason for a demographic differential between developed and developing countries? Why was it significant?

SECTION 2 THE SECOND INDUSTRIAL REVOLUTION

FOCUS QUESTION

How did the second Industrial Revolution transform European life?

Impact of the Second Industrial Revolution on European Life	
Development	**Impact**
Steel	
Chemicals	
Electricity	
Oil	
Globalization	
Urbanization	

Using the information in your table, write a brief answer to the Focus Question.

OUTLINE

Read the section topic entitled "New Industries" and create an outline of the section below. Note the key words that reflect the main ideas in each paragraph as well as the key words that inform those ideas.

I. New Industries
  A. Third quarter of nineteenth century
    1.
    2.
    3.
    4.
  B.
    1.
    2.
    3.
    4.
  C.
    1.
    2.
    3.
    4.
    5.
  D.
    1.
    2.
    3.
    4.
    5.
  E.
    1.
    2.
    3.
    4.

REVIEW QUESTIONS

Write a brief answer to the following questions. Remember, each answer should highlight a primary idea using key words and supporting details.

1. How did the Second Industrial Revolution transform European society?

2. What new industries developed, and which do you think had the greatest impact in the twentieth century?

3. Why did European economic growth slacken in the second half of the nineteenth century?

SECTION 3 THE MIDDLE CLASSES IN ASCENDANCY

FOCUS QUESTION

What explains the prominence of the middle class in late-nineteenth-century Europe?

Why Middle Class Was Prominent		
•	•	•

Using the information in your table, write a brief answer to the Focus Question.

OUTLINE

Read the section topic entitled "Social Distinctions Within the Middle Classes" and create an outline of the section below. Note the key words that reflect the main ideas in each paragraph as well as the key words that inform those ideas.

I. Social Distinctions Within the Middle Classes
   A. Owners and managers of great businesses and banks
      1.
      2.
      3.
      4.
      5.
   B.
      1.
      2.
      3.
   C.
      1.
      2.
      3.
      4.
      5.
   D.
      1.
      2.

Review Questions

Write a brief answer to the following questions. Remember, each answer should highlight a primary idea using key words and supporting details.

1. What was the significance of the revolutions of 1848 to the ascendancy of the middle class?

2. What distinguished the petite bourgeoisie from professionals, shopkeepers, and schoolteachers?

SECTION 4 LATE-NINETEENTH-CENTURY URBAN LIFE

FOCUS QUESTION

What forces shaped the development of European cities?

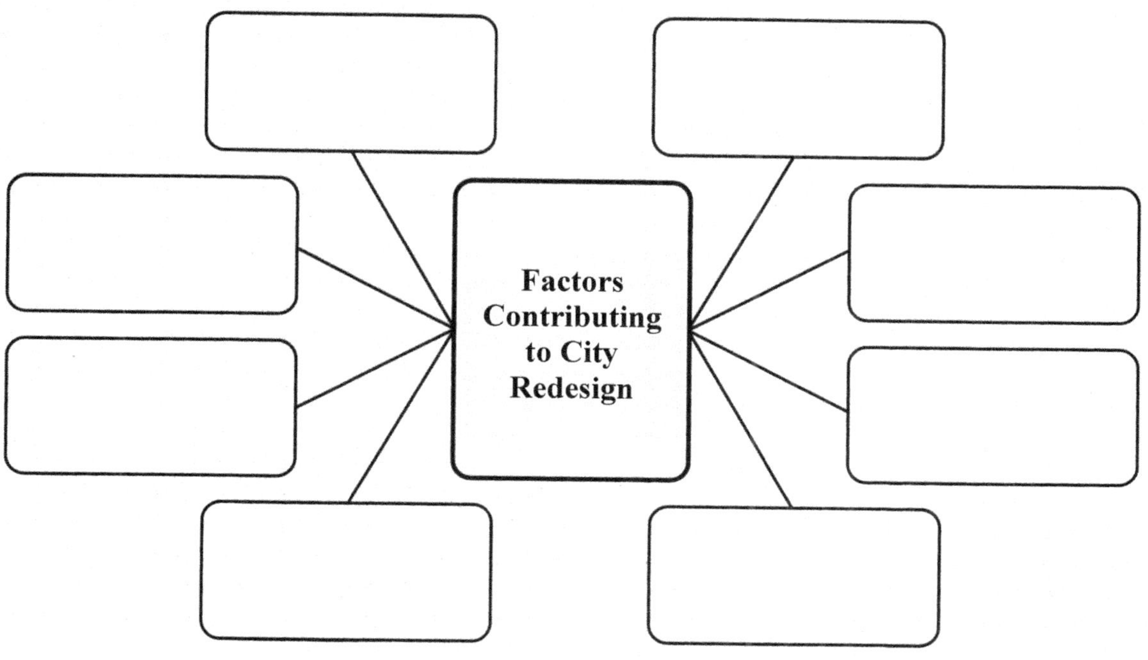

Using the information in your concept web, write a brief answer to the Focus Question.

OUTLINE

Read the section topic entitled "Urban Sanitation" and create an outline of the section below. Note the key words that reflect the main ideas in each paragraph as well as the key words that inform those ideas.

I. Urban Sanitation

A. Concern with health, housing result of cholera epidemics of 1830s, 1840s

1.

2.

3.

4.

5.

6.

B.

1.

2.

3.

4.

5.

C.

1.

2.

3.

D.

1.

2.

3.

Review Questions

Write a brief answer to the following questions. Remember, each answer should highlight a primary idea using key words and supporting details.

1. Why were European cities redesigned during the late nineteenth century?

2. Why were housing and health key issues for urban reform?

SECTION 5 VARIETIES OF LATE-NINETEENTH-CENTURY WOMEN'S EXPERIENCES

FOCUS QUESTION

What was life like for women in late-nineteenth-century Europe?

Lives of European Women in the Late Nineteenth Century			
All Women	**Middle Class Women**	**Working Women**	**Poor Women**

Using the information in your table, write a brief answer to the Focus Question.

OUTLINE

Read the section topic entitled "Women of the Middle Class" and create an outline of the section below. Note the key words that reflect the main ideas in each paragraph as well as the key words that inform those ideas.

I. Women of the Middle Class
   A. The Cult of Domesticity
      1.
      2.
      3.
      4.
      5.
   B.
      1.
      2.
   C.
      1.
      2.
   D.
      1.
      2.
      3.
      4.
      5.
      6.
   E.
      1.
      2.
      3.
   F.
      1.
      2.
      3.
      4.
      5.

Review Questions

Write a brief answer to the following questions. Remember, each answer should highlight a primary idea using key words and supporting details.

1. What was the status of European women in the second half of the nineteenth century? Why did they grow discontented with their lot? What factors led to change?

2. To what extent had they improved their position by 1914? What tactics did they use to effect change?

3. Was the emancipation of women inevitable?

4. How did women approach their situation differently from country to country?

SECTION 6 JEWISH EMANCIPATION

FOCUS QUESTION

How did Jewish life in Europe change in the late nineteenth century?

Change in Jewish Life in the Late Nineteenth Century	
Before	**After**
•	•
•	•
•	•

Using the information in your table, write a brief answer to the Focus Question.

OUTLINE

Read the section topic entitled "Broadened Opportunities" and create an outline of the section below. Note the key words that reflect the main ideas in each paragraph as well as the key words that inform those ideas.

I. Broadened Opportunities

A. Western Europe generally

1.

2.

3.

4.

5.

6.

7.

8.

9.

B.

1.

2.

3.

4.

C.

1.

2.

3.

4.

5.

6.

REVIEW QUESTIONS

Write a brief answer to the following questions. Remember, each answer should highlight a primary idea using key words and supporting details.

1. What were the major characteristics of Jewish emancipation in the nineteenth century?

2. What stimulated vast numbers of Jews from leaving their homelands during the late nineteenth century? Where did they go?

Section 7 Labor, Socialism, and Politics to World War I

Focus Question

What role did the Socialist and labor movements play in late-nineteenth-century politics?

Role of Socialist and Labor Movements in Politics	
Movement	**Role**

Using the information in your table, write a brief answer to the Focus Question.

OUTLINE

Read the section topic entitled "Great Britain: Fabianism and Early Welfare Programs" and create an outline of the section below. Note the key words that reflect the main ideas in each paragraph as well as the key words that inform those ideas.

I. Great Britain: Fabianism and Early Welfare Programs
    A. Labor organizing in Britain
        1.
        2.
        3.
        4.
        5.
        6.
        7.
    B.
        1.
        2.
    C.
        1.
        2.
        3.
    D.
        1.
        2.
        3.
        4.
    E.
        1.
        2.
        3.
        4.

READING SKILL: SUMMARIZE

Complete the chart below identifying the key events characterizing the Russian Revolution of 1905 and its aftermath.

Revolution of 1905 and Its Aftermath	
Event	**Characteristics**
Bloody Sunday	
Soviets	
October Manifesto	
Stolypin's Ministry	

Review Questions

Write a brief answer to the following questions. Remember, each answer should highlight a primary idea using key words and supporting details.

1. What was the status of the European working classes in 1860? Had it improved by 1914? Why did trade unions and organized mass political parties grow?

2. Why were the debates over "opportunism" and "revisionism" important to the Western European socialist parties?

3. What were the benefits and drawbacks of industrialization for Russia? Were the tsars wise to attempt to modernize their country, or should they have left it as it was?

4. How did Lenin's view of socialism differ from that of the Socialists in Western Europe?

Review: Key Terms and People

Complete your review of the chapter by writing a brief definition of the following terms and people.

Demographic
Second Industrial Revolution
Henry Bessemer
Gottlieb Daimler
London Great Exhibition of 1851
W. H. Smith
Petite bourgeoisie
Georges Haussmann
Miasma
Louis René Villermé
Albert Embankment
Jules Simon
1882 Married Woman's Property Act
University of Zurich
Cult of Domesticity
Harriet Taylor
Emmeline Pankhurst
Suffragettes
Trade Unionism
First International
Syndicalism
Revisionism
Sergei Witte
Kulaks
Bolsheviks
Duma
Pogroms
Lionel Rothschild
Anti-Semitism

My Key Terms

Write down terms that are unfamiliar. How are the words used? Do other words or examples reveal their meaning? Try to figure out meaning from the context.

CHAPTER 16
THE BIRTH OF MODERN EUROPEAN THOUGHT

Complete the following exercises in order *as you read* this chapter.

SECTION 1 THE NEW READING PUBLIC

FOCUS QUESTION

What effect did state-financed education have on literacy in late-nineteenth-century Europe?

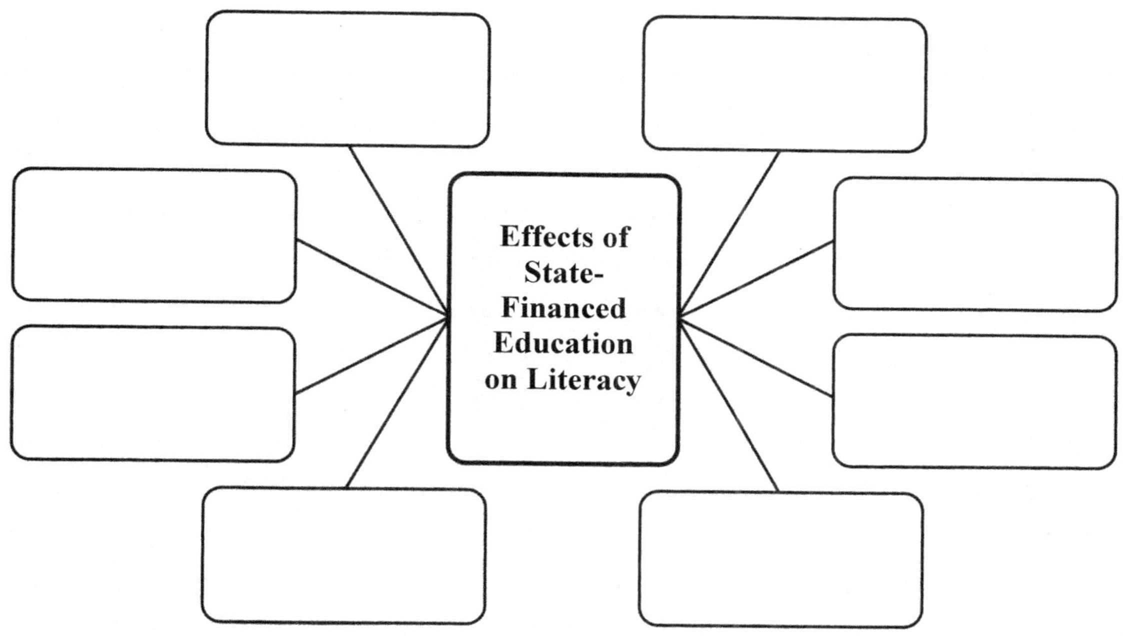

Using the information in your concept web, write a brief answer to the Focus Question.

OUTLINE

Read the section topic entitled "Advances in Primary Education" and create an outline of the section below. Note the key words that reflect the main ideas in each paragraph as well as the key words that inform those ideas.

I. Advances in Primary Education
   A. State-sponsored primary education advances literacy
      1.
      2.
      3.
      4.
      5.
   B.
      1.
      2.
      3.
   C.
      1.
      2.
      3.
      4.

Review Questions

Write a brief answer to the following questions. Remember, each answer should highlight a primary idea using key words and supporting details.

1. Why did some governments have to give further attention to secondary education by the time of World War I?

2. Why was the new literacy the intellectual parallel of the railroad and the steamship?

SECTION 2 SCIENCE AT MIDCENTURY

FOCUS QUESTION

What role did science play in the second half of the nineteenth century?

Role of Science in the Second Half of the Nineteenth Century	
Role	**Description**

Using the information in your table, write a brief answer to the Focus Question.

OUTLINE

Read the section topic entitled "Science at Midcentury" and create an outline of the section below. Note the key words that reflect the main ideas in each paragraph as well as the key words that inform those ideas.

I. Science at Midcentury

  A. Comte, Positivism, and the Prestige of Science

    1.

    2.

    3.

    4.

  B.

    1.

    2.

    3.

    4.

    5.

    6.

    7.

  C.

    1.

    2.

    3.

    4.

    5.

REVIEW QUESTIONS

Write a brief answer to the following questions. Remember, each answer should highlight a primary idea using key words and supporting details.

1. Why was science dominant in the second half of the nineteenth century?

2. How did the scientific outlook change between 1850 and 1914?

3. What was positivism?

4. How did Darwin's and Wallace's theory of natural selection affect ethics, Christianity, and European views of human nature?

Section 3 Christianity and the Church Under Siege

Focus Question

What challenges did European Christianity face in the late nineteenth century?

Intellectual Skepticism		

Using the information in your chart, write a brief answer to the Focus Question.

Outline

Read the section topic entitled "Intellectual Skepticism" and create an outline of the section below. Note the key words that reflect the main ideas in each paragraph as well as the key words that inform those ideas.

I. Intellectual Skepticism
   A. Intellectuals challenge Christianity
      1.
      2.
      3.
   B.
      1.
      2.
      3.
      4.
      5.
      6.
      7.
      8.
      9.
   C.
      1.
      2.
      3.
      4.
      5.
      6.
      7.
      8.
   D.
      1.
      2.
      3.
      4.
      5.
   E.
      1.
      2.

Review Questions

Write a brief answer to the following questions. Remember, each answer should highlight a primary idea using key words and supporting details.

1. Why was Christianity attacked in the late nineteenth century?

2. Why was Leo XIII regarded as a liberal Pope? Why was the papacy itself so resilient?

3. Why did Europeans feel superior toward Islam?

4. How did Islamic thinkers respond to the European challenge?

Section 4 Toward a Twentieth-Century Frame of Mind

Focus Question

How did developments in science, literature, and art reflect a profound shift in Western thought?

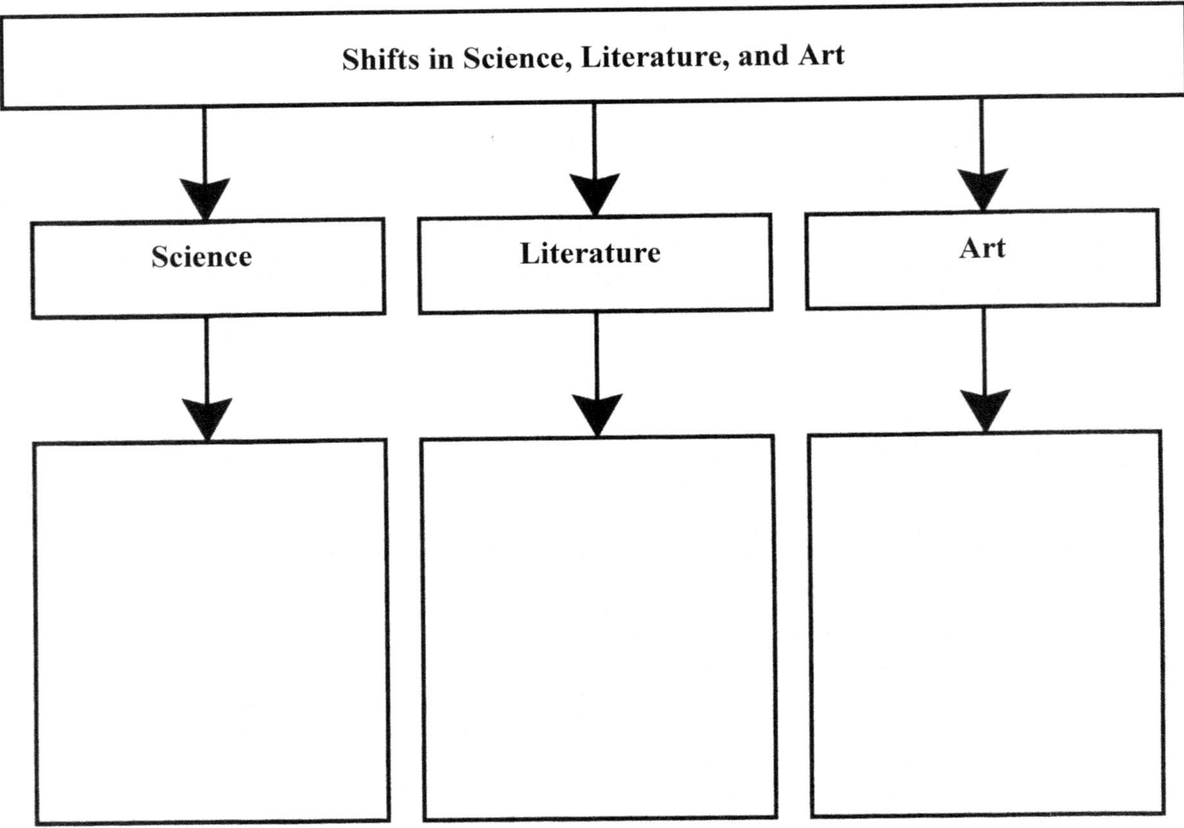

Using the information in your table, write a brief answer to the Focus Question.

OUTLINE

Read the section topic entitled "The Coming of Modern Art" and create an outline of the section below. Note the key words that reflect the main ideas in each paragraph as well as the key words that inform those ideas.

I. The Coming of Modern Art

A. Impressionism; See: Manet, Monet, Pissarro, Renoir, Degas

1.
2.
3.
4.
5.
6.
7.
8.
9.
10.

B.

1.
2.
3.
4.
5.
6.
7.
8.
9.

C.

1.
2.
3.
4.
5.
6.

Reading Skill: Summarize

Complete the table below identifying the primary themes of Freudian psychology.

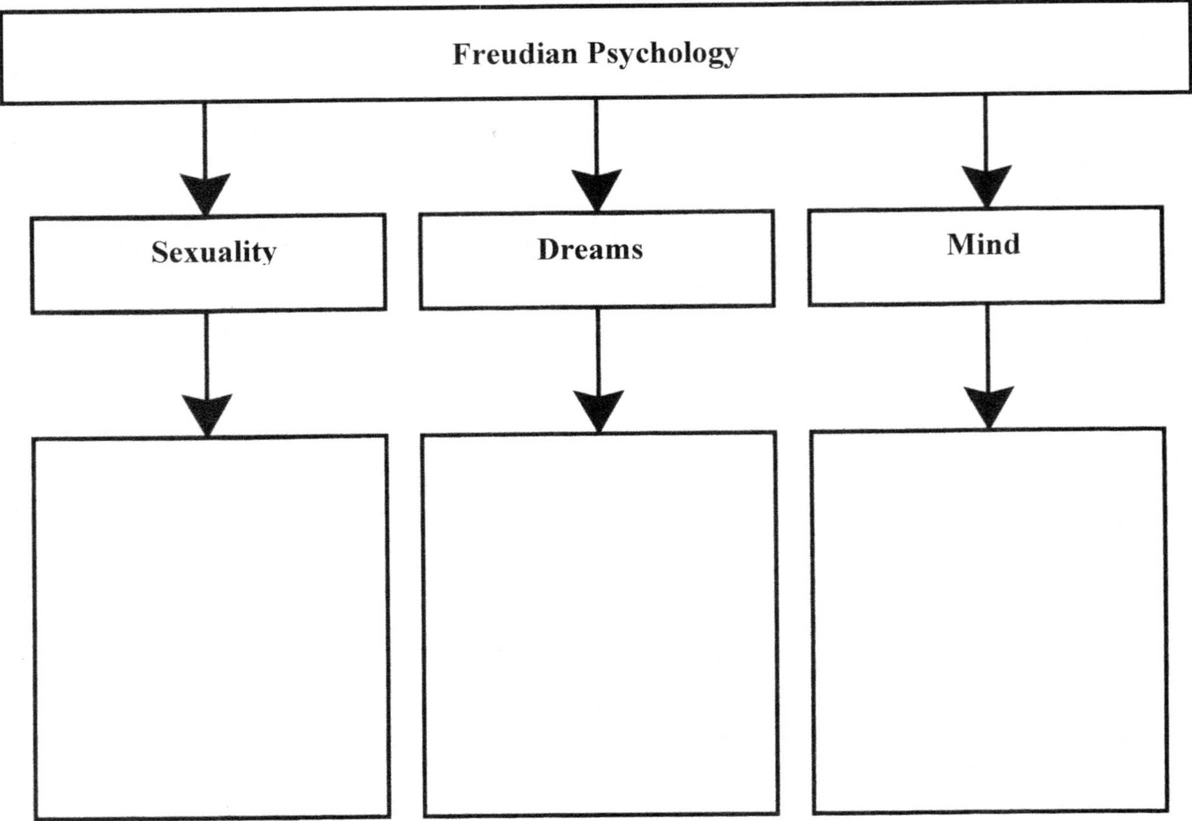

Review Questions

Write a brief answer to the following questions. Remember, each answer should highlight a primary idea using key words and supporting details.

1. How did the realists undermine middle-class morality? How did literary modernism differ from realism?

2. What were the major movements associated with the rise of modern art?

3. How did Nietzsche and Freud challenge traditional morality?

4. What was the character of late-nineteenth-century racism? How did it become associated with anti-Semitism?

SECTION 5 WOMEN AND MODERN THOUGHT

FOCUS QUESTION

How did women challenge gender stereotypes in the late nineteenth and early twentieth centuries?

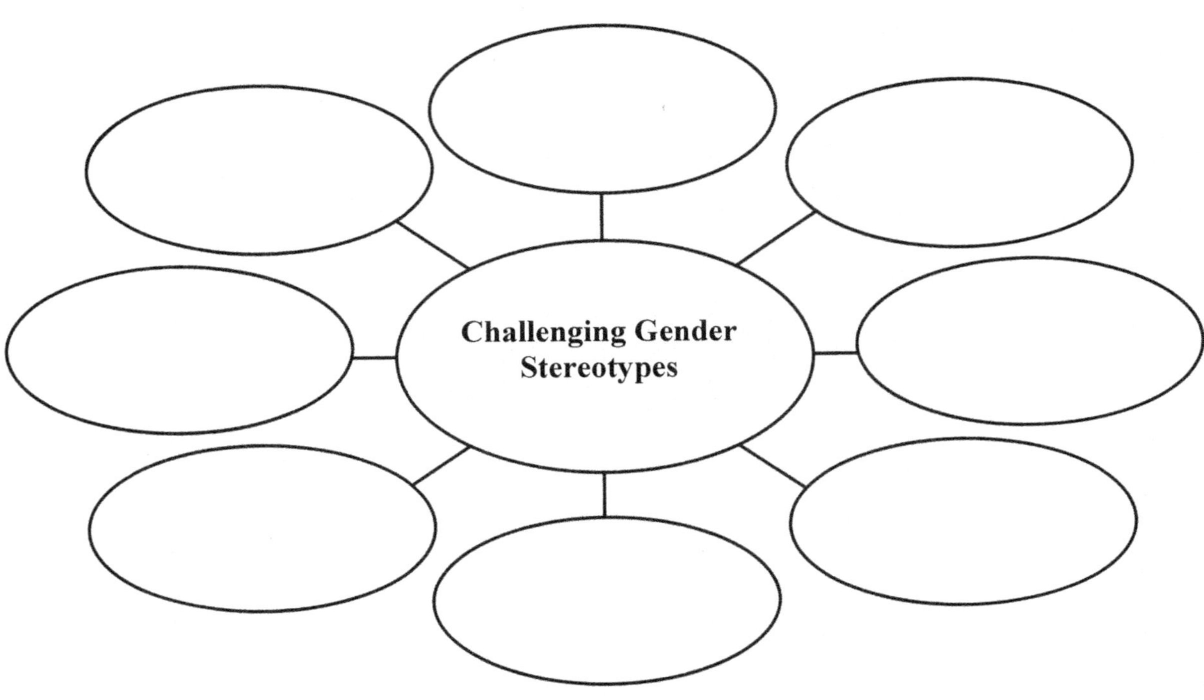

Using the information in your concept web, write a brief answer to the Focus Question.

Outline

Read the section topic entitled "New Directions in Feminism" and create an outline of the section below. Note the key words that reflect the main ideas in each paragraph as well as the key words that inform those ideas.

I. New Directions in Feminism
   A. Feminists of the age primarily focused on obtaining the franchise
      1.
      2.
   B.
      1.
      2.
      3.
      4.
      5.
      6.
      7.
      8.
      9.
   C.
      1.
      2.
      3.
   D.
      1.
      2.
   E.
      1.
      2.
      3.
   F.
      1.
      2.
      3.
      4.

Review Questions

Write a brief answer to the following questions. Remember, each answer should highlight a primary idea using key words and supporting details.

1. Why were many late-nineteenth-century intellectuals afraid of and hostile to women?

2. What social and political issues affected women in the late nineteenth and early twentieth centuries?

3. What were new departures in turn-of-the-century feminism?

4. How did many ideas associated with modernism conflict with feminist goals?

Review: Key Terms and People

Complete your review of the chapter by writing a brief definition of the following terms and people.

Literacy
William Whewell
Positivism
Charles Darwin
Herbert Spencer
Social Darwinism
T. H. Huxley
Charles Lyell
Friedrich Nietzsche
Kulturkampf
First Vatican Council
Ernest Renan
Salafi
Wahhabi movement
Ernst Mach
Uncertainty principle
Naturalism
Modernism
Keynesian economics
Postimpressionism
Sigmund Freud
Max Weber
Racism
Zionism
Ethnological Society
Karl Vogt
Karen Horney
Contagious Diseases Acts
Ellen Key
Virginia Woolf

My Key Terms

Write down terms that are unfamiliar. How are the words used? Do other words or examples reveal their meaning? Try to figure out meaning from the context.

CHAPTER 17
THE AGE OF WESTERN IMPERIALISM

Complete the following exercises *as you read* this chapter.

SECTION 1 THE CLOSE OF THE AGE OF EARLY MODERN COLONIZATION

FOCUS QUESTION

How did early modern colonization differ from nineteenth-century Western imperialism?

Comparing Early Modern and Nineteenth Century Imperialism	
Early Modern Imperialism	**Nineteenth Century Imperialism**

Using the information in your table, write a brief answer to the Focus Question.

OUTLINE

Read the section topic entitled "The Close of the Age of Early Modern Colonization" and create an outline of the section below. Note the key words that reflect the main ideas in each paragraph as well as the key words that inform those ideas.

I. The Close of the Age of Early Modern Colonization

A. Late fifteenth to late eighteenth century European expansion

1.

2.

3.

4.

5.

6.

B.

1.

2.

3.

4.

5.

6.

7.

8.

9.

10.

READING SKILL: SUMMARIZE

Complete the chart below identifying the key regional political transformations that occurred between the mid-eighteenth and early nineteenth centuries.

Regional Political Transformations	
Region	**Transformation**

Review Questions

Write a brief answer to the following questions. Remember, each answer should highlight a primary idea using key words and supporting details.

1. How did European imperial interests shift geographically in the nineteenth century?

2. How did the elimination of slavery represent a significant shift from early modern to nineteenth century imperialism?

Section 2 The Age of British Imperial Dominance

Focus Question

How did Britain use its economic might to extend its influence around the world?

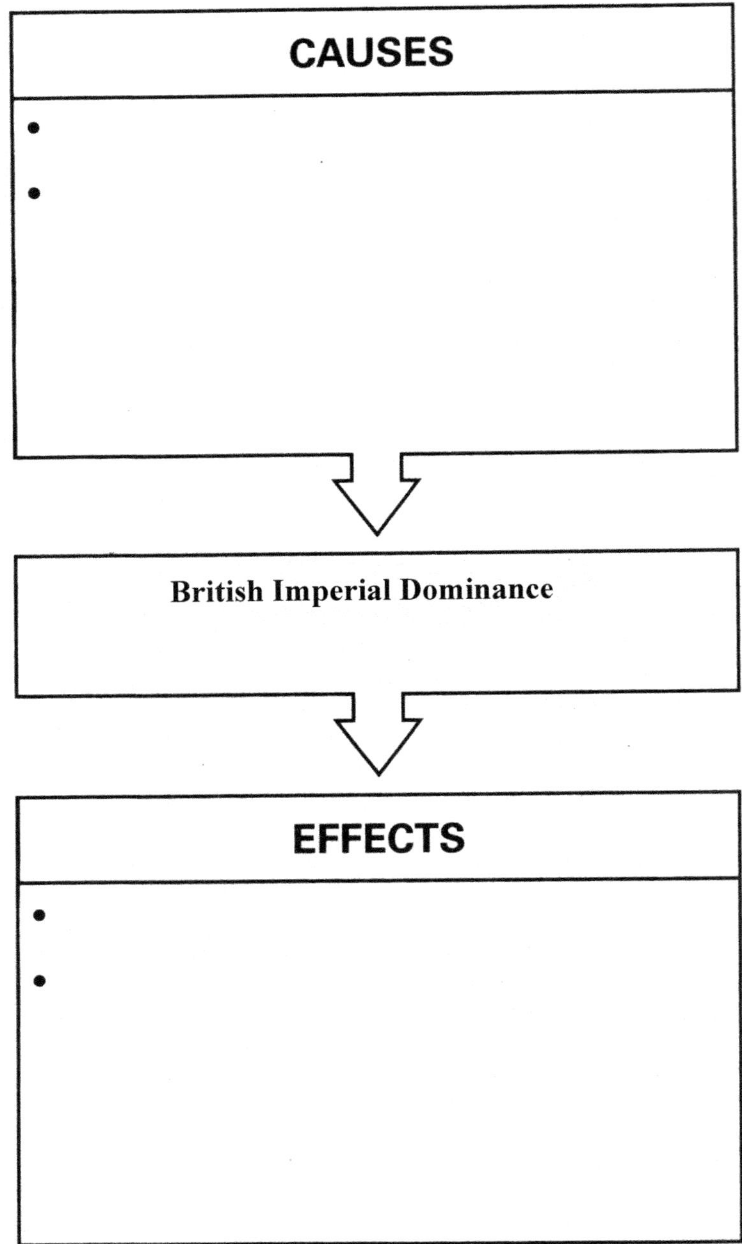

Using the information in your chart, write a brief answer to the Focus Question.

OUTLINE

Read the section topic entitled "The Imperialism of Free Trade" and create an outline of the section below. Note the key words that reflect the main ideas in each paragraph as well as the key words that inform those ideas.

I. The Imperialism of Free Trade
   A. Mercantilist origins of empire
      1.
      2.
   B.
      1.
      2.
      3.
      4.
   C.
      1.
      2.
      3.
      4.
      5.
   D.
      1.
      2.
      3.
      4.
      5.
      6.
   E.
      1.
      2.
      3.
      4.
      5.
   F.
      1.
      2.

Reading Skill: Summarize

Complete the chart below contrasting mercantilism with free trade economics.

Contrasting Economic Assumptions	
Mercantilism	**Free Trade**
• • •	• • •

Review Questions

Write a brief answer to the following questions. Remember, each answer should highlight a primary idea using key words and supporting details.

1. What was free-trade imperialism?

2. Why was Britain the dominant world power until the late nineteenth century?

3. How was free trade related to the expansion of European influence around the globe?

4. What were the Opium Wars?

SECTION 3 INDIA—THE JEWEL IN THE CROWN OF THE BRITISH EMPIRE

FOCUS QUESTION

Why was India such an important part of the British Empire?

Causes	Events	Effect
• • • • •	• • • • •	**India became a British base for military and commercial dominance throughout Asia**

Using the information in your flowchart, write a brief answer to the Focus Question.

OUTLINE

Read the section topic entitled "India—The Jewel in the Crown of the British Empire" and create an outline of the section below. Note the key words that reflect the main ideas in each paragraph as well as the key words that inform those ideas.

I. India—The Jewel in the Crown of the British Empire
   A. Britain lost North America (except Canada); gained India
      1.
      2.
      3.
      4.
   B.
      1.
      2.
   C.
      1.
      2.
      3.
      4.
   D.
      1.
      2.
      3.
   E.
      1.
      2.
      3.
      4.
      5.
      6.
   F.
      1.
      2.
      3.

Review Questions

Write a brief answer to the following questions. Remember, each answer should highlight a primary idea using key words and supporting details.

1. How did the British come to dominate India?

2. What were the causes of the Indian rebellion of 1857?

3. How did British rule in India change after the rebellion?

4. Why was India so important to Britain?

Section 4 The "New Imperialism," 1870–1914

Focus Question

What was new about the "New Imperialism?"

New Imperialism	
Characteristics	**Methods**
•	•
•	•
•	•

Using the information in your chart, write a brief answer to the Focus Question.

OUTLINE

Read the section topic entitled The "New Imperialism," (1870–1914) and create an outline of the section below. Note the key words that reflect the main ideas in each paragraph as well as the key words that inform those ideas.

I. The New Imperialism, (1870–1914)
   A. 1870–1914 Europe, the United States, Japan engage in imperial expansion
      1.
      2.
   B.
   C.
      1.
      2.
      3.
      4.
      5.
      6.
   D.
      1.
      2.
      3.
   E.
      1.
      2.
   F.
      1.
      2.
   G.
      1.
      2.
   H.
      1.
      2.

Reading Skill: Summarize

Complete the concept web below identifying the distinguishing characteristics of the New Imperialism.

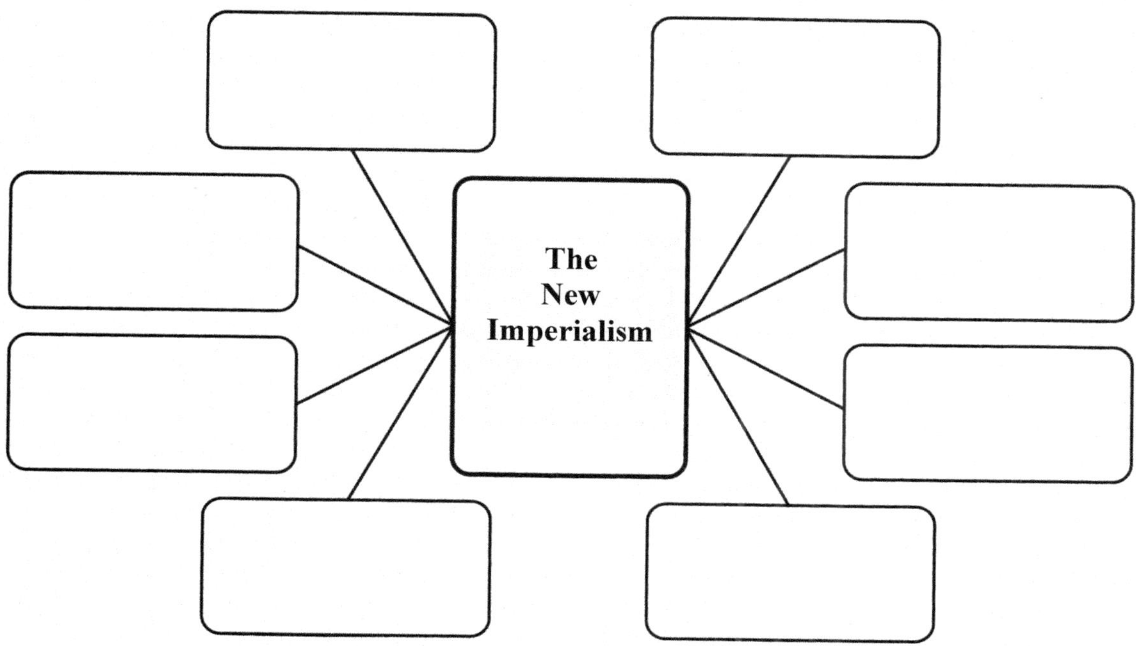

Review Questions

Write a brief answer to the following questions. Remember, each answer should highlight a primary idea using key words and supporting details.

1. Why was it significant that multiple nations were involved in the New Imperialism? Which nations were they?

2. What was a protectorate? What distinguishes it from the free trade imperialism of the past?

SECTION 5 MOTIVES FOR THE NEW IMPERIALISM

FOCUS QUESTION

What were the motives for the New Imperialism?

Economic Motives for the New Imperialism	
Possible economic motives	**Evaluation of those motives**
•	•
•	•
•	•

Using the information in your chart, write a brief answer to the Focus Question.

OUTLINE

Read the section topic entitled "Motives for the New Imperialism" and create an outline of the section below. Note the key words that reflect the main ideas in each paragraph as well as the key words that inform those ideas.

I. Motives for the New Imperialism
   A. Economic motive primary explanation until mid-twentieth century
      1.
      2.
      3.
      4.
   B.
      1.
      2.
      3.
      4.
      5.
   C.
      1.
      2.
   D.
      1.
      2.
      3.
      4.
      5.
      6.
   E.
      1.
      2.
      3.
      4.
      5.
   F.
      1.
      2.
      3.
      4.

READING SKILL: SUMMARIZE

Complete the chart below identifying the primary motives guiding the New Imperialism.

Primary Motives for the New Imperialism			
Great Powers	**Power Vacuums**	**Geopolitical Assumptions**	**Contemporary Justifications**

Review Questions

Write a brief answer to the following questions. Remember, each answer should highlight a primary idea using key words and supporting details.

1. What were the motives of the New Imperialism?

2. To what extent was the New Imperialism related to the capitalist search for higher profits and new markets?

3. How did colonial officials and businesspeople influence the growth of colonial empires?

Section 6 The Partition of Africa

Focus Question

How did European politics contribute to the "Scramble for Africa"?

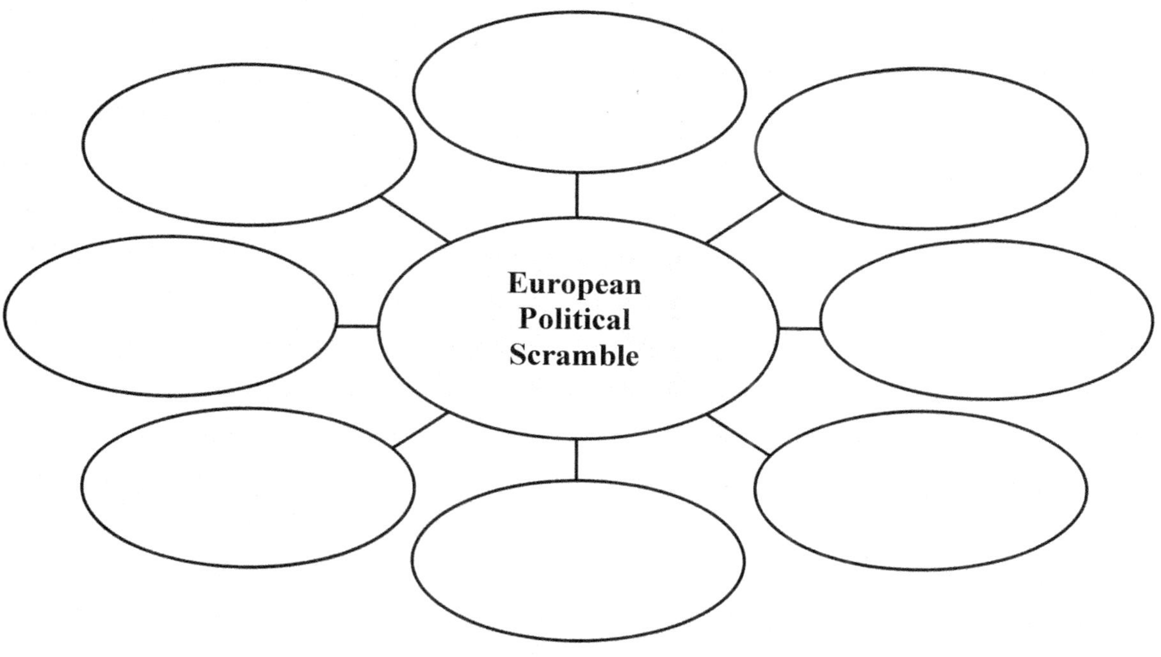

Using the information in your concept web, write a brief answer to the Focus Question.

Outline

Read the section topic entitled "The Belgian Congo" and create an outline of the section below. Note the key words that reflect the main ideas in each paragraph as well as the key words that inform those ideas.

I. The Belgian Congo
   A. King Leopold II of Belgium appropriated the Congo
      1.
      2.
      3.
      4.
      5.
      6.
      7.
      8.
      9.
      10.
      11.
      12.
   B.
      1.
      2.
      3.
   C.
      1.
      2.
      3.
      4.

REVIEW QUESTIONS

Write a brief answer to the following questions. Remember, each answer should highlight a primary idea using key words and supporting details.

1. Why was Algeria the most important part of the French Empire?

2. What parts of the Ottoman Empire fell under European rule between the 1880s and 1914? Why did Britain come to dominate Egypt?

3. Why did Germany and Italy acquire colonies?

4. Why did Leopold II build an empire in the Congo?

5. What was the "Scramble for Africa"?

Section 7 Russian Expansion in Mainland Asia

Focus Question

How did Russia come to control a vast and diverse Asian empire, and what developments facilitated Western penetration and control of Asia?

Tsars shift to "inorodtsy" policy in late eighteenth century
• • • •

Using the information in your flowchart, write a brief answer to the Focus Question.

OUTLINE

Read the section topic entitled "Russian Expansion in Mainland Asia" and create an outline of the section below. Note the key words that reflect the main ideas in each paragraph as well as the key words that inform those ideas.

I. Russian Expansion in Mainland Asia
   A. Russian empire up to eighteenth century
      1.
      2.
   B.
      1.
      2.
   C.
      1.
      2.
   D.
      1.
      2.
      3.
      4.
   E.
      1.
      2.
      3.
      4.
   F.
      1.
      2.
      3.
   G.
      1.
      2.

Review Questions

Write a brief answer to the following questions. Remember, each answer should highlight a primary idea using key words and supporting details.

1. Where did Russia expand in mainland Asia?

2. Why was nineteenth- century and early twentieth-century Russian imperial conquest fraught with difficulties felt even today?

SECTION 8 WESTERN POWERS IN ASIA

FOCUS QUESTION

What role did Western powers such as France and the United States play in Asia?

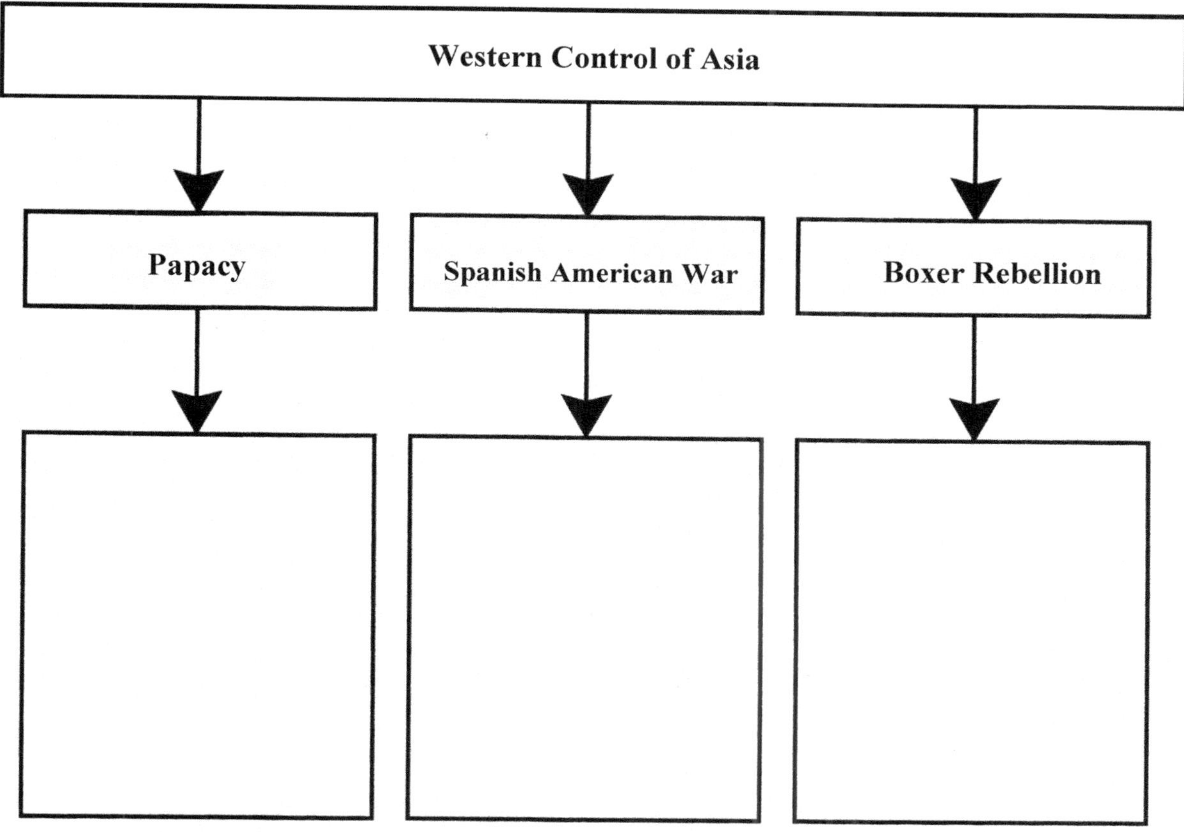

Using the information in your chart, write a brief answer to the Focus Question.

Outline

Read the section topic entitled "France in Asia" and create an outline of the section below. Note the key words that reflect the main ideas in each paragraph as well as the key words that inform those ideas.

I. France in Asia
  A. French presence in Indochina and elsewhere in Asia
    1.
    2.
    3.
  B.
    1.
    2.
    3.
  C.
    1.
    2.
  D.
    1.
    2.
    3.
    4.
    5.
    6.

REVIEW QUESTIONS

Write a brief answer to the following questions. Remember, each answer should highlight a primary idea using key words and supporting details.

1. How did the United States become an imperial power?

2. What were the consequences of Western imperialism in China?

SECTION 9 TOOLS OF IMPERIALISM

FOCUS QUESTION

How did technological innovations make nineteenth-century imperialism possible?

Effects of Technological Innovations	
Innovation	**Effect**
•	•
•	•
•	•

Using the information in your table, write a brief answer to the Focus Question.

Outline

Read the section topic entitled "Firearms" and create an outline of the section below. Note the key words that reflect the main ideas in each paragraph as well as the key words that inform those ideas.

I. Firearms

  A. Firearms: overwhelming Western advantage

    1.

    2.

    3.

    4.

    5.

    6.

  B.

    1.

    2.

  C.

    1.

    2.

  D.

    1.

    2.

    3.

    4.

  E.

    1.

    2.

REVIEW QUESTIONS

Write a brief answer to the following questions. Remember, each answer should highlight a primary idea using key words and supporting details.

1. What were the "tools of imperialism"? How did these technological improvements enable Western powers to dominate so much of the non-Western world?

2. Why was quinine so important for the spread of empires?

Section 10 The Missionary Factor

Focus Question

What was the relationship between missionaries and their home governments?

Missionaries and Home Governments	
Conflict	**Accord**
•	•
•	•
•	•

Using the information in your table, write a brief answer to the Focus Question.

OUTLINE

Read the section topic entitled "Missionaries and Indigenous Religious Movements" and create an outline of the section below. Note the key words that reflect the main ideas in each paragraph as well as the key words that inform those ideas.

I. Missionaries and Indigenous Religious Movements
   A. African and Asian Christian Churches
      1.
      2.
   B.
      1.
      2.
      3.
      4.
   C.
      1.
      2.
      3.
      4.

REVIEW QUESTIONS

Write a brief answer to the following questions. Remember, each answer should highlight a primary idea using key words and supporting details.

1. Why did Western missionary efforts expand in the nineteenth century?

2. Why was the relationship between Western missionaries and colonial officials so complicated?

3. Why did Africans want to found their own churches?

4. How has the spread of Christianity in the non-Western world affected the Christian churches?

Section 11 Science and Imperialism

Focus Question

How did science increase imperialism's appeal to domestic audiences in Europe?

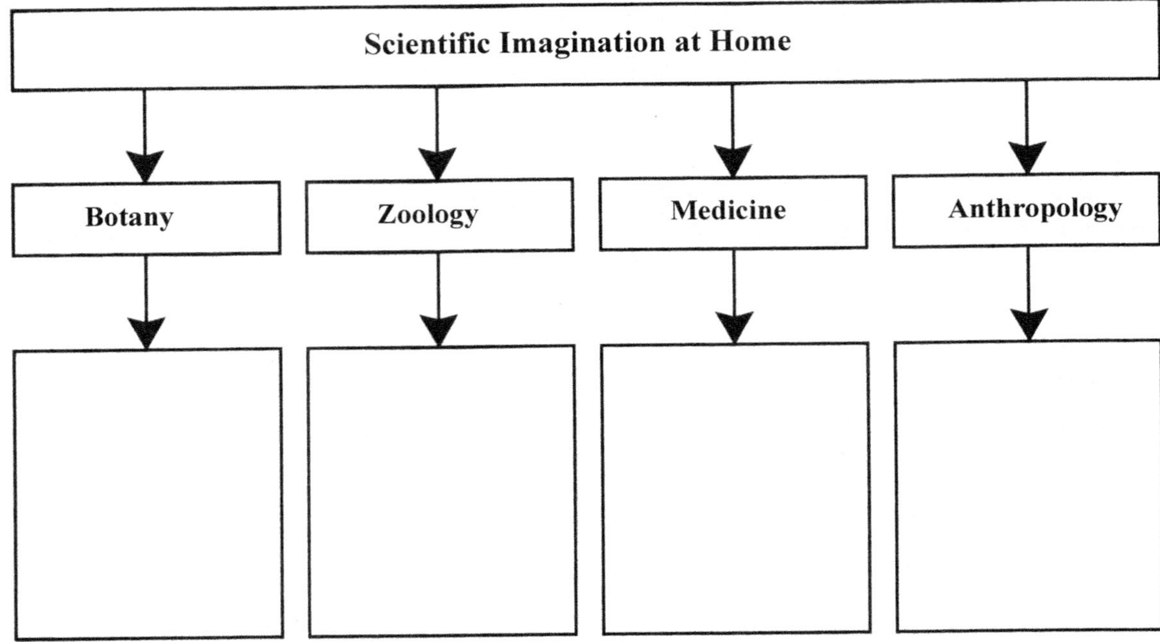

Using the information in your chart, write a brief answer to the Focus Question.

OUTLINE

Read the section topic entitled "Botany" and create an outline of the section below. Note the key words that reflect the main ideas in each paragraph as well as the key words that inform those ideas.

I. Botany
   A. Botany reflecting, nurturing a vast expansion of agriculture worldwide
      1.
      2.
      3.
      4.
      5.
      6.
   B.
      1.
      2.
   C.
      1.
      2.
      3.
      4.
      5.
      6.
      7.
      8.
      9.
      10.
      11.
      12.

Review Questions

Write a brief answer to the following questions. Remember, each answer should highlight a primary idea using key words and supporting details.

1. What sciences were most associated with the New Imperialism? Why was science significant?

2. What role did racism play in the New Imperialism?

REVIEW: KEY TERMS AND PEOPLE

Complete your review of the chapter by writing a brief definition of the following terms and people.

New Imperialism
Imperialism
Monroe Doctrine
Imperialism of Free Trade
Opium Wars
Mughal Empire
maharajahs
East India Company
Sepoy Rebellion
Protectorates
Spheres of Influence
Khedives
The Mahdi
Anglo-French Entente
Leopold II
Berlin Conference
Herero people
Great Trek
Khedives
Apartheid
Afrikaaner
Apartheid
Inorodtsy
Transcaucasus
Kazakhs
Anglo-Russian Convention
Napoleon III
Indochina
Robert Fulton
Nemesis
Quinine
Submarine cables
Enfield rifle
Evangelical
The Society for the Propagation of the Faith

Mangena Makone
William Carey
David Livingstone
Pasteur Institute
Royal Botanical Garden at Kew
Carlos Finley
Paul Broca
Royal Museum for Central Africa

My Key Terms

Write down terms that are unfamiliar. How are the words used? Do other words or examples reveal their meaning? Try to figure out meaning from the context.

CHAPTER 18
ALLIANCES, WAR, AND A TROUBLED PEACE

Complete the following exercises *as you read* this chapter.

SECTION 1 EMERGENCE OF THE GERMAN EMPIRE AND THE ALLIANCE SYSTEMS (1873–1890)

FOCUS QUESTION

Why did the alliance system fail?

1888: William II came to the German throne
•   •   •   •

Using the information in your chart, write a brief answer to the Focus Question.

Outline

Read the section topic entitled "Bismarck's Leadership" and create an outline of the section below. Note the key words that reflect the main ideas in each paragraph as well as the key words that inform those ideas.

I. Bismarck's Leadership
   A. 1871–1890, Bismarck's goals: protect new Germany, no war, no colonies
      1.
      2.
   B.
      1.
      2.
   C.
      1.
      2.
      3.
      4.
      5.
      6.
      7.
   D.
      1.
      2.
      3.
   E.
      1.
      2.
      3.
      4.
   F.
      1.
      2.
   G.
      1.
      2.
      3.

Review Questions

Write a brief answer to the following questions. Remember, each answer should highlight a primary idea using key words and supporting details.

1. What role in the world did Bismarck envisage for the new Germany after 1871?

2. How successful was he in carrying out his vision? Was he wise to tie Germany to Austria-Hungary?

3. Why and in what stages did Britain abandon its policy of "splendid isolation" at the turn of the century? Were the policies it pursued instead wise ones, or should Britain have followed a different course altogether?

SECTION 2 WORLD WAR I

FOCUS QUESTION

How did conflict in the Balkans lead to the outbreak of general war in Europe?

1888: Young Turks seized power in the Ottoman Empire
• • • •

Using the information in your flowchart, write a brief answer to the Focus Question.

Outline

Read the section topic entitled "Strategies and Stalemate: 1914–1917" and create an outline of the section below. Note the key words that reflect the main ideas in each paragraph as well as the key words that inform those ideas.

I. Strategies and Stalemate: 1914–1917
    A. Outbreak of war
        1.
        2.
        3.
        4.
    B.
        1.
        2.
        3.
        4.
        5.
        6.
    C.
        1.
        2.
        3.
        4.
        5.
        6.
    D.
        1.
        2.
    E.
        1.
        2.
    F.
        1.
        2.
        3.

Reading Skill: Summarize

Complete the chart below identifying the interests of each of the great powers and Balkan countries at the advent of WWI.

National Interests	
Nation	**Interests**

Review Questions

Write a brief answer to the following questions. Remember, each answer should highlight a primary idea using key words and supporting details.

1. How did developments in the Balkans lead to the outbreak of World War I?

2. What was the role of Serbia? Of Austria? Of Russia?

3. What was the aim of German policy in July 1914?

4. Did Germany want a general war?

Section 3 The Russian Revolution

Focus Question

What factors made the rise of the Bolsheviks to power in Russia possible?

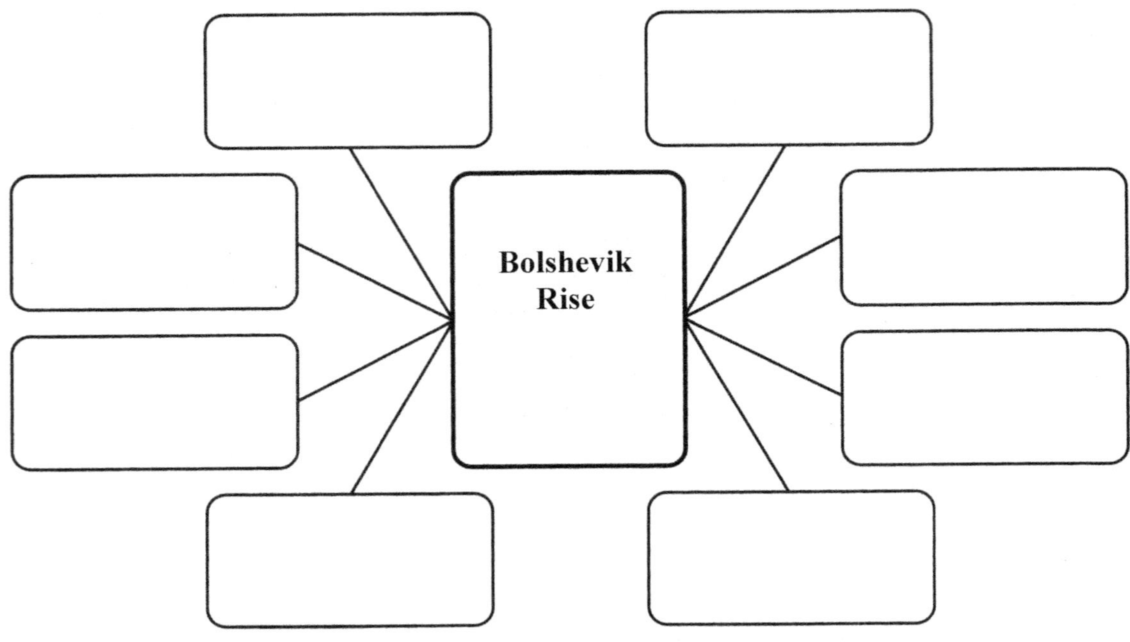

Using the information in your concept web, write a brief answer to the Focus Question.

OUTLINE

Read the section topic entitled "The Communist Dictatorship" and create an outline of the section below. Note the key words that reflect the main ideas in each paragraph as well as the key words that inform those ideas.

I. The Communist Dictatorship
   A. Bolsheviks secure their victory
      1.
      2.
      3.
      4.
   B.
      1.
      2.
      3.
   C.
      1.
      2.
      3.
   D.
      1.
      2.
      3.
      4.
      5.
   E.
      1.
      2.
      3.
      4.
      5.

Reading Skill: Summarize

Complete the concept web below identifying the key reasons the Bolsheviks gained enough support to stage a successful coup.

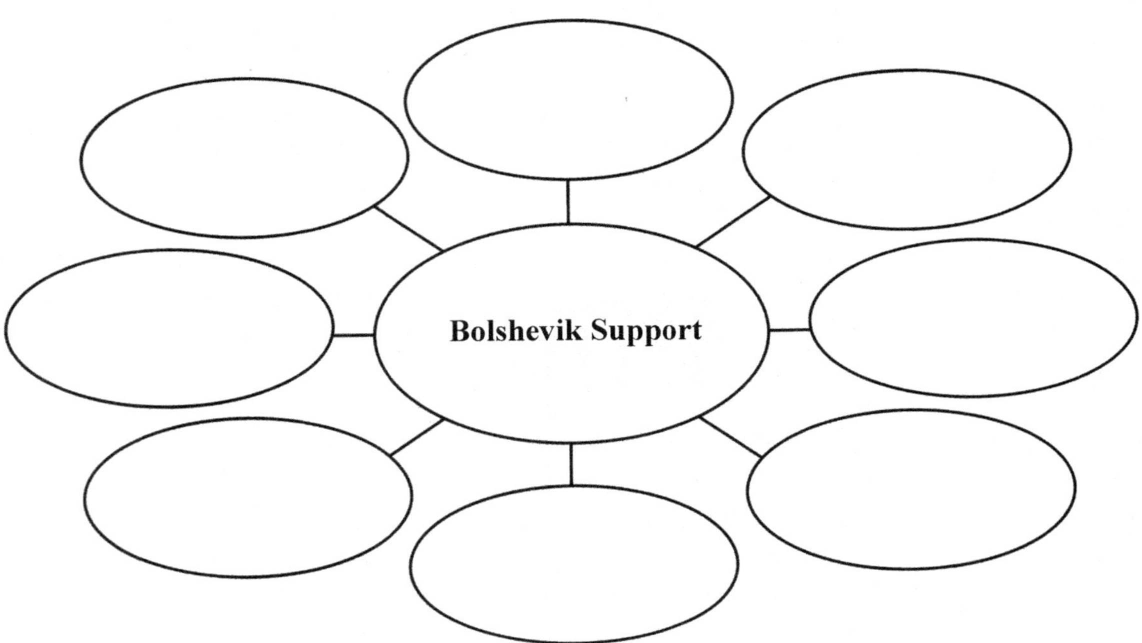

Review Questions

Write a brief answer to the following questions. Remember, each answer should highlight a primary idea using key words and supporting details.

1. Why did Lenin succeed in establishing Bolshevik rule in Russia?

2. What role did Trotsky play?

3. Was it wise policy for Lenin to take Russia out of the war?

Section 4 The End of World War I

Focus Question

What were the immediate consequences of the end of World War I?

Immediate Consequences of the End of World War I	
Political	**Psychological**

Using the information in your table, write a brief answer to the Focus Question.

OUTLINE

Read the section topic entitled "The End of the Ottoman Empire" and create an outline of the section below. Note the key words that reflect the main ideas in each paragraph as well as the key words that inform those ideas.

I. The End of the Ottoman Empire
    A. At outbreak of war
        1.
        2.
    B.
        1.
        2.
        3.
        4.
    C.
        1.
        2.
        3.
    D.
        1.
        2.
        3.
        4.
        5.
    E.
        1.
        2.

Review Questions

Write a brief answer to the following questions. Remember, each answer should highlight a primary idea using key words and supporting details.

1. Why did Germany lose World War I? Could Germany have won, or was victory never a possibility?

2. What were the benefits of Versailles to Europe, and what were its drawbacks? Was the settlement too harsh or too conciliatory? Could it have secured lasting peace in Europe? How might it have been improved?

SECTION 5 THE SETTLEMENT AT PARIS

FOCUS QUESTION

What were the key weaknesses of the Paris peace settlement?

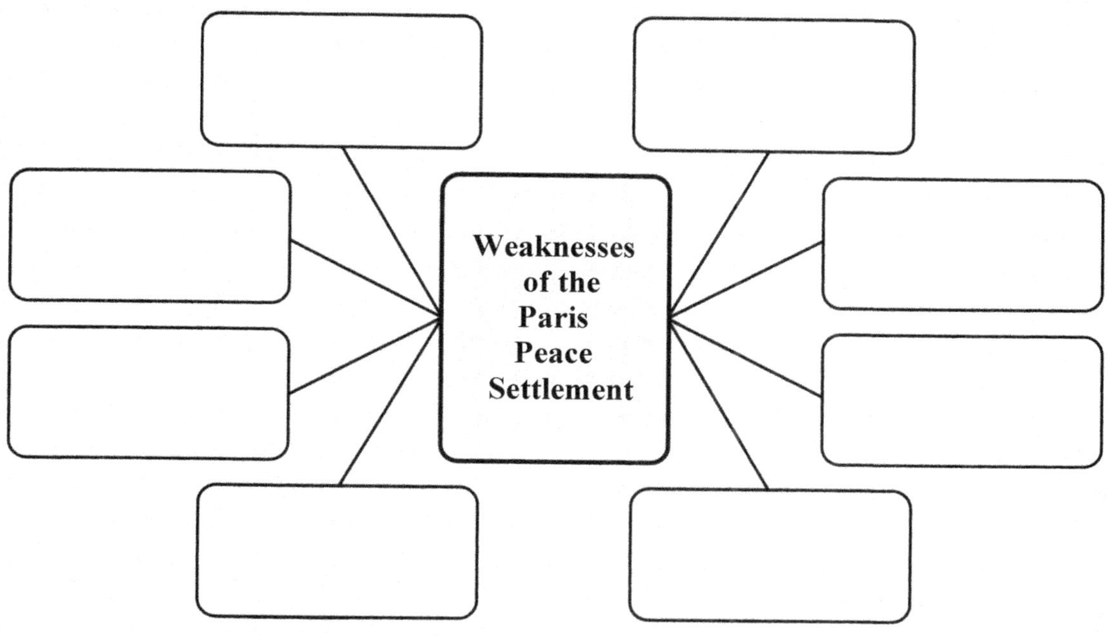

Using the information in your concept web, write a brief answer to the Focus Question.

Outline

Read the section topic entitled "Obstacles the Peacemakers Faced" and create an outline of the section below. Note the key words that reflect the main ideas in each paragraph as well as the key words that inform those ideas.

I. Obstacles the Peacemakers Faced
    A. Multiple difficulties facing representatives of democratic governments
        1.
        2.
        3.
        4.
        5.
    B.
        1.
        2.
        3.
        4.
    C.
        1.
        2.
        3.
        4.
    D.
        1.
        2.
        3.
        4.
        5.
    E.
        1.
        2.
        3.

Review Questions

Write a brief answer to the following questions. Remember, each answer should highlight a primary idea using key words and supporting details.

1. How had imperialism contributed to pre-World War I rivalries?

2. How did the war and the peace settlement change European colonialism and plant seeds for further colonial discontent?

REVIEW: KEY TERMS AND PEOPLE

Complete your review of the chapter by writing a brief definition of the following terms and people.

Three Emperor's League
Treaty of San Stefano
Congress of Berlin
Triple Alliance
Reinsurance Treaty
William II
Entente Cordial
Triple Entente
Panther
Archduke Francis Ferdinand
Schlieffen Plan
Trench warfare
Battle of Tannenberg
Battle at Verdun
Lusitania
Nicholas II
Bolshevik Party
V. I. Lenin
March Revolution
Mensheviks
Provisional Government
Treaty of Brest-Litovsk
White Russians
Paul von Hindenburg
Erich Ludendorff
Fourteen Points
Social Democratic Party
Sharif
Mandates
Ataturk
David Lloyd George
Georges Clemenceau
Woodrow Wilson
Balfour Declaration
Spartacus group

League of Nations
Reparations
War guilt clause

My Key Terms

Write down terms that are unfamiliar. How are the words used? Do other words or examples reveal their meaning? Try to figure out meaning from the context.

Chapter 19
The Interwar Years: The Challenge of Dictators and Depression

Complete the following exercises *as you read* this chapter.

Section 1 After Versailles: Demands for Revision and Enforcement

Focus Question

Why did the Paris settlement fail to bring peace and prosperity to Europe?

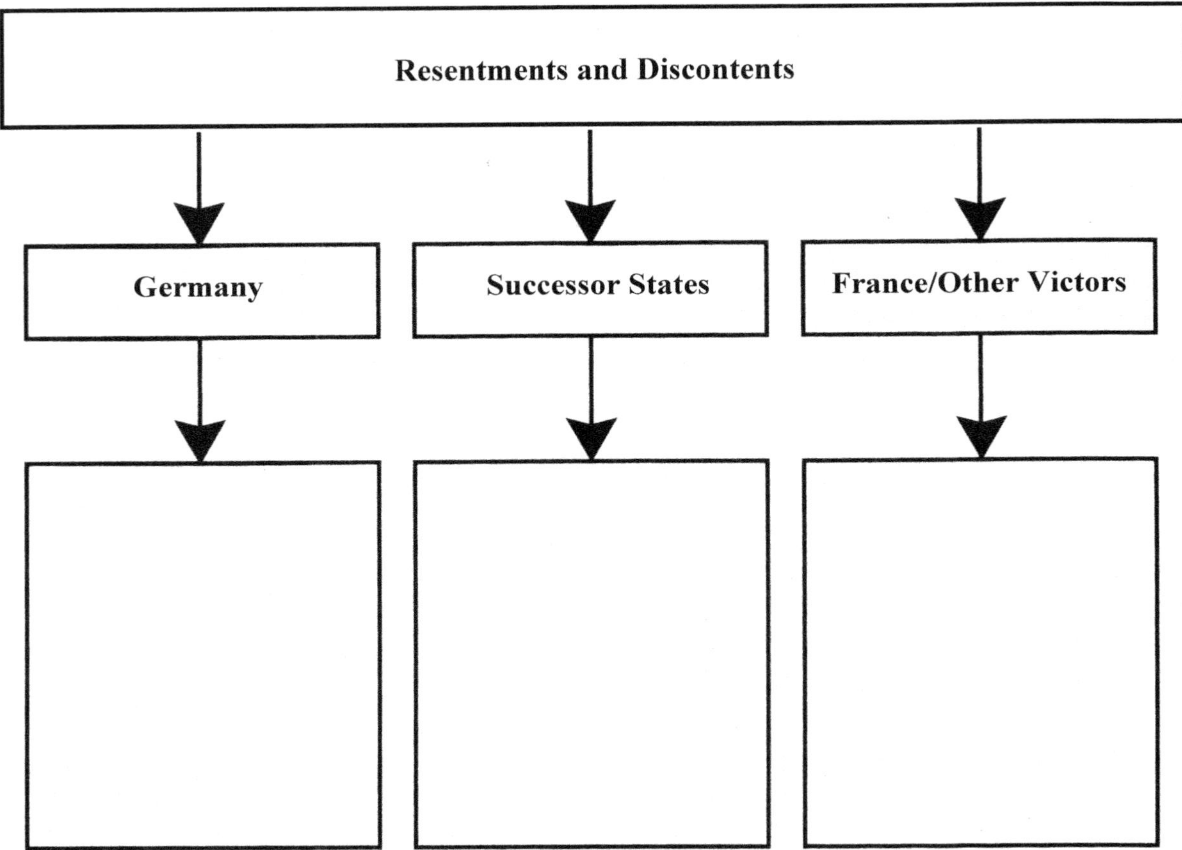

Using the information in your chart, write a brief answer to the Focus Question.

OUTLINE

Read the section topic entitled "After Versailles: Demands for Revision and Enforcement" and create an outline of the section below. Note the key words that reflect the main ideas in each paragraph as well as the key words that inform those ideas.

I. After Versailles: Demands for Revision and Enforcement

  A. Resentments and Discontents

    1.

    2.

    3.

    4.

    5.

    6.

Review Questions

Write a brief answer to the following questions. Remember, each answer should highlight a primary idea using key words and supporting details.

1. Why would the issue of enforcement of the Paris treaties be a cause for political turmoil in France during the 1920s and 1930s?

2. How could a German politician guarantee himself a seat in parliament during the 1920s and 1930s?

SECTION 2 TOWARD THE GREAT DEPRESSION IN EUROPE

FOCUS QUESTION

What key factors combined to produce the Great Depression?

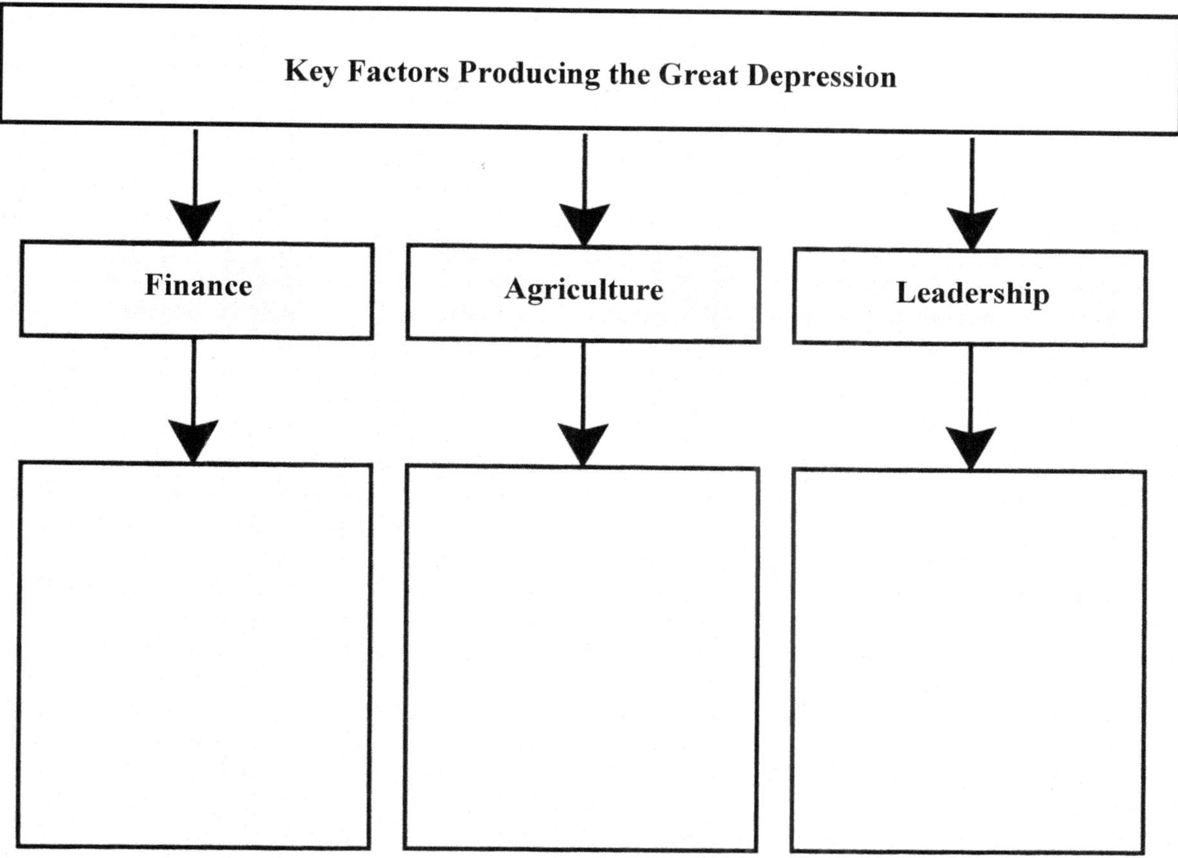

Using the information in your chart, write a brief answer to the Focus Question.

OUTLINE

Read the section topic entitled "Problems in Agricultural Commodities" and create an outline of the section below. Note the key words that reflect the main ideas in each paragraph as well as the key words that inform those ideas.

I. Problems in Agricultural Commodities
   A. Effect of world grain production on European farmers (1920s)
      1.
      2.
      3.
      4.
      5.
      6.
      7.
      8.
      9.
   B.
      1.
      2.
      3.
      4.
      5.
   C.
      1.
      2.
      3.
      4.
      5.

Review Questions

Write a brief answer to the following questions. Remember, each answer should highlight a primary idea using key words and supporting details.

1. What caused the Great Depression?

2. Why was it more severe and why did it last longer than previous economic downturns? Could it have been avoided?

Section 3 The Soviet Experiment

Focus Question

What was the relationship between politics and economics in the early decades of the Soviet Union?

Politics and Economics in the Early Soviet Union		
Type	**Economics**	**Politics**
War Communism		
New Economic Policy		

Using the information in your table, write a brief answer to the Focus Question.

OUTLINE

Read the section topic entitled "The New Economic Policy" and create an outline of the section below. Note the key words that reflect the main ideas in each paragraph as well as the key words that inform those ideas.

I. The New Economic Policy
   A. Distinguishing public and private enterprise
      1.
      2.
      3.
   B.
      1.
      2.
      3.
   C.
      1.
      2.
      3.

READING SKILL: SUMMARIZE

Complete the chart below identifying the steps Stalin took to consolidate his personal rule over the Soviet Union.

Stalin in Control
Stalin's steps to consolidate personal rule • • • •

Review Questions

Write a brief answer to the following questions. Remember, each answer should highlight a primary idea using key words and supporting details.

1. How did Stalin achieve supreme power in the Soviet Union?

2. Why did he decide that Russia had to industrialize rapidly? Why did this require the collectivization of agriculture? Was the policy a success? How did it affect the Russian people?

3. Why did Stalin carry out the great purges?

Section 4 The Fascist Experiment in Italy

Focus Question

What did Fascism mean to Mussolini and his supporters?

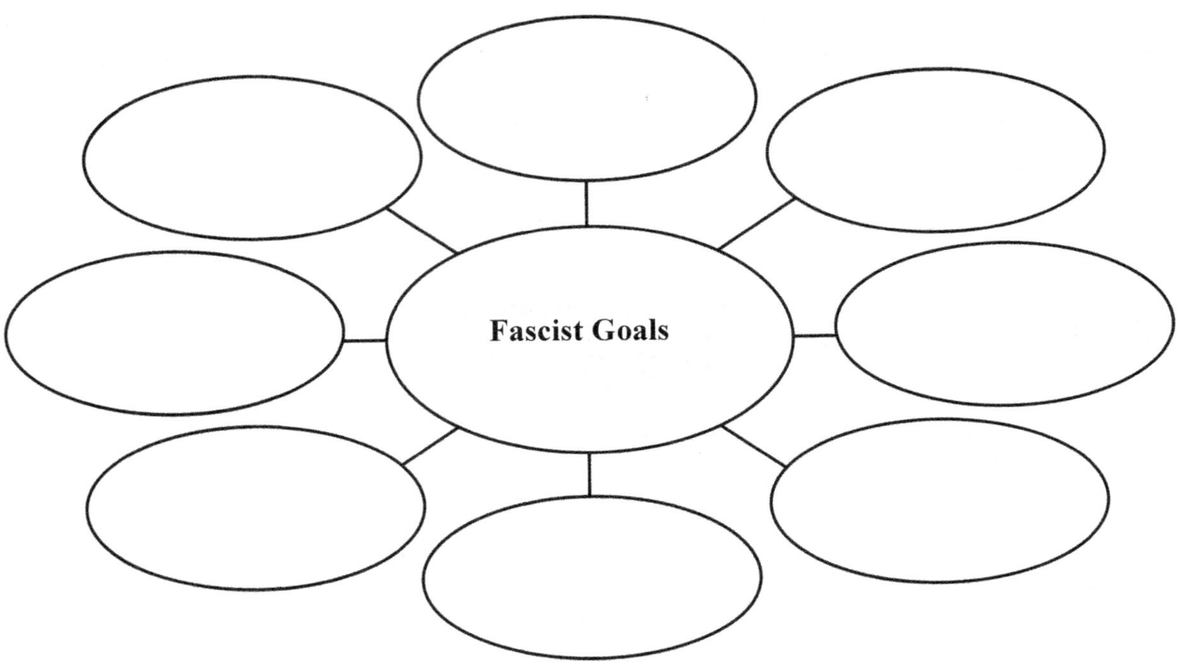

Using the information in your concept web, write a brief answer to the Focus Question.

OUTLINE

Read the section topic entitled "The Fascists in Power" and create an outline of the section below. Note the key words that reflect the main ideas in each paragraph as well as the key words that inform those ideas.

I. The Fascists in Power

  A. Mussolini appointed prime minister of Italy

    1.

    2.

  B.

    1.

    2.

    3.

    4.

  C.

    1.

    2.

    3.

    4.

    5.

    6.

    7.

  D.

    1.

    2.

    3.

    4.

    5.

    6.

    7.

Reading Skill: Summarize

Complete the concept web below identifying the provisions of the Lateran Accord.

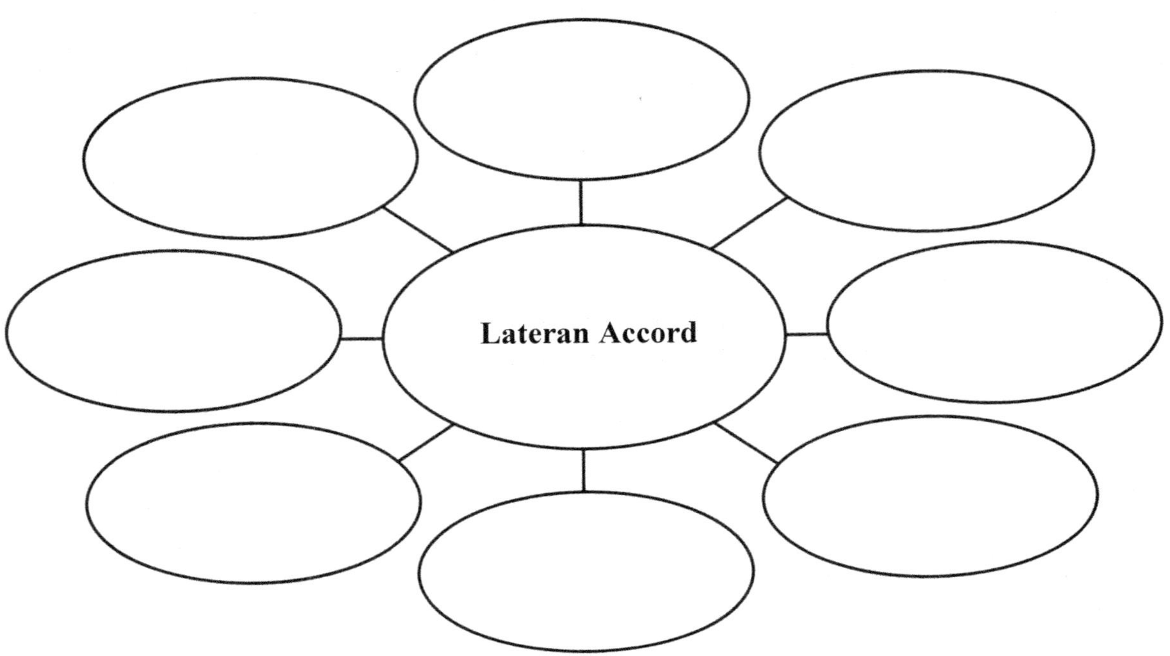

Review Questions

Write a brief answer to the following questions. Remember, each answer should highlight a primary idea using key words and supporting details.

1. Why was Italy dissatisfied and unstable after World War I?

2. How did Mussolini achieve power?

3. What were the characteristics of the Fascist state?

SECTION 5 GERMAN DEMOCRACY AND DICTATORSHIP

FOCUS QUESTION

Why did democracy fail to thrive in postwar Germany?

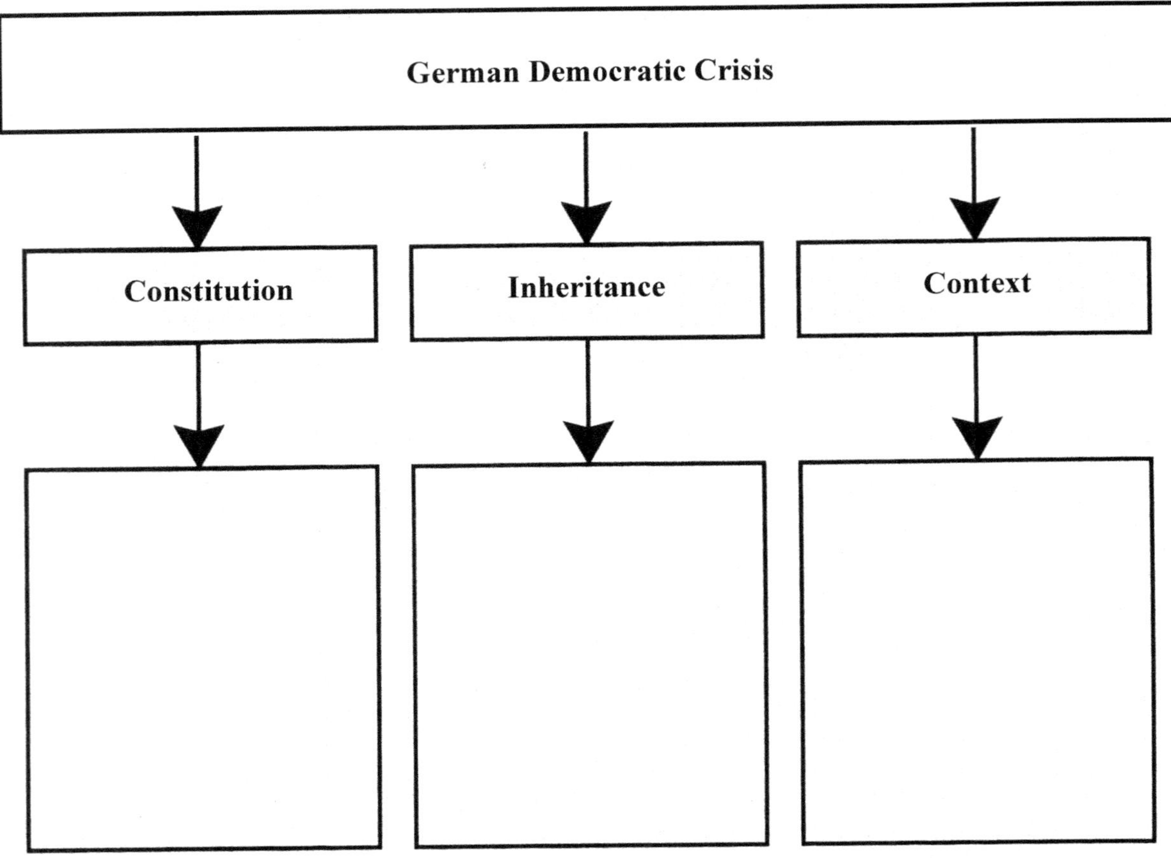

Using the information in your chart, write a brief answer to the Focus Question.

OUTLINE

Read the section topic entitled "Hitler's Consolidation of Power" and create an outline of the section below. Note the key words that reflect the main ideas in each paragraph as well as the key words that inform those ideas.

I. Hitler's Consolidation of Power

  A. Full legal authority

    1.

    2.

    3.

    4.

    5.

  B.

    1.

    2.

    3.

    4.

  C.

    1.

    2.

    3.

    4.

    5.

    6.

  D.

    1.

    2.

    3.

    4.

    5.

    6.

  E.

    1.

    2.

Review Questions

Write a brief answer to the following questions. Remember, each answer should highlight a primary idea using key words and supporting details.

1. Why did the Weimar Republic collapse in Germany?

2. How did Hitler come to power?

3. Which groups in Germany supported Hitler and why were they pro-Nazi?

4. How did he consolidate his power?

5. Why was anti-Semitism central to Nazi policy?

Section 6 Trials of the Successor States in Eastern Europe

Focus Question

What shared challenges did the successor states face in eastern Europe?

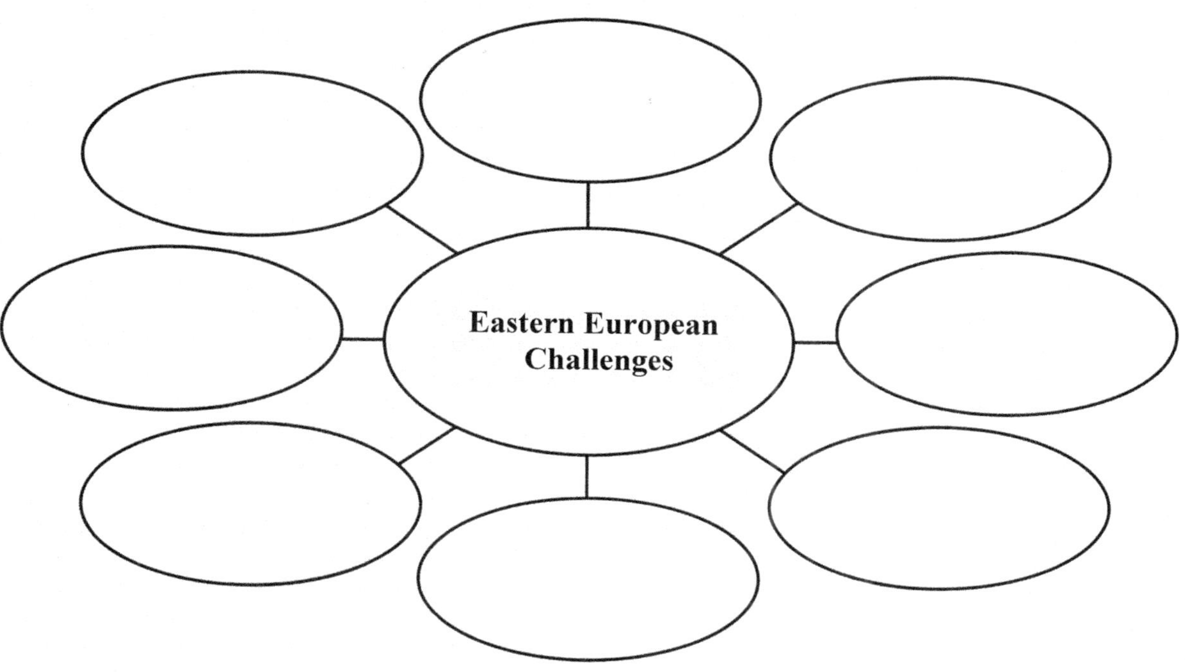

Using the information in your concept web, write a brief answer to the Focus Question.

OUTLINE

Read the section topic entitled "Hungary: Turn to Authoritarianism" and create an outline of the section below. Note the key words that reflect the main ideas in each paragraph as well as the key words that inform those ideas.

I. Hungary: Turn to Authoritarianism
   A. Hungarian Soviet Republic
      1.
      2.
      3.
   B.
      1.
      2.
      3.
      4.
      5.
   C.
      1.
      2.
   D.
      1.
      2.
      3.
      4.
      5.
      6.

Reading Skill: Summarize

Complete the chart below identifying the authoritarian turns of the successor states in Eastern Europe.

Eastern European Authoritarianism	
Country	**Turn to Authoritarianism**

REVIEW QUESTIONS

Write a brief answer to the following questions. Remember, each answer should highlight a primary idea using key words and supporting details.

1. What characteristics did the authoritarian regimes in the Soviet Union, Italy, and Germany have in common? What role did terror play in each?

2. Why did liberal democracy fail in the successor states of Eastern Europe?

3. What made Czechoslovakia an exception?

Review: Key Terms and People

Complete your review of the chapter by writing a brief definition of the following terms and people.

Great Depression
Weimar Republic
Lausanne Conference
Sinn Fein
Popular Front
War Communism
Kronstadt mutiny
Comintern
Joseph Stalin
Gosplan
Collectivization
Great Purges
Benito Mussolini
Fascism
Gabriele D'Annunzio
Coalition government
Lateran Accord
Weimar Republic
Kapp Putsch
Nazi
SA
Mein Kampf
Gustav Stresemann
Locarno Agreements
Article 48
SS
Kristallnacht
Hermann Göring
Josef Pilsudski
Thomas Masaryk
Bela Kun

My Key Terms

Write down terms that are unfamiliar. How are the words used? Do other words or examples reveal their meaning? Try to figure out meaning from the context.

CHAPTER 20
WORLD WAR II

Complete the following exercises *as you read* this chapter.

SECTION 1 AGAIN THE ROAD TO WAR (1933–1939)

FOCUS QUESTION

How did World War I sow the seeds of World War II?

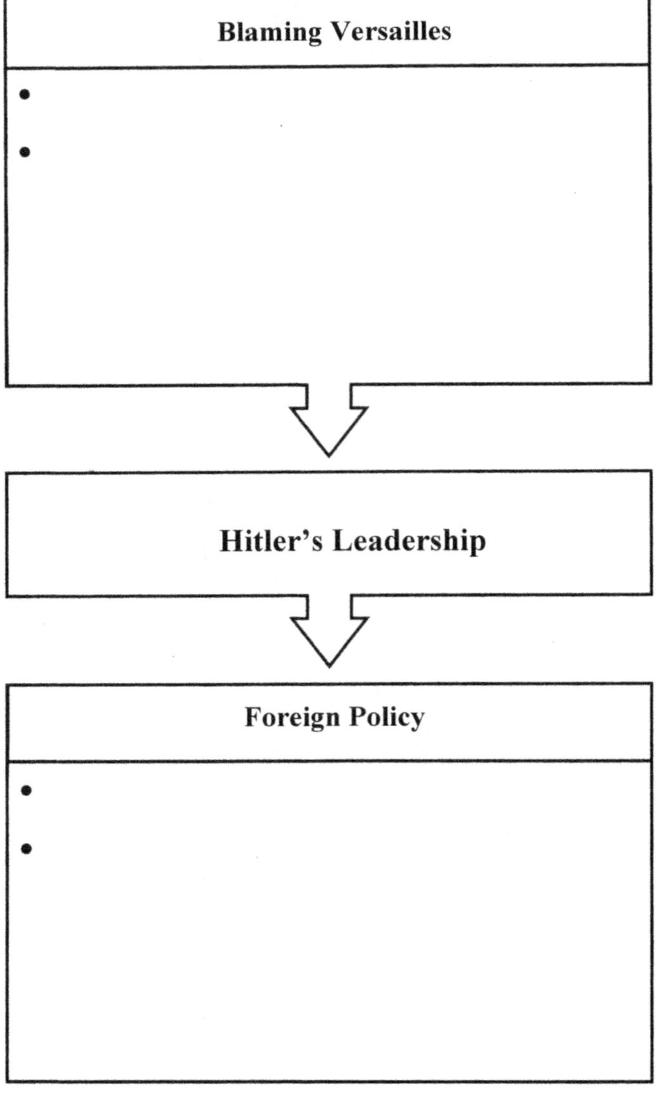

Using the information in your chart, write a brief answer to the Focus Question.

OUTLINE

Read the section topic entitled "Hitler's Goals" and create an outline of the section below. Note the key words that reflect the main ideas in each paragraph as well as the key words that inform those ideas.

I. Hitler's Goals

    A. Consistent racial theory and goals

        1.

        2.

    B.

        1.

        2.

        3.

        4.

    C.

        1.

        2.

        3.

        4.

        5.

        6.

        7.

    D.

        1.

        2.

        3.

        4.

    E.

        1.

        2.

        3.

Review Questions

Write a brief answer to the following questions. Remember, each answer should highlight a primary idea using key words and supporting details.

1. What were Hitler's foreign policy aims? Was he bent on conquest, or did he simply want to return Germany to its 1914 boundaries?

2. Why did Britain and France adopt a policy of appeasement in the 1930s? Did the West buy valuable time to rearm at Munich in 1938?

SECTION 2 WORLD WAR II (1939–1945)

FOCUS QUESTION

In what ways was World War II a "total" war?

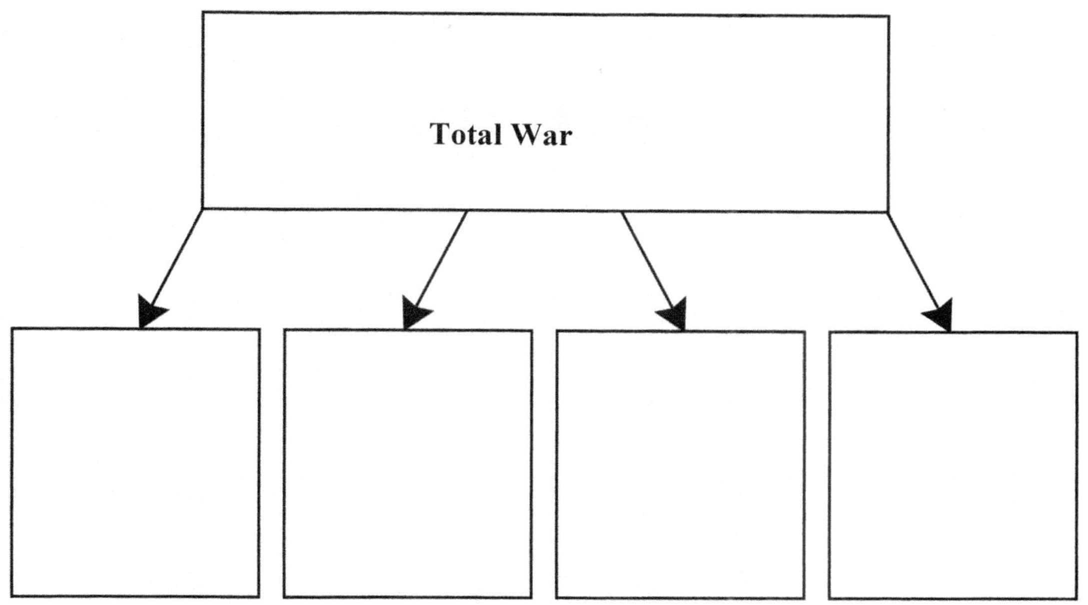

Using the information in your chart, write a brief answer to the Focus Question.

OUTLINE

Read the section topic entitled "The German Attack on Russia" and create an outline of the section below. Note the key words that reflect the main ideas in each paragraph as well as the key words that inform those ideas.

I. The German Attack on Russia
   A. Operation Barbarossa
      1.
      2.
      3.
   B.
      1.
      2.
      3.
      4.
      5.
      6.
      7.
   C.
      1.
      2.
      3.
   D.
      1.
      2.
      3.
      4.
      5.

Review Questions

Write a brief answer to the following questions. Remember, each answer should highlight a primary idea using key words and supporting details.

1. How was Hitler able to defeat France so easily in 1940?

2. Why did the air war against Britain fail?

3. Why did Hitler invade Russia? Could the invasion have succeeded?

4. Why did Japan attack the United States at Pearl Harbor?

5. How important was American intervention in the war?

6. Why did the United States drop atomic bombs on Japan? Was President Truman right to use the bombs?

Section 3 Racism and the Holocaust

Focus Question

What was the Holocaust?

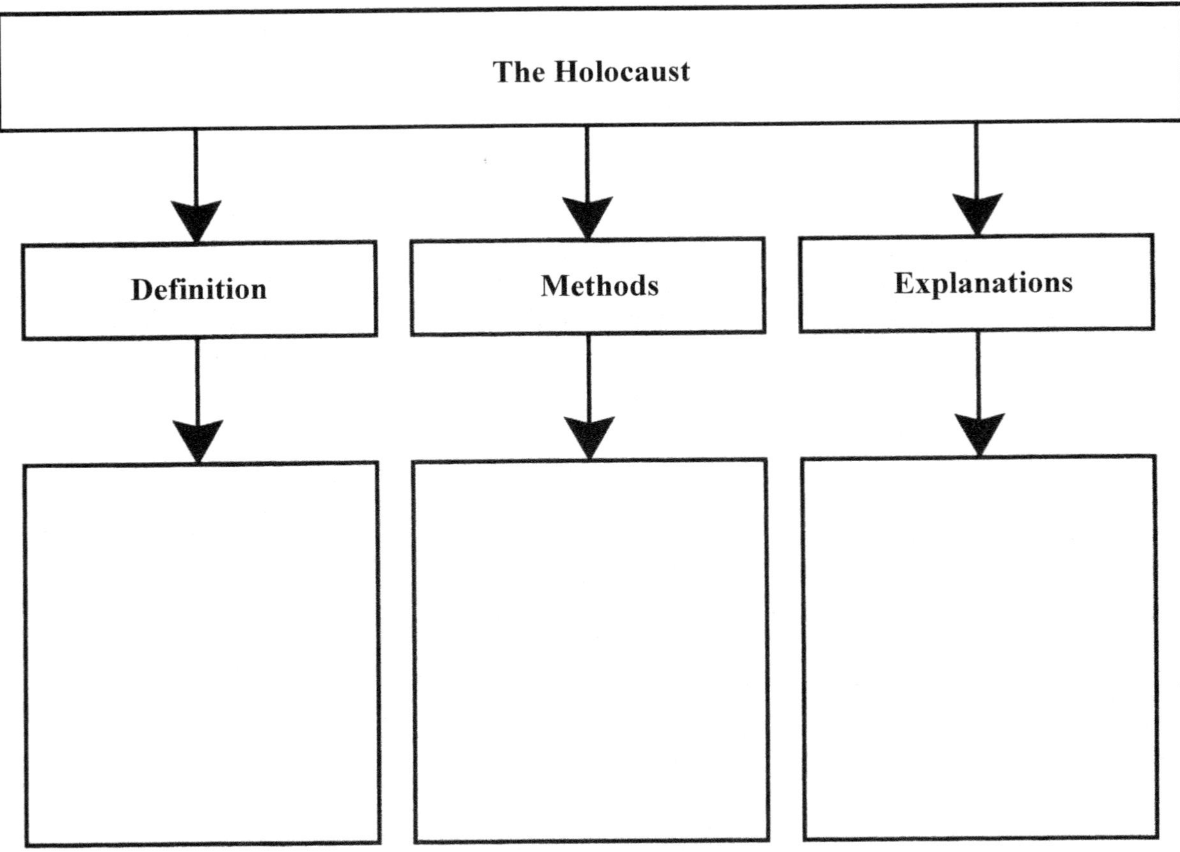

Using the information in your chart, write a brief answer to the Focus Question.

OUTLINE

Read the section topic entitled "The Nazi Assault on the Jews of Poland" and create an outline of the section below. Note the key words that reflect the main ideas in each paragraph as well as the key words that inform those ideas.

I. The Nazi Assault on the Jews of Poland
  A. Nazi antipathy for Polish Jews in particular
    1.
    2.
    3.
  B.
    1.
    2.
    3.
    4.
    5.
    6.
    7.
  C.
    1.
    2.
    3.
    4.
    5.
  D.
    1.
    2.
    3.
    4.
    5.
  E.
    1.
    2.

Reading Skill: Summarize

Complete the chart below identifying the nature of Polish citizenship as it was defined between the eighteenth and twentieth centuries.

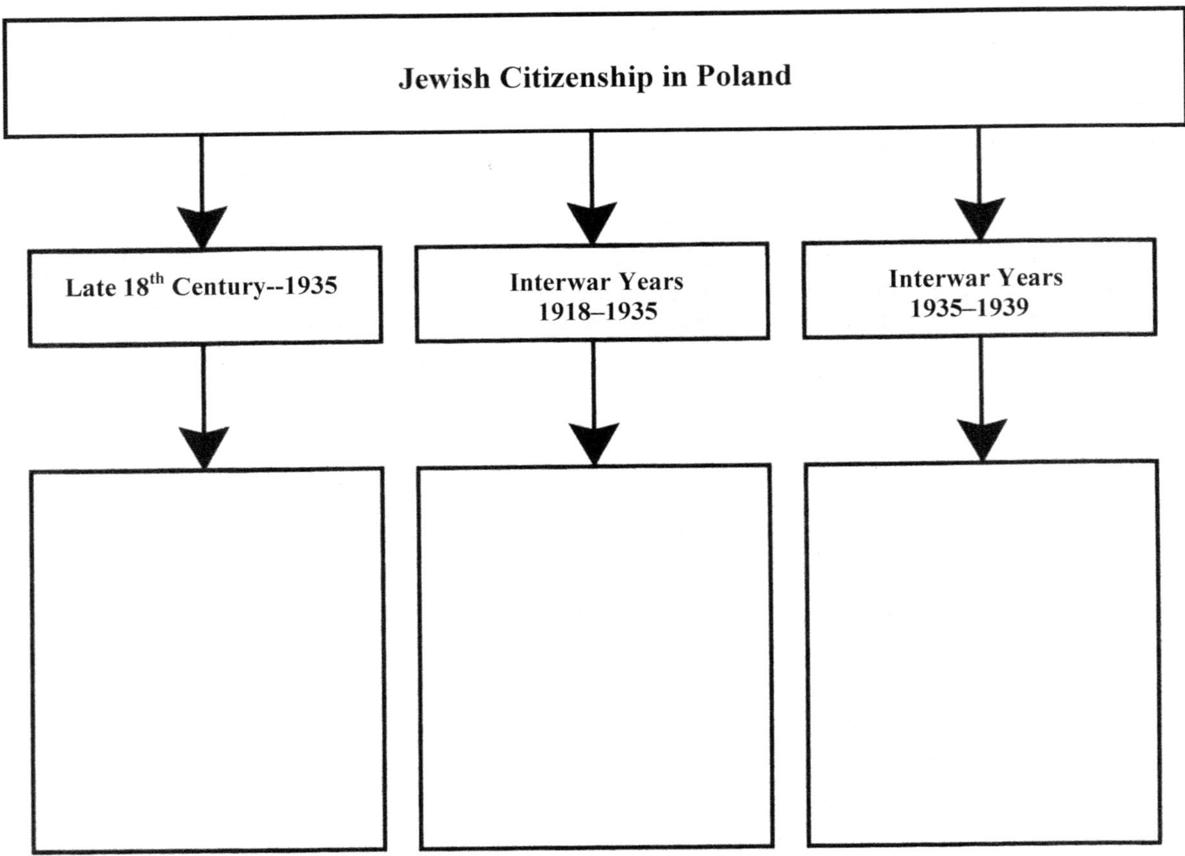

Review Questions

Write a brief answer to the following questions. Remember, each answer should highlight a primary idea using key words and supporting details.

1. What was Hitler's "final solution" to the Jewish question?

2. Why did he want to eliminate Slavs as well?

3. To what extent can it be said that the Holocaust was the defining event of the twentieth century?

SECTION 4 THE DOMESTIC FRONTS

FOCUS QUESTION

What impact did World War II have on European society?

Impact of World War II on European Society			
Country	**Production and Sacrifice**	**Propaganda and Politics**	**Civilian Casualties and Disruption**
Germany			
France			
Britain			
Soviet Union			

Using the information in your table, write a brief answer to the Focus Question.

Outline

Read the section topic entitled "France: Defeat, Collaboration, and Resistance" and create an outline of the section below. Note the key words that reflect the main ideas in each paragraph as well as the key words that inform those ideas.

I. France: Defeat, Collaboration, and Resistance
   A. Terms of 1940 armistice between France and Germany
      1.
      2.
      3.
      4.
      5.
      6.
   B.
      1.
      2.
      3.
   C.
      1.
      2.
      3.
      4.
      5.
      6.
   D.
      1.
      2.
      3.
      4.

Reading Skill: Summarize

Complete the concept web below identifying the measures the British took to organize for victory.

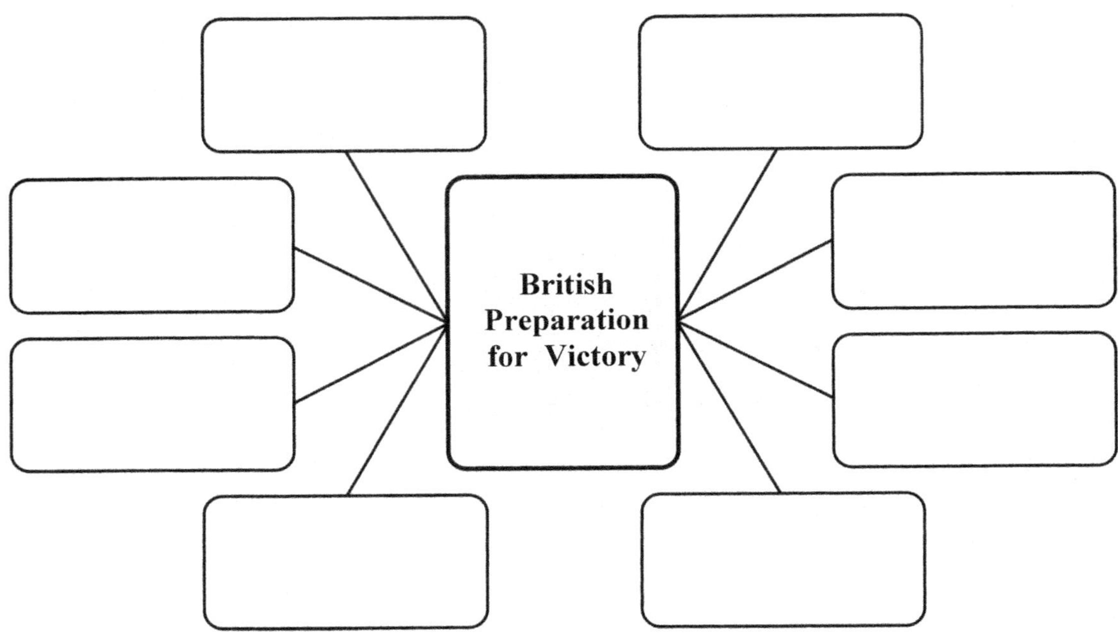

REVIEW QUESTIONS

Write a brief answer to the following questions. Remember, each answer should highlight a primary idea using key words and supporting details.

1. How did experiences on the domestic front in Britain differ from those in Germany and France?

2. What impact did "The Great Patriotic War" have on the people of the Soviet Union?

SECTION 5 PREPARATIONS FOR PEACE

FOCUS QUESTION

How did the Allies prepare for a postwar Europe?

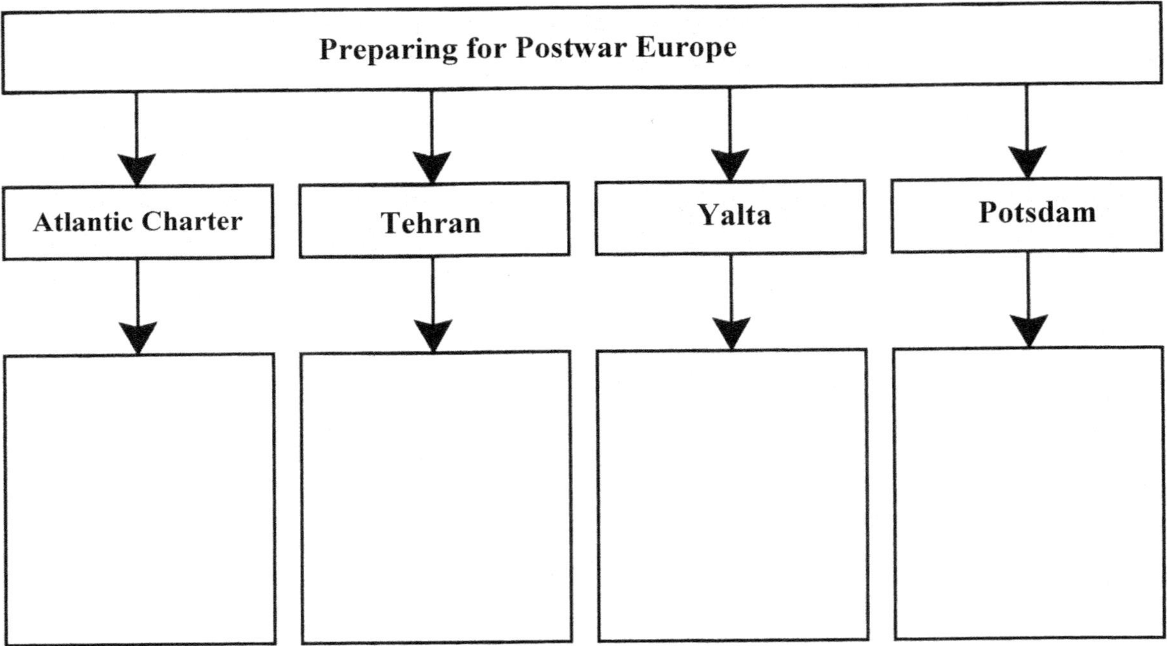

Using the information in your chart, write a brief answer to the Focus Question.

OUTLINE

Read the section topic entitled "Tehran: Agreement on a Second Front" and create an outline of the section below. Note the key words that reflect the main ideas in each paragraph as well as the key words that inform those ideas.

I. Tehran: Agreement on a Second Front
   A. In 1943 the "Big Three" (USSR, Britain, US) met in Tehran
      1.
      2.
      3.
      4.
      5.
      6.
      7.
      8.
   B.
      1.
      2.
      3.
      4.
      5.
      6.
   C.
      1.
      2.
      3.
      4.
   D.
      1.
      2.
      3.

Review: Key Terms and People

Complete your review of the chapter by writing a brief definition of the following terms and people.

Lebensraum
Lytton Report
Stresa Front
Axis
Falangists
Neville Chamberlain
Nazi-Soviet Pact
Blitzkrieg
Winston Churchill
Luftwaffe
Operation Barbarossa
Erwin Rommel
Third Reich
Battle of Stalingrad
Dresden
Battle of the Bulge
Untermenschen
Heinrich Himmler
Judenrein
Holocaust
Warsaw
Treblinka
Jedwabne
Josef Goebbels
Vichy
Charles de Gaulle
Dimitri Shostakovitch
Atlantic Charter
Tehran Conference
Yalta
Potsdam

My Key Terms

Write down terms that are unfamiliar. How are the words used? Do other words or examples reveal their meaning? Try to figure out meaning from the context.

CHAPTER 21
THE COLD WAR ERA, DECOLONIZATION, AND THE EMERGENCE OF A NEW EUROPE

Complete the following exercises *as you read* this chapter.

SECTION 1 THE EMERGENCE OF THE COLD WAR

FOCUS QUESTION

What were the origins of the Cold War?

Origins of the Cold War		
	Ideology	**Interests**
Soviet Union		
United States		

Using the information in your table, write a brief answer to the Focus Question.

OUTLINE

Read the section topic entitled "NATO and the Warsaw Pact" and create an outline of the section below. Note the key words that reflect the main ideas in each paragraph as well as the key words that inform those ideas.

I. NATO and the Warsaw Pact
   A. Creating a Western bloc
      1.
      2.
      3.
   B.
      1.
      2.
      3.
      4.
      5.
      6.
   C.
      1.
      2.
   D.
      1.
      2.
      3.
      4.
      5.
      6.
   E.
      1.
      2.
      3.

READING SKILL: SUMMARIZE

Complete the chart below identifying the primary reasons for Germany's partition into two separate countries.

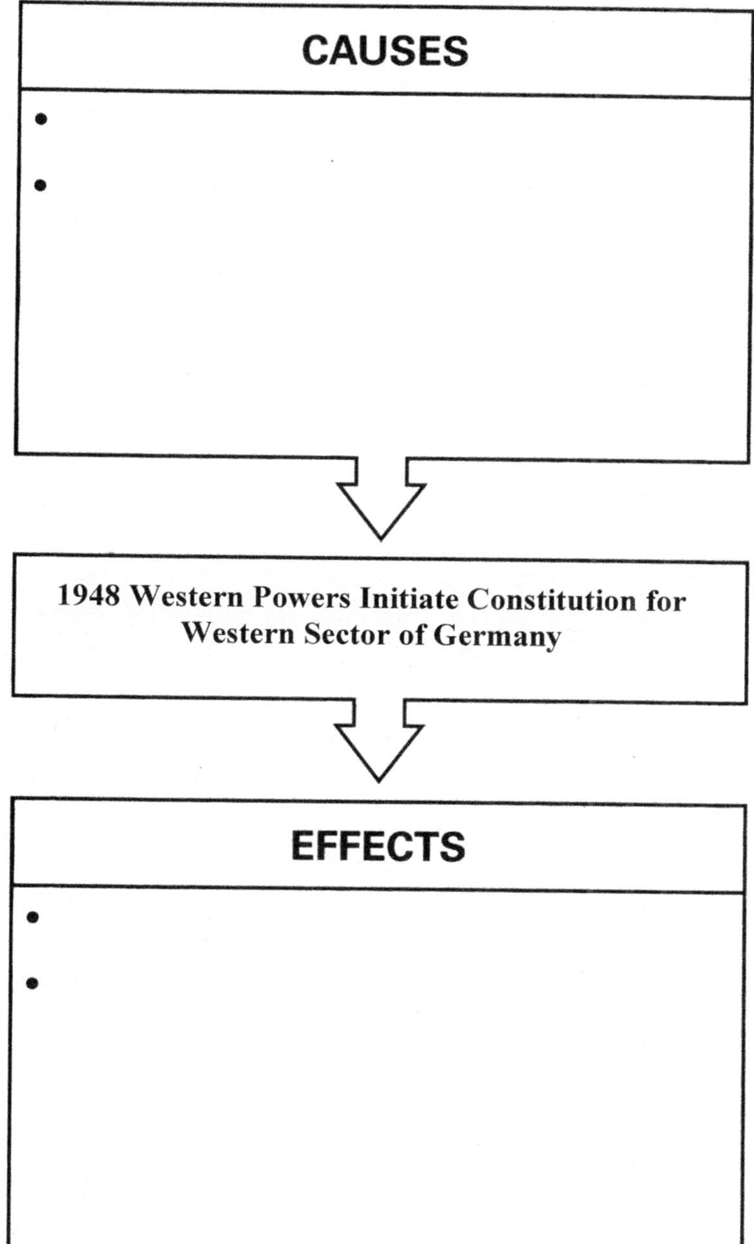

Review Questions

Write a brief answer to the following questions. Remember, each answer should highlight a primary idea using key words and supporting details.

1. How did the United States and the Soviet Union come to dominate Europe after 1945?

2. How would you define the policy of containment?

3. In what areas of the world did the United States specifically try to contain Soviet power from 1945 to 1982?

4. Why were 1956 and 1962 crucial years in the Cold War?

Section 2 The Khrushchev Era in the Soviet Union

Focus Question

What domestic policies did Khrushchev pursue?

1956: Khrushchev denounced Stalin in secret speech at Twentieth Congress of the Communist Party
•   •   •

Using the information in your flowchart, write a brief answer to the Focus Question.

Outline

Read the section topic entitled "Khrushchev's Domestic Policies" and create an outline of the section below. Note the key words that reflect the main ideas in each paragraph as well as the key words that inform those ideas.

I. Khrushchev's Domestic Policies
    A. Nikita Khrushchev
        1.
        2.
        3.
        4.
    B.
        1.
        2.
        3.
    C.
        1.
        2.
    D.
        1.
        2.
        3.
        4.
    E.
        1.
        2.
        3.
        4.
        5.

REVIEW QUESTIONS

Write a brief answer to the following questions. Remember, each answer should highlight a primary idea using key words and supporting details.

1. How did Khrushchev's policies and reforms change the Soviet state after the repression of Stalin?

2. What made the Suez crisis significant for future European foreign policy?

SECTION 3 LATER COLD WAR CONFRONTATIONS

FOCUS QUESTION

How did the Berlin Wall and the Cuban Missile Crisis strain relations between the United States and the Soviet Union?

U.S./Soviet Relations 1956–1962		
Event	**Description**	**Effect**
Berlin Wall		
Cuban Missile Crisis		

Using the information in your table, write a brief answer to the Focus Question.

OUTLINE

Read the section topic entitled "The Berlin Wall" and create an outline of the section below. Note the key words that reflect the main ideas in each paragraph as well as the key words that inform those ideas.

I. The Berlin Wall
    A. 1960 Paris Summit Conference aborted
        1.
        2.
    B.
        1.
        2.
        3.
    C.
        1.
        2.
    D.
        1.
        2.

Review Questions

Write a brief answer to the following questions. Remember, each answer should highlight a primary idea using key words and supporting details.

1. Why did Khrushchev destroy the Paris Summit Conference of 1960?

2. Why did the Soviet Union and United States conclude a nuclear test ban treaty in 1963?

Section 4 The Brezhnev Era

Focus Question

What impact did Brezhnev have on the Soviet Union and Eastern Europe?

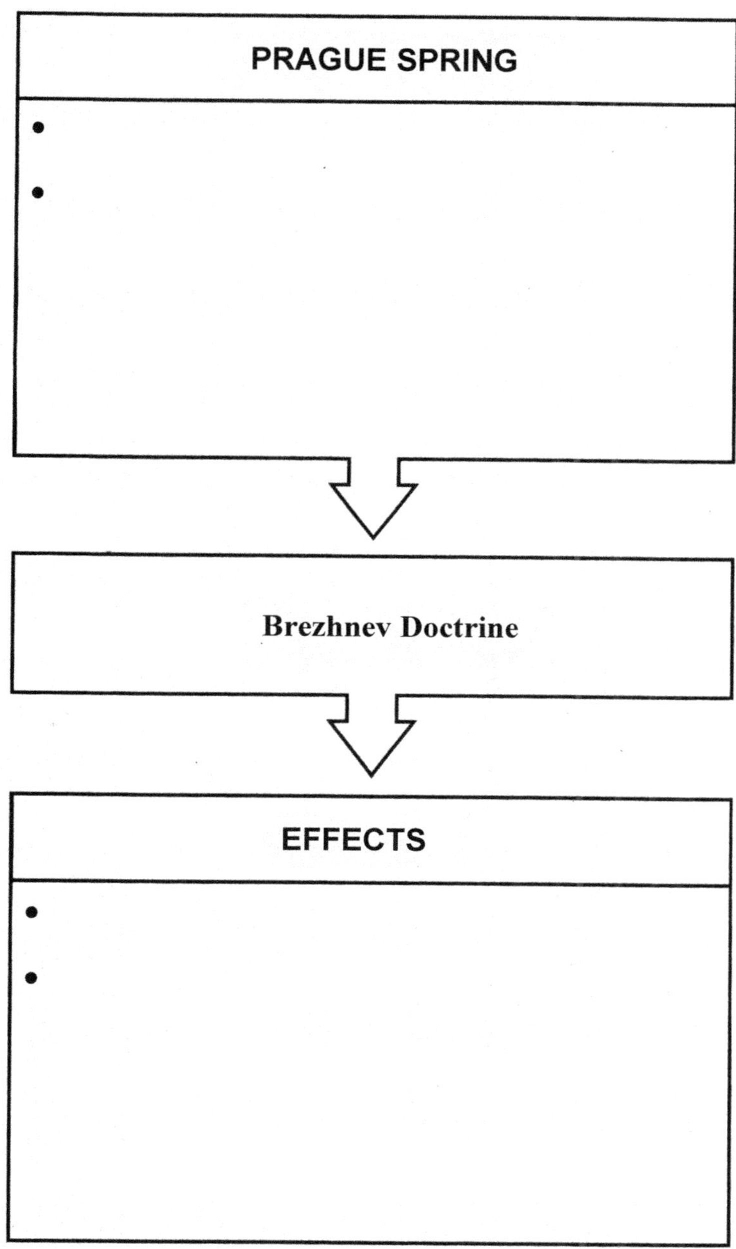

Using the information in your chart, write a brief answer to the Focus Question.

OUTLINE

Read the section topic entitled "The Invasion of Afghanistan" and create an outline of the section below. Note the key words that reflect the main ideas in each paragraph as well as the key words that inform those ideas.

I. The Invasion of Afghanistan
   A. 1979 Soviets invade Afghanistan
      1.
      2.
      3.
      4.
      5.
   B.
      1.
      2.
      3.
      4.
      5.
      6.
      7.
   C.
      1.
      2.
      3.
      4.
      5.
      6.

REVIEW QUESTIONS

Write a brief answer to the following questions. Remember, each answer should highlight a primary idea using key words and supporting details.

1. In what way were the Truman and Brezhnev Doctrines similar or different?

2. In what way did Brezhnev's leadership of the Soviet Union contribute to Reagan's foreign policy?

Section 5 Decolonization: The European Retreat from Empire

Focus Question

How was World War II a catalyst for decolonization?

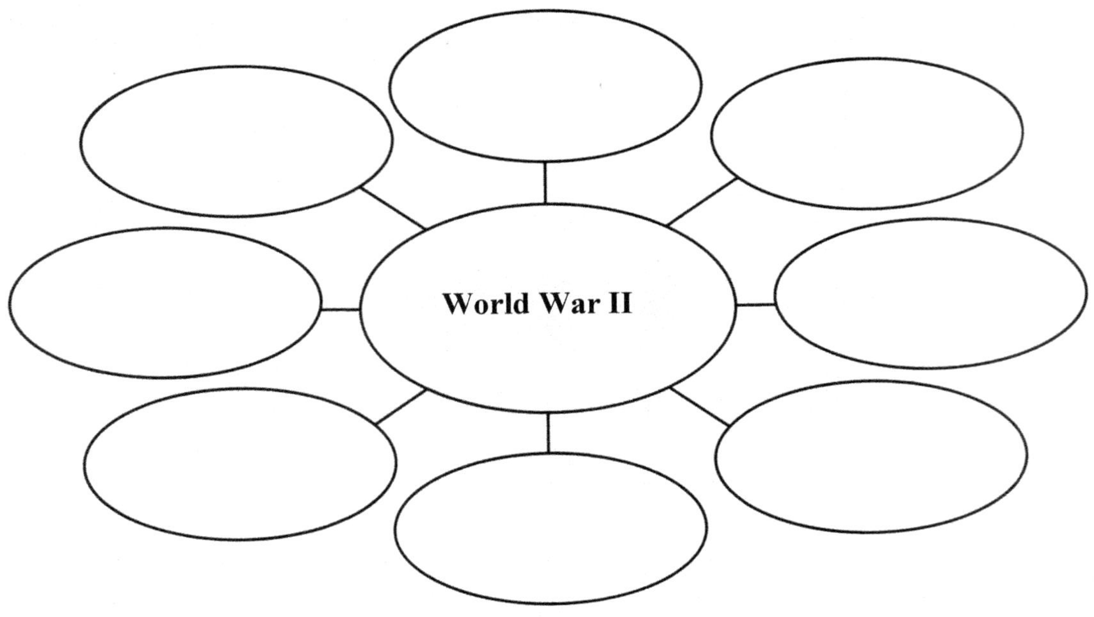

Using the information in your concept web, write a brief answer to the Focus Question.

OUTLINE

Read the section topic entitled "Further British Retreat from Empire" and create an outline of the section below. Note the key words that reflect the main ideas in each paragraph as well as the key words that inform those ideas.

I. Further British Retreat from Empire
   A. British surrender of India: beginning of end of empire
      1.
      2.
      3.
      4.
      5.
      6.
      7.
   B.
      1.
      2.
      3.
      4.
   C.
      1.
      2.
   D.
      1.
      2.

Reading Skill: Summarize

Complete the concept web below identifying the primary goals and tactics Gandhi used to liberate India from British colonial rule.

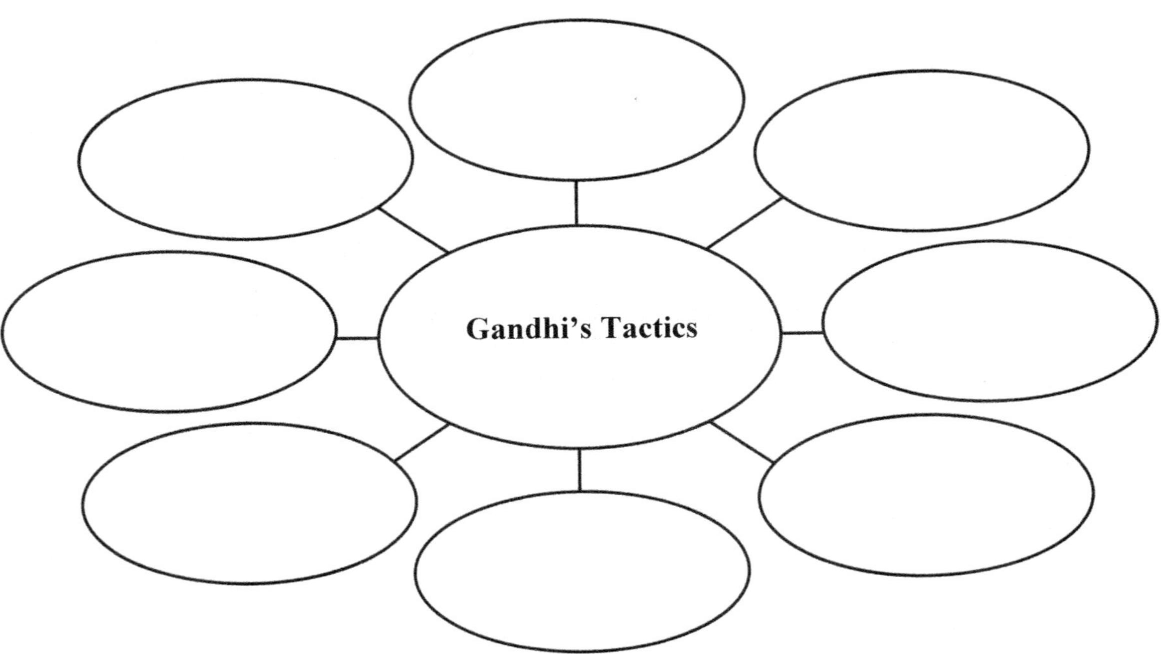

Review Questions

Write a brief answer to the following questions. Remember, each answer should highlight a primary idea using key words and supporting details.

1. Why did the nations of Europe give up their empires?

2. How did World War II affect the movement toward decolonization?

3. How did Gandhi lead India toward independence?

SECTION 6 THE TURMOIL OF FRENCH DECOLONIZATION

FOCUS QUESTION

Why was France so reluctant to decolonize?

French Resistance to Decolonization	
Algeria	**Vietnam**
•	•
•	•
•	•

Using the information in your table, write a brief answer to the Focus Question.

OUTLINE

Read the section topic entitled "France and Vietnam" and create an outline of the section below. Note the key words that reflect the main ideas in each paragraph as well as the key words that inform those ideas.

I. France and Vietnam
   A. Pre-WWII and French Indochina
      1.
      2.
      3.
   B.
      1.
      2.
      3.
   C.
      1.
      2.
   D.
      1.
      2.
      3.
   E.
      1.
      2.
      3.
      4.
      5.
      6.
      7.

REVIEW QUESTIONS

Write a brief answer to the following questions. Remember, each answer should highlight a primary idea using key words and supporting details.

1. How did French decolonization policies differ from Britain's policies?

2. How did the United States become involved in Vietnam?

SECTION 7 THE COLLAPSE OF EUROPEAN COMMUNISM

FOCUS QUESTION

Why did European communism collapse?

Brezhnev's repressive policies gave rise to dissent movement
• • • • • •

Using the information in your chart, write a brief answer to the Focus Question.

Outline

Read the section topic entitled "Gorbachev Attempts to Reform the Soviet Union" and create an outline of the section below. Note the key words that reflect the main ideas in each paragraph as well as the key words that inform those ideas.

I. Gorbachev Attempts to Reform the Soviet Union
   A. Lingering problems in the Soviet Union
      1.
      2.
      3.
   B.
      1.
      2.
   C.
      1.
      2.
      3.
      4.
   D.
      1.
      2.
      3.
      4.
      5.
      6.
   E.
      1.
      2.
      3.
      4.

Review Questions

Write a brief answer to the following questions. Remember, each answer should highlight a primary idea using key words and supporting details.

1. What internal political pressures did the Soviet Union experience in the 1970s and early 1980s? What steps did the Soviet government take to repress those protests?

2. What role did Gorbachev's attempted reforms play in the collapse of the Soviet Union?

3. What were the major events in Eastern Europe—particularly Poland--that contributed to the collapse of communism?

4. What were the major domestic challenges to the new Confederation of Independent States?

Section 8 The Collapse of Yugoslavia and Civil War

Focus Question

How did ethnic tensions lead to civil war in Yugoslavia?

Ethnic Tensions and Civil War		
Ethnic Group Characteristics	**National Complaint**	**Action**

Using the information in your table, write a brief answer to the Focus Question.

OUTLINE

Read the section topic entitled "The Collapse of Yugoslavia and Civil War" and create an outline of the section below. Note the key words that reflect the main ideas in each paragraph as well as the key words that inform those ideas.

I. The Collapse of Yugoslavia and Civil War

A. Yugoslavia

1.

2.

3.

4.

5.

6.

B. Ethnic divisions come to the fore

1.

2.

3.

4.

5.

6.

7.

8.

9.

10.

11.

12.

13.

14.

15.

REVIEW QUESTIONS

Write a brief answer to the following questions. Remember, each answer should highlight a primary idea using key words and supporting details.

1. Was the former Yugoslavia a national state?

2. Why did it break apart and slide into civil war?

3. How did the West respond to this crisis?

SECTION 9 PUTIN AND THE RESURGENCE OF RUSSIA

FOCUS QUESTION

What vision does Putin have of Russia's place in the world?

Russia as a World Power		

=

Using the information in your chart, write a brief answer to the Focus Question.

OUTLINE

Read the section topic entitled "Putin and the Resurgence of Russia" and create an outline of the section below. Note the key words that reflect the main ideas in each paragraph as well as the key words that inform those ideas.

I. Putin and the Resurgence of Russia
   A. Vladimir Putin
      1.
      2.
   B.
      1.
      2.
   C.
      1.
      2.
      3.
   D.
      1.
      2.
      3.
   E.
      1.
      2.
      3.
      4.
      5.
      6.
      7.
   F.
      1.
      2.

Review Questions

Write a brief answer to the following questions. Remember, each answer should highlight a primary idea using key words and supporting details.

1. What were the major difficulties that the Russian Federation faced in the 1990s and beyond? How did the policies of Yeltsin and Putin address them?

2. How has Putin attempted to preside over a resurgence of Russian great power influence? How do his goals in part reflect concern over the example of the political disintegration of Yugoslavia?

SECTION 10 THE RISE OF RADICAL POLITICAL ISLAMISM

FOCUS QUESTION

What forces gave rise to radical political Islamism?

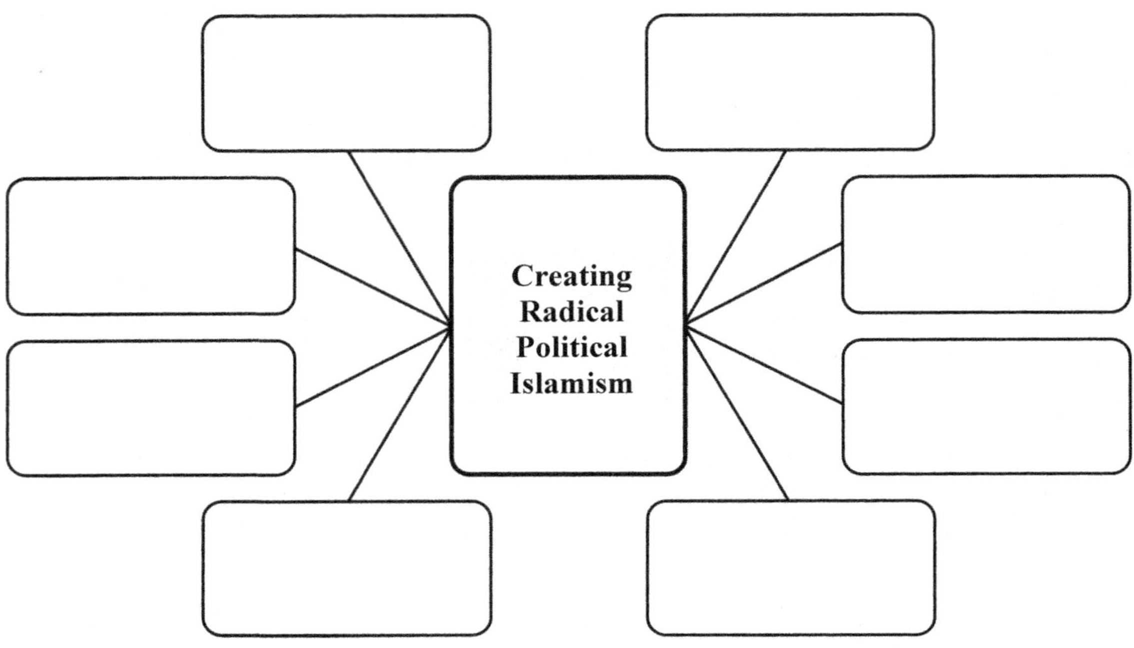

Using the information in your concept web, write a brief answer to the Focus Question.

OUTLINE

Read the section topic entitled "The Iranian Revolution" and create an outline of the section below. Note the key words that reflect the main ideas in each paragraph as well as the key words that inform those ideas.

I. The Iranian Revolution

  A. Ayatollah Ruhollah Khomeini and the Revolution of 1979

    1.

    2.

    3.

  B.

    1.

    2.

    3.

    4.

  C.

    1.

    2.

    3.

    4.

    5.

    6.

    7.

  D.

    1.

    2.

Review Questions

Write a brief answer to the following questions. Remember, each answer should highlight a primary idea using key words and supporting details.

1. What were the major causes for the rise of radical political Islamism?

2. In what ways is the present U.S. intervention in the Middle East a result of decolonization, and in what ways are other factors at work?

SECTION 11 A TRANSFORMED WEST

FOCUS QUESTION

How did the events of September 11, 2001 transform the West?

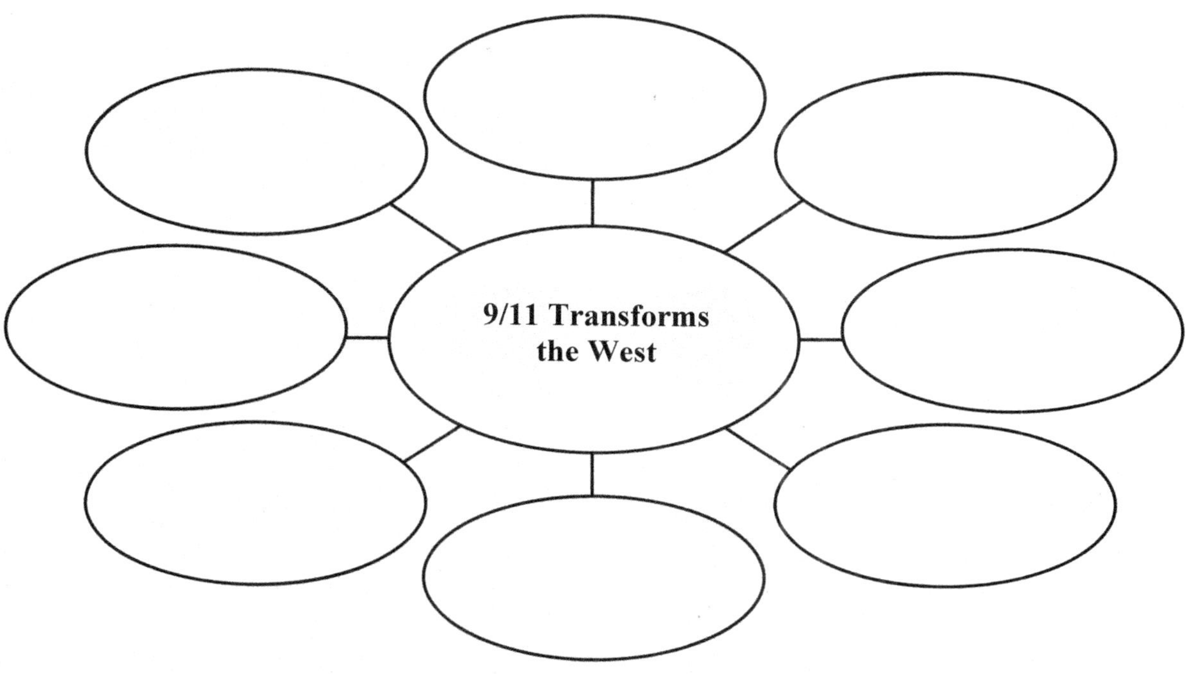

Using the information in your concept web, write a brief answer to the Focus Question.

Outline

Read the section topic entitled "A Transformed West" and create an outline of the section below. Note the key words that reflect the main ideas in each paragraph as well as the key words that inform those ideas.

I. A Transformed West
    A. "War on Terrorism" in response to attacks of September 11, 2001
        1.
        2.
        3.
        4.
    B.
        1.
        2.
        3.
        4.
        5.
        6.
        7.
    C.
        1.
        2.
        3.
        4.
    D.
        1.
        2.
    E.
        1.
        2.
        3.
        4.

REVIEW QUESTIONS

Write a brief answer to the following questions. Remember, each answer should highlight a primary idea using key words and supporting details.

1. How did the American response to the attacks of September 11, 2001, divide the NATO alliance?

2. Why do some European nations feel able to dissent from the U.S. position in the Middle East when they rarely did so during the Cold War?

Review: Key Terms and People

Complete your review of the chapter by writing a brief definition of the following terms and people.

Cold War
Containment
Truman Doctrine
Marshall Plan
Berlin Blockade
NATO
The thirty-eighth parallel
Nikita Khrushchev
Aleksandr Solzhenitsyn
Secret Speech
Hungarian Uprising
Sputnik
U-2 aircraft
Berlin Wall
People's Republic of China
Fulgencio Batista
Fidel Castro
Cuban Missile Crisis
Prague Spring
Brezhnev Doctrine
Détente
Helsinki Accords
Karol Wojtyla
Lech Walesa
Strategic Defense Initiative
Decolonization
Mohandas Gandhi
Doctrine of Nonviolence
Bangladesh
National Liberation Front
Organization Armé Secrète
Ho Chi Minh
Viet Minh
SEATO
Nguyen Van Thieu

Vietnamization
Andrei Sakharov
Mikhail Gorbachev
Perestroika
Glasnost
Velvet Revolution
Boris Yeltsin
Vladimir Putin
Tito
Slobodan Milosevic
Ethnic Cleansing
International War Crimes Tribunal
Kosovo
Russian Federation
Chechnya
Georgia
Iranian Revolution
Ayatollah Ruhollah Khomeini
Theocracy
Muslim reformism
Muslim Brotherhood
September 11, 2001
Al Qaeda
George W. Bush
Saddam Hussein
War on Terrorism

My Key Terms

Write down terms that are unfamiliar. How are the words used? Do other words or examples reveal their meaning? Try to figure out meaning from the context.

CHAPTER 22
SOCIAL, CULTURAL, AND ECONOMIC CHALLENGES IN THE WEST TO THE PRESENT

Complete the following exercises *as you read* this chapter.

SECTION 1 THE TWENTIETH-CENTURY MOVEMENT OF PEOPLES

FOCUS QUESTION

How has migration changed the face of Europe?

European Migration	
Migration	**Effect**

Using the information in your table, write a brief answer to the Focus Question.

OUTLINE

Read the section topic entitled "Displacement through War" and create an outline of the section below. Note the key words that reflect the main ideas in each paragraph as well as the key words that inform those ideas.

I. Displacement Through War

A. 1938–1948 46 million displaced: Central, Eastern Europe, Soviet Union

1.

2.

3.

4.

5.

B.

1.

2.

3.

4.

5.

6.

7.

Review Questions

Write a brief answer to the following questions. Remember, each answer should highlight a primary idea using key words and supporting details.

1. How did migration affect twentieth-century European social life? What internal and external forces led to migration?

2. How has Islamic migration into Europe affected social tensions on the continent? How did the migration come about?

3. What are the incidents occurring in Europe that have raised resentment within the Islamic world?

Section 2 Toward a Welfare State Society

Focus Question

What effect did the Great Depression and World War II have on the way Europeans viewed the role of government in social and economic life?

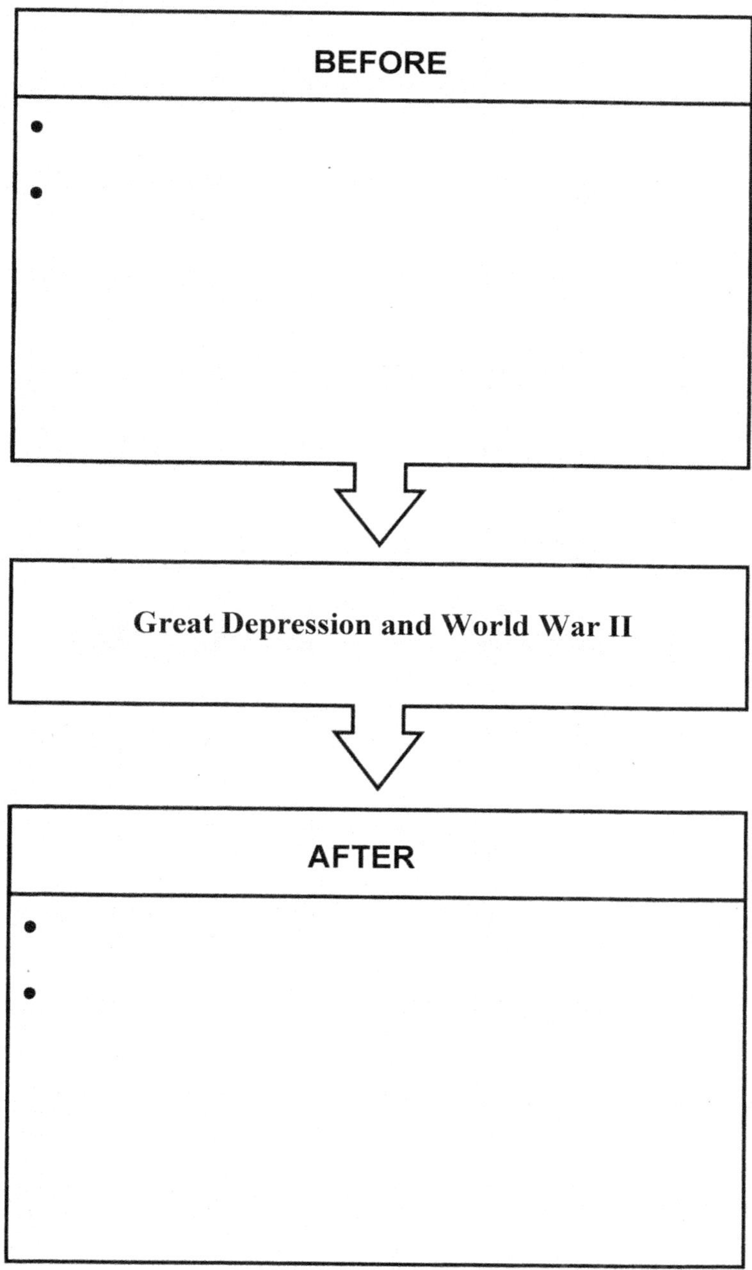

Using the information in your chart, write a brief answer to the Focus Question.

OUTLINE

Read the section topic entitled "The Creation of Welfare States" and create an outline of the section below. Note the key words that reflect the main ideas in each paragraph as well as the key words that inform those ideas.

I. The Creation of Welfare States
  A. Rethinking social welfare
    1.
    2.
    3.
    4.
    5.
  B.
    1.
    2.
  C.
    1.
    2.
    3.
    4.
    5.
    6.
  D.
    1.
    2.
    3.
    4.
    5.
    6.
    7.
  E.
    1.
    2.
    3.

REVIEW QUESTIONS

Write a brief answer to the following questions. Remember, each answer should highlight a primary idea using key words and supporting details.

1. Other than the British Labor Party, who was responsible for introducing social welfare policy into Europe in the post-war years? Why?

2. What forces have threatened the stability of social welfare in Europe since the late 1970s, and especially since the 1990s?

SECTION 3 NEW PATTERNS IN WORK AND EXPECTATIONS OF WOMEN

FOCUS QUESTION

How has the status of women changed in Europe since the end of World War II?

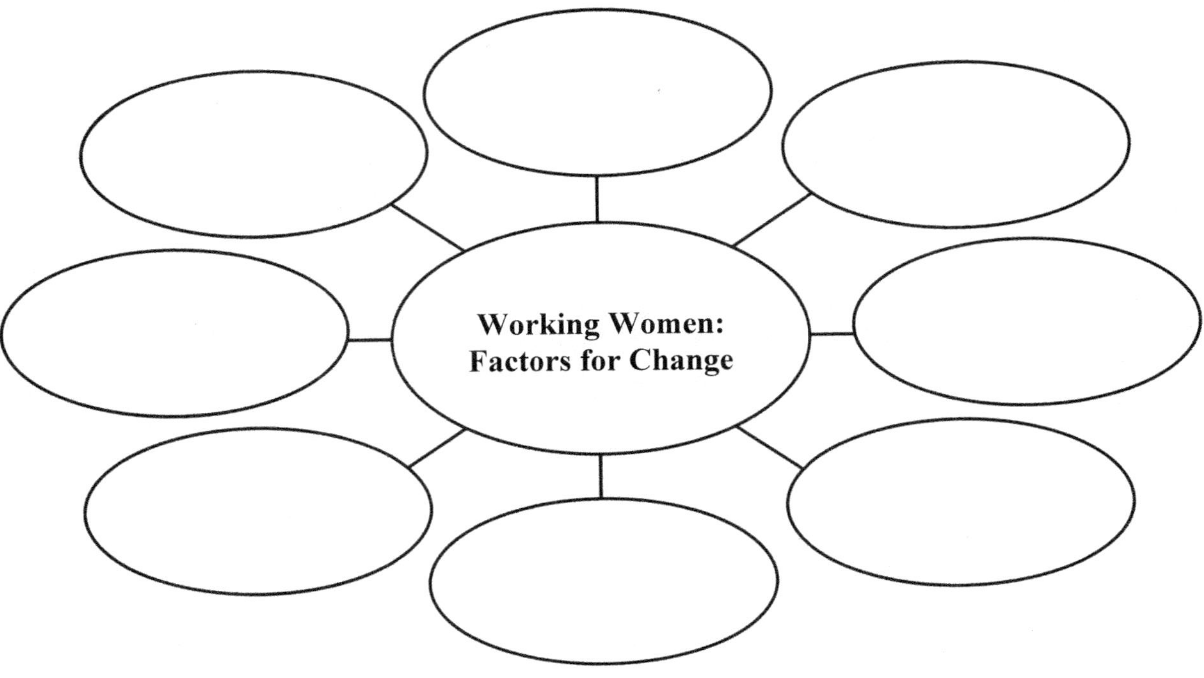

Using the information in your concept web, write a brief answer to the Focus Question.

Outline

Read the section topic entitled "Feminism" and create an outline of the section below. Note the key words that reflect the main ideas in each paragraph as well as the key words that inform those ideas.

I. Feminism

   A. Post-war exploration of female experience of the world

      1.

      2.

      3.

      4.

      5.

   B.

      1.

      2.

      3.

      4.

Review Questions

Write a brief answer to the following questions. Remember, each answer should highlight a primary idea using key words and supporting details.

1. How did women's social and economic roles change in the second half of the twentieth century?

2. What changes and problems have women faced since the fall of communism in Eastern Europe?

SECTION 4 TRANSFORMATIONS IN KNOWLEDGE AND CULTURE

FOCUS QUESTION

How was cultural and intellectual life transformed in Europe during the twentieth century?

European Cultural and Intellectual Life in the Twentieth Century	
Movement	**Transformation**

Using the information in your table, write a brief answer to the Focus Question.

OUTLINE

Read the section topic entitled "Environmentalism" and create an outline of the section below. Note the key words that reflect the main ideas in each paragraph as well as the key words that inform those ideas.

I. Environmentalism
   A. Postwar economic boom fueled by shortages of consumer goods
      1.
      2.
      3.
      4.
      5.
   B.
      1.
      2.
      3.
      4.
      5.
      6.
   C.
      1.
      2.
   D.
      1.
      2.
      3.
   E.
      1.
      2.

REVIEW QUESTIONS

Write a brief answer to the following questions. Remember, each answer should highlight a primary idea using key words and supporting details.

1. How did the pursuit and diffusion of knowledge change in the twentieth century? What have been the effects of the communications revolutions?

2. Has Western intellectual life become more unified or less so? Why?

3. What did Nietzsche and Kierkegaard contribute to existentialism? How was existentialism a response to the crises of the twentieth century?

4. In what specific ways was Europe Americanized in the second half of the twentieth century? How do you explain the trend toward a consumer society?

SECTION 5 ART SINCE WORLD WAR II

FOCUS QUESTION

How did the Cold War shape Western art in the second half of the twentieth century?

Art and the Cold War	
Realism	**Abstraction**
• • •	• • •

Using the information in your table, write a brief answer to the Focus Question.

Outline

Read the section topic entitled "Cultural Divisions and the Cold War" create an outline of the section below. Note the key words that reflect the main ideas in each paragraph as well as the key words that inform those ideas.

I. Cultural Divisions and the Cold War
   A. Socialist realism
      1.
      2.
      3.
      4.
      5.
      6.
   B.
      1.
      2.
      3.
      4.
   C.
      1.
      2.
   D.
      1.
      2.
      3.

Review Questions

Write a brief answer to the following questions. Remember, each answer should highlight a primary idea using key words and supporting details.

1. Why did New York City emerge as the international center for modern art after World War II?

2. Why is Rachel Whiteread's *Nameless Library* an apt memorial to the Holocaust?

Section 6 The Christian Heritage

Focus Question

How has the Christian heritage of the West been affected by events of the twentieth century?

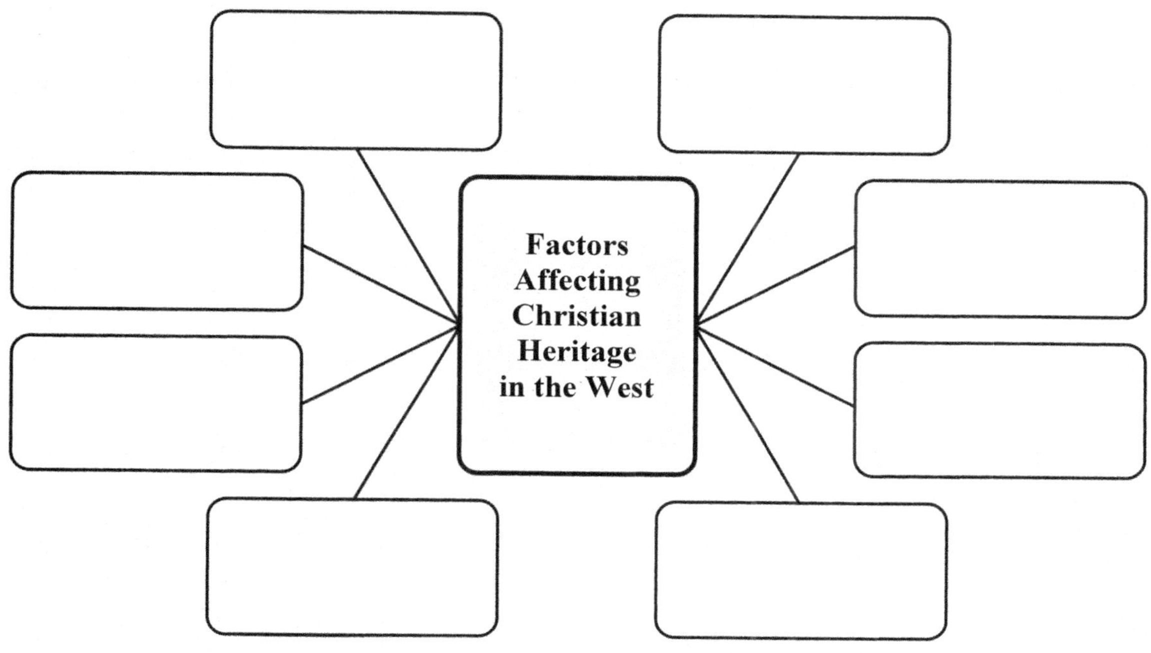

Using the information in your concept web, write a brief answer to the Focus Question.

OUTLINE

Read the section topic entitled "Roman Catholic Reform" and create an outline of the section below. Note the key words that reflect the main ideas in each paragraph as well as the key words that inform those ideas.

I. Roman Catholic Reform
    A. 1959 Vatican II: most extensive changes since Council of Trent
        1.
        2.
    B.
        1.
        2.
        3.
        4.
    C.
        1.
        2.
        3.
        4.
        5.
    D.
        1.
        2.
        3.
        4.
        5.
    E.
        1.
        2.
        3.
        4.

Review Questions

Write a brief answer to the following questions. Remember, each answer should highlight a primary idea using key words and supporting details.

1. How might post-war religious theologies and interpretations have influenced the state and society?

2. How did the work of Pope John Paul II change the Catholic Church and, by extension, the world?

SECTION 7 LATE-TWENTIETH-CENTURY TECHNOLOGY: THE ARRIVAL OF THE COMPUTER

FOCUS QUESTION

What impact has the computer had on twentieth-century society?

Impact of the Computer on Twentieth Century Society	
Category	**Impact**

Using the information in your table, write a brief answer to the Focus Question.

Outline

Read the section topic entitled "The Development of Desktop Computers" and create an outline of the section below. Note the key words that reflect the main ideas in each paragraph as well as the key words that inform those ideas.

I. The Development of Desktop Computers
   A. 1950s transistor revolution
      1.
      2.
   B.
      1.
      2.
      3.
      4.
   C.
      1.
      2.
      3.
   D.
      1.
      2.
      3.
      4.
      5.

READING SKILL: SUMMARIZE

Complete the concept web below identifying the primary technological developments of the twentieth century prior to desktop computing.

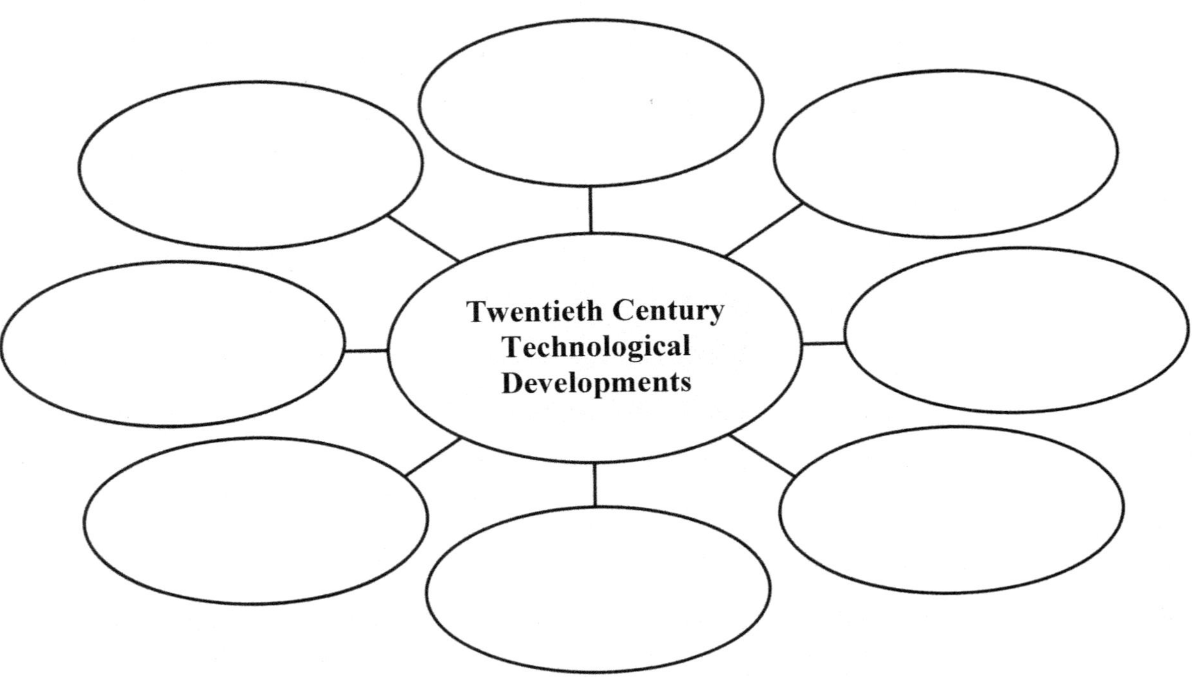

REVIEW QUESTIONS

Write a brief answer to the following questions. Remember, each answer should highlight a primary idea using key words and supporting details.

1. What were the technological steps in the emergence of the computer?

2. What changes will computers bring in the next decade?

SECTION 8 THE CHALLENGES OF EUROPEAN UNIFICATION

FOCUS QUESTION

What led to Western European unification following World War II?

Western European Unification	
Category	**Factors**
Encouragement and Necessity	
Political Determination	

Using the information in your table, write a brief answer to the Focus Question.

OUTLINE

Read the section topic entitled "The European Economic Community" and create an outline of the section below. Note the key words that reflect the main ideas in each paragraph as well as the key words that inform those ideas.

I. The European Economic Community (EEC)
   A. 1957 Treaty of Rome creation of EEC
      1.
      2.
      3.
      4.
   B.
      1.
      2.
   C.
      1.
      2.
      3.
      4.
      5.
      6.
   D.
      1.
      2.
   E.
      1.
      2.
      3.

Reading Skill: Summarize

Complete the concept web below identifying the primary issues causing discord in the European Union during the 2000s.

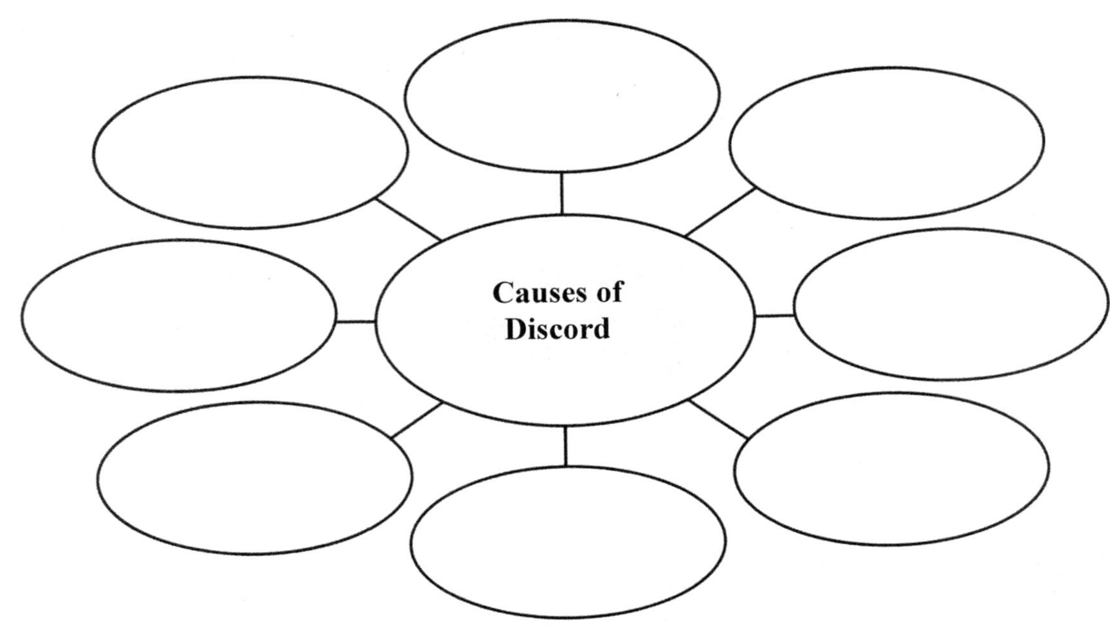

Review Questions

Write a brief answer to the following questions. Remember, each answer should highlight a primary idea using key words and supporting details.

1. What were the major steps in the emergence of the European Union?

2. Why is the Union now facing a crisis?

Section 9 New American Leadership and Financial Crisis

Focus Question

How did the year 2008 impact the relationship between the United States and Europe, and how have recent developments affected this relationship?

2008 Turning Point?		
•	•	•

Using the information in your chart, write a brief answer to the Focus Question.

OUTLINE

Read the section topic entitled "New American Leadership and Financial Crisis" and create an outline of the section below. Note the key words that reflect the main ideas in each paragraph as well as the key words that inform those ideas.

I. New American Leadership and Financial Crisis
   A. New American Leadership
      1.
      2.
      3.
      4.
      5.
   B.
      1.
      2.
   C.
      1.
      2.
      3.
      4.
   D.
      1.
      2.
      3.
      4.

Review Questions

Write a brief answer to the following questions. Remember, each answer should highlight a primary idea using key words and supporting details.

1. Why did Europeans have high hopes for the presidency of Barack Obama?

2. Why are world markets a primary area for concern regarding European relations with the United States in the future?

Review: Key Terms and People

Complete your review of the chapter by writing a brief definition of the following terms and people.

Forced migration
National Front
Guest worker
Social Welfare
Christian Democratic Parties
William Beveridge
Clement Attlee
Margaret Thatcher
German Social Democratic Party
Simone de Beauvoir
Arthur Koestler
George Orwell
Existentialism
Soren Kierkegaard
Jean-Paul Sartre
Green Party
Chernobyl
Jackson Pollock
Social realism
Abstract art
Rachel Whiteread
Neo-Orthodoxy
Liberal theology
Vatican II
Pope John Paul II
Pope Benedict XVI
European Coal and Steel Community
European Economic Community
Common Market
European Union
Barack Obama

My Key Terms

Write down terms that are unfamiliar. How are the words used? Do other words or examples reveal their meaning? Try to figure out meaning from the context.